New Finnish Architecture

Egon Tempel **New Finnish Architecture**

The Architectural Press London

For Özgen

85139 473 6

Published in the U.K. and Commonwealth by
The Architectural Press London 1968
Copyright by Verlag Gerd Hatje, Stuttgart 1968
Printed in Germany

Translation into English by James C. Palmes

Contents · Inhalt

Rovaniemi

Kemi

Oulu

Pietarsaari

Vaasa

Jyväskylä

Tampere

Imatra

Lahti

Hamina

Turku

Hyvinkää

Porvoo

Helsinki

Salo

Hanko

6

Introduction

Einleitung

Historical

Lying on the outermost edge of the European continent, Finland lingered untouched by Western civilization until the twelfth century, when the influence of Sweden and the Roman church penetrated the country from the West and missionaries from Novgorod and Byzantium came from the East. By 1300 most of Finland had been converted to Christianity from Scandinavia, with only the extreme Eastern region remaining under Russo-Byzantine ascendancy, and the frontier between the two cultural entities was thus finally established.

The influence of the West appeared first in the Åland Isles lying between Sweden and Finland, where the twelfth and fourteenth century churches clearly reflect Gotlandic Swedish models. In the South and South-East of the Finnish mainland the first major buildings appeared soon after 1300, the most important being the cathredral and castle of Turku, at that time the capital.

The very close links between North and Central Europe in the middle ages grew weaker as the country sank progressively into a politically distinct, provincial, isolation during the Reformation. Indeed it was not until the second half of the 18th century that buildings began to appear again — like the fortress of Suomenlinna — comparable in significance and architectural quality with the cathedral and castle of Turku. While Europe experienced the majestic progression of Renaissance and Baroque, nothing occurred in Finland of similar importance. Almost unaffected by European stylistic developments, Finnish endeavours were directed towards opening up the central hinterland of the Ödmark.

The 17th century saw the foundation of many towns, but as most construction was of wood, they were often completely destroyed by fires. Until the beginning of the nineteenth century Finland's architecture retained its anonymous character and paid no heed to ornamental refinements. No fundamental change took place until the Empire period when, favoured by the newly-acquired political autonomy inside the Russian state which transferred the province from Sweden, Finland emerged as a Russian grand duchy from her provincial isolation and embraced the architectural manners of Central Europe. Helsinki took shape as the new capital, a splendid monument to these events, while Empire became the national architectural style which gives Finnish towns their particular flavour.

Industrialization, germinating in the nineteenth century and drawing its sustenance from Sweden, stimulated as everywhere else the quest for new architectural forms, the escape into a national romanticism showing only the inability of architecture to synthesize and express contemporary ideas. In Finland also, the breakthrough to modern was the result of world-wide changes in social and political structure after the first world war. Modern architecture of the twenties owed much of its impetus to Finland and today the work of Finnish architects can be found in many countries.

Geschichtlicher Überblick

Finnland liegt am äußersten Rand des europäischen Kontinents. So kam es erst im 12. Jahrhundert mit der abendländischen Kultur in Berührung. Von Westen her wirkten der Einfluß Schwedens und der römischen Kirche; Nowgorod und Byzanz missionierten das Land von Osten. Um 1300 war der größte Teil Finnlands von Skandinavien her christianisiert; nur das östliche Randgebiet blieb unter byzantinisch-russischem Einfluß. Die Grenze zwischen den beiden Kulturbereichen war damit endgültig festgelegt.

Der Einfluß westlicher Kultur zeigt sich zuerst auf den zwischen Schweden und Finnland liegenden Ålandinseln. Die Kirchenbauten aus dem 12. und 14. Jahrhundert folgen deutlich gotländisch-schwedischen Vorbildern. Im Süden und Südosten des finnischen Festlandes entstehen die ersten größeren Bauwerke bald nach 1300; unter ihnen sind die Kathedrale und die Burg der damaligen Hauptstadt Turku die bedeutendsten.

Die im Mittelalter sehr engen Bindungen zu Nord- und Mitteleuropa wurden schwächer, als das Land während der Reformation zunehmend in eine politisch bedingte provinzielle Isolierung zurücksank. Bezeichnend dafür ist, daß erst in der zweiten Hälfte des 18. Jahrhunderts wieder Bauwerke errichtet wurden — wie etwa die Festung Suomenlinna —, die in Bedeutung und architektonischer Qualität an die Kathedrale oder das Schloß von Turku heranreichen. Während Europa mit Renaissance und Barock Höhepunkte der architektonischen Entwicklung erlebte, entstand in Finnland kein Bauwerk von vergleichbarer Bedeutung. Nahezu unberührt von der europäischen Stilentwicklung gingen die Finnen daran, das Landesinnere, die Ödmark, zu erschließen.

Das 17. Jahrhundert war die große Zeit der Stadtgründungen. Da die meisten Bauten aus Holz bestanden, wurden diese Städte oft durch Großfeuer vollkommen zerstört. Bis zum Beginn des 19. Jahrhunderts bewahrt die Baukunst Finnlands ihren anonymen Charakter und verzichtet auf üppige Zierformen. Erst in der Stilperiode des Empire vollzieht sich ein grundsätzlicher Wandel. Begünstigt durch die neugewonnene staatliche Autonomie innerhalb des Russischen Reiches, das 1809 die Provinz von Schweden übernahm, tritt Finnland als russisches Großfürstentum aus seiner provinziellen Isolierung heraus und öffnet sich zentraleuropäischen Stilrichtungen. Es entsteht die junge Hauptstadt Helsinki, das großartige Denkmal einer neuen Entwicklung. Das Empire wird zum nationalen Baustil, der vor allem den Städten ihr typisches Gepräge gibt.

Die im 19. Jahrhundert beginnende Industrialisierung, deren Impulse von Schweden ausgingen, gab wie überall auf der Welt den Anstoß zu neuen Stilformen. Bezeichnend für das damalige Unvermögen der Architektur, Synthese und Ausdruck der Zeitströmungen zu sein, war die Flucht in die Nationalromantik. Der Durchbruch zur Moderne erfolgte auch in Finnland auf Grund der weltweiten gesellschaftspolitischen Strukturwandlung nach dem ersten Weltkrieg.

Die moderne Architektur des zwanzigsten Jahrhunderts hat aus Finnland viele Anregungen und Impulse bekommen, und heute sind Werke finnischer Architekten in zahlreichen Ländern der Erde zu finden.

1. Sketch map showing the most important places mentioned in the selected examples.

1. Kartenskizze mit den wichtigsten im Beispielteil genannten Orten.

Geography

Finland has 4,600,000 inhabitants. With an area of 305,500 sq km excluding lakes, this means 13,7 per sq km. In the German Federal Republic 50 million people occupy 245,300 sq km, corresponding to a density of 202 per sq km. In England about 52 million live in an area of 243,990 sq km, or 216 per sq km. Even in the thickly populated South and South-West coastal regions the proportion of inhabitants to the sq km is much smaller than in a comparable European country. Central Finland is riddled with lakes. A network of waterways links them together and with the Gulfs of Finland in the South and Bothnia in the West. The principal raw material is wood. In the summer the trees are felled in the North and then begin a yearlong journey through lakes and rivers to the cellulose factories on the coast. The landscape of North Finland and Lapland is marked by short summers and everlasting winters, loneliness and great distances. The population density is no more than two persons per sq km.

2. Die Landschaft.
2. The landscape.

Geographie

Finnland hat 4,6 Millionen Einwohner. Das sind bei einer Bodenfläche von 305 500 qkm, ohne Seen, pro Quadratkilometer 13,7 Einwohner. In der Bundesrepublik Deutschland wohnen 50 Millionen auf 245 300 qkm, das entspricht einer Bevölkerungsdichte von 202 Menschen pro Quadratkilometer. England hat bei 243 990 qkm rund 52 Millionen Einwohner, das heißt pro Quadratkilometer 216. Selbst in den dicht besiedelten südlichen und südwestlichen Küstengebieten Finnlands ist der Bevölkerungsanteil auf den Quadratkilometer viel geringer als in einem vergleichbaren europäischen Land (Bild 1, 2). Mittelfinnland wird von zahlreichen Seen durchzogen. Ein Netz von Wasseradern verbindet sie untereinander und mit dem Finnischen Meerbusen im Süden und dem Bottnischen Meerbusen im Westen. Wichtigstes Rohmaterial des Landes ist das Holz. Im Sommer werden die Bäume im Norden gefällt und treten dann eine einjährige Reise durch Seen und Flüsse bis zu den Zellulosefabriken der Küstengebiete an. Die Landschaften Nordfinnlands und Lapplands werden durch kurze Sommer und endlos dauernde Winter, Einsamkeit und weite Entfernungen geprägt. Die Wohndichte beträgt dort zwei Menschen auf einen Quadratkilometer.

Anonymous Vernacular Architecture

The influences of West and East are most clearly apparent in vernacular building. The farmsteads and settlements of West Finland have a defensive, enclosed, character. In the East, on the other hand, a more open type is generally preferred, with outbuildings grouped loosely around the main structure. The dwellings represent various types of two-room house. Family and animals lived in a single-storey building under one roof. The enclosed rectangular yard usually led to the byre and the sauna (ill. 3-5). By the end of the 18th century a two-storey one-room house with a separate section for stock was common, originating from the single-room house with ground-level fireplace and smoke-opening in the roof.

Most manor houses of the late middle ages, like the farmsteads, were built on log-cabin principles. The farm premises were on the ground floor, living rooms on the first floor and dining hall above. Two single-storey wings with servants' quarters, barn and byre flanked the courtyard, and this arrangement superseded the older type of rectangular yard enclosed on all sides.

The first stone churches were built in the 13th century on the Åland Isles (ill. 7, 8). The earliest churches on the mainland rose in the newly-settled Western coastal regions. Before Turku became a bishopric, the main centres lay in the districts North-East of the old capital in Nousiainen and later Koroinen. Towards the end of the 14th century a few three-aisle hall-type churches were built, which clearly reflect Germano-Baltic influence. The markedly horizontal ornamentation of the stone churches from the end of the 15th century is traceable to Danish influences (ill. 9, 10).

Among the most distinctive examples of Finnish architecture are the wooden churches. Those still preserved today were for the most part built between the 17th and the beginning of the 19th centuries. This wood church architecture, largely the work of native master-builders, exploits — like all Finnish 17th century timber building — the structural methods of the log-house. The commonest types are single-nave hall churches and churches of cruciform plan, the favourite form being the Greek cross plan composed of five equal squares. The wood churches of Finland of the 17th and 18th centuries, like the mediaeval stone churches, all have a free-standing bell tower.

The fortresses of Finland were strongholds of the Swedish empire and at the same time seats of government. They were generally built on islands or cliff tops and were surrounded by moats. A typical example is Olavinlinna in the Kyrönsalmi-Sund (ill. 11-13) built on a rocky island at the end of the 15th century. Next to the castle of Turku, among the grandest is the stronghold of Viipuri. The island fortress of Suomenlinna erected by the Swedes, with its ring wall seven kilometres long, is one of the largest Baroque strongholds in Europe. After the great Nordic war and the loss of Viipuri, the frontier town of Hamina was constructed as a defence against the East. Its star-shaped street system spreading out from the market place is unique in North Europe (ill. 14).

Anonyme bodenständige Architektur

In der anonymen Baukunst sind die Einflüsse von Westen und Osten am deutlichsten spürbar. So zeigen die Gehöfte und Siedlungen Westfinnlands einen wehrhaften, geschlossenen Charakter. In Ostfinnland dagegen wird allgemein eine offenere Bauweise bevorzugt: Die Nebengebäude gruppieren sich lose um das Hauptgebäude. Die Wohnbauten sind verschiedene Typen des Zweistubenhauses. Wohn- und Stallteil liegen in dem eingeschossigen Gebäude unter einem Dach. Zum geschlossenen Hofviereck gehören meist Scheune und Sauna (Bild 3-5). Um das Ende des 18. Jahrhunderts verbreitet sich das zweigeschossige Einstubenhaus mit einem separaten Stallteil, das auf den Urtyp des Einraumhauses mit ebenerdiger Feuerstelle und Rauchöffnung im Dach zurückgeht.

Die meisten Herrenhöfe des Spätmittelalters wurden ähnlich wie die Bauernhöfe nach dem Konstruktionssystem des Blockhauses errichtet. Im Erdgeschoß liegen die Wirtschaftsräume, im ersten Stock die Wohnräume und darüber der Festsaal. Den Hofraum flankieren zwei eingeschossige Flügelbauten mit Gesindewohnungen, Scheune und Stall. Diese Hofform löst den älteren Typ des allseitig umschlossenen Hofvierecks ab.

Die ersten Steinkirchen wurden im 13. Jahrhundert auf der Insel Åland gebaut (Bild 7, 8). Auf dem Festland entstanden die frühesten Kirchen in den neu besiedelten westlichen Küstengebieten. Bevor Turku Bischofssitz wurde, lag das Schwergewicht auf den Gebieten nordöstlich der alten Hauptstadt in Nousiainen und später in Koroinen. Gegen Ende des 14. Jahrhunderts wurden einige große dreischiffige Hallenkirchen gebaut, die deutlich deutschbaltischen Einfluß erkennen lassen. Die strenge horizontale Ornamentik der Steinkirchen vom Ausgang des 15. Jahrhunderts wird auf dänische Einflüsse zurückgeführt (Bild 9, 10).

Zu den erlesensten Beispielen finnischer Baukunst gehören die Holzkirchen. Die heute noch erhaltenen wurden großenteils in der Zeit vom 17. bis zum Beginn des 19. Jahrhunderts erbaut. Diese Holzkirchenarchitektur, die vorwiegend von ländlichen Meistern stammt, benutzt wie alle finnischen Holzbauten des 17. Jahrhunderts das Konstruktionssystem des Blockhauses. Die häufigsten Typen sind einschiffige Hallenkirchen und Kirchen auf kreuzförmigem Grundriß. Bevorzugt wird, bis in das Empire hinein, die aus fünf gleichen Quadraten gebildete Grundrißform des griechischen Kreuzes. Wie die mittelalterlichen Steinkirchen Finnlands haben auch die Holzkirchen des 17. und 18. Jahrhunderts immer einen frei stehenden Glockenturm.

Die Burgen Finnlands waren schwedische Reichsburgen und zugleich Sitz der Verwaltung. Sie wurden meist auf Inseln oder Felshöhen angelegt und sind von Wassergräben umgeben. Ein typisches Beispiel ist die Ende des 15. Jahrhunderts auf einer Klippeninsel errichtete Burg Olavinlinna im Kyrönsalmi-Sund (Bild 11-13). Zu den stattlichsten Anlagen gehört neben der Burg von Turku die Festung von Viipuri. Die von den Schweden erbaute Inselfestung Suomenlinna ist mit ihren sieben Kilometer langen Ringmauern eine der größten Barockfestungen Europas. Nach dem großen Nordischen Krieg und dem Verlust Viipuris wurde die Grenzstadt Hamina als Festung gegen den Osten ausgebaut. Ihr sternförmiges, vom Marktplatz ausgehendes Straßennetz ist für Nordeuropa einmalig (Bild 14).

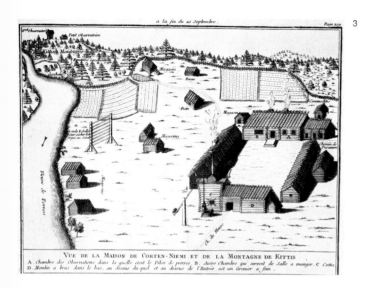

3

VUE DE LA MAISON DE CORTEN-NIEMI ET DE LA MONTAGNE DE KITTIS

A. Chambre des Observations dans la quelle etoit le Polre de pierres. B. Autre Chambre qui servoit de Salle a manger. C. Cotta.
D. Moulin a bras dans le bas, au dessus du quel et au dessus de l'Entrée est un Grenier a foin.

4

5

6

7

8

9

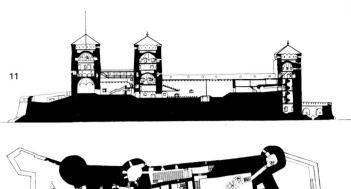

11

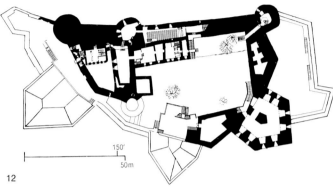

12

10

13

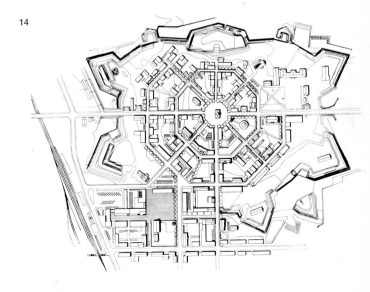

14

3. Korteniemi farm-house, Kittilä.
4. Farm-house at Seurasaari open-air museum.
5. Living-room of Kanajärvi farm-house, Häme.
6. Porvoo.
7, 8. Sund church, Åland isles, 13th century.
9, 10. Church at Inkoo, 15th century.
11-13. Olavinlinna castle, near Savonlinna, 1475.
14. Hamina, plan of centre.

3. Bauernhof Korteniemi, Kittilä.
4. Bauernhof im Freiluftmuseum von Seurasaari.
5. Wohnstube im Bauernhof Kanajärvi, Häme.
6. Porvoo.
7, 8. Kirche in Sund auf Åland, 13. Jahrhundert.
9, 10. Kirche in Inkoo, 15. Jahrhundert.
11-13. Burg Olavinlinna bei Savonlinna, 1475.
14. Hamina, Zentralplan.

Empire in Helsinki

A few years after Finland had become an independent Russian grand duchy, Helsinki replaced Turku as the capital. The political and cultural centre now shifted towards Russia and the metropolis of Petrograd. When Helsinki was burnt in 1808, the reconstruction was undertaken to a different and more comprehensive plan. The politician and diplomat, Johann Albrecht Ehrenström, one of the city's great citizens and a man of wide vision, supervised operations as chairman of a planning committee, contriving a town of straight roads and open squares. Thanks also to him, Carl Ludwig Engel, a fellow student of Schinkel, was invited to Helsinki. In 1824 Engel succeeded Charles Bassi as Controller of Public Works and assumed responsibility for the capital's further development. Within twenty-five years he had completed the largest architectural group in the North designed as a single conception: the Senate Square (ill. 17) with its splendid Empire buildings. Gently sloping towards the South, the square is bordered on the west side by the university (ill. 15) and on the east by the Senate House. The cathedral (ill. 18), raised on a platform and with a lofty portico, dominates the Northern end. Engel's most important creation is the library (ill. 16) with a high-domed reading-room, standing next to the university and adjoining the former military hospital. By no means all this great architect's work was done in Helsinki: other buildings including churches, civic buildings, manor houses and mansions are to be found throughout the land.

Empire in Helsinki

Einige Jahre nachdem Finnland autonomes russisches Großfürstentum wurde, trat Helsinki als Hauptstadt an die Stelle des alten Turku: Das politische und kulturelle Zentrum verschob sich in Richtung Rußlands und seiner Metropole Petersburg. Nach dem Brand Helsinkis im Jahre 1808 ging man nach veränderten und erweiterten Plänen an den Wiederaufbau. Der Politiker und Diplomat Johann Albrecht Ehrenström, einer der großen Bürger dieser Stadt und ein Mann von visionärer Weitsicht, überwachte als Vorsitzender eines Planungskomitees die Arbeiten. Er schlug eine Stadt mit geraden Straßen und offenen Plätzen vor. Sein Verdienst war es auch, daß man Carl Ludwig Engel, einen Studienkollegen Schinkels, nach Helsinki rief. 1824 wurde Engel als Nachfolger von Charles Bassi zum Generalintendanten des Landesbauwesens ernannt und übernahm die Verantwortung für den weiteren Ausbau der Hauptstadt. Innerhalb eines Vierteljahrhunderts realisierte er den größten, nach einer einheitlichen Vorstellung entwickelten architektonischen Komplex der nordischen Länder: den Senatsplatz (Bild 17) mit seinen großartigen Empirebauwerken. Der leicht nach Süden abfallende Platz wird im Westen von der Universität (Bild 15) und im Osten vom Senatsgebäude begrenzt. Die erhöht stehende Domkirche (Bild 18) mit dem hohen Säulenportal bildet den Abschluß nach Norden. Die bedeutendste Schöpfung Engels ist die neben der Universität errichtete Bibliothek (Bild 16) mit ihrem hohen Kuppelsaal, an die sich das ehemalige Militärhospital anschließt. Nur ein Teil des Lebenswerkes dieses großen Architekten steht in Helsinki; weitere Bauten wie Kirchen, Herrenhöfe, Residenzen und Wohnhäuser finden sich im ganzen Land.

9

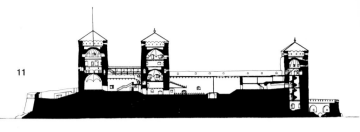

11

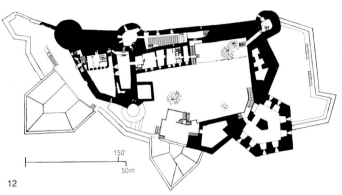

12

10

13

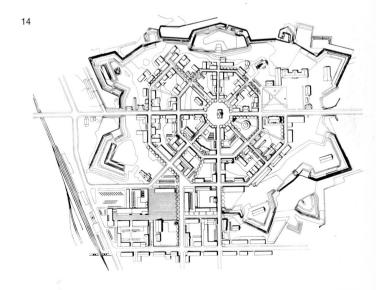

14

3. Korteniemi farm-house, Kittilä.
4. Farm-house at Seurasaari open-air museum.
5. Living-room of Kanajärvi farm-house, Häme.
6. Porvoo.
7, 8. Sund church, Åland isles, 13th century.
9, 10. Church at Inkoo, 15th century.
11-13. Olavinlinna castle, near Savonlinna, 1475.
14. Hamina, plan of centre.

3. Bauernhof Korteniemi, Kittilä.
4. Bauernhof im Freiluftmuseum von Seurasaari.
5. Wohnstube im Bauernhof Kanajärvi, Häme.
6. Porvoo.
7, 8. Kirche in Sund auf Åland, 13. Jahrhundert.
9, 10. Kirche in Inkoo, 15. Jahrhundert.
11-13. Burg Olavinlinna bei Savonlinna, 1475.
14. Hamina, Zentralplan.

Empire in Helsinki

A few years after Finland had become an independent Russian grand duchy, Helsinki replaced Turku as the capital. The political and cultural centre now shifted towards Russia and the metropolis of Petrograd. When Helsinki was burnt in 1808, the reconstruction was undertaken to a different and more comprehensive plan. The politician and diplomat, Johann Albrecht Ehrenström, one of the city's great citizens and a man of wide vision, supervised operations as chairman of a planning committee, contriving a town of straight roads and open squares. Thanks also to him, Carl Ludwig Engel, a fellow student of Schinkel, was invited to Helsinki. In 1824 Engel succeeded Charles Bassi as Controller of Public Works and assumed responsibility for the capital's further development. Within twenty-five years he had completed the largest architectural group in the North designed as a single conception: the Senate Square (ill. 17) with its splendid Empire buildings. Gently sloping towards the South, the square is bordered on the west side by the university (ill. 15) and on the east by the Senate House. The cathedral (ill. 18), raised on a platform and with a lofty portico, dominates the Northern end. Engel's most important creation is the library (ill. 16) with a high-domed reading-room, standing next to the university and adjoining the former military hospital. By no means all this great architect's work was done in Helsinki: other buildings including churches, civic buildings, manor houses and mansions are to be found throughout the land.

Empire in Helsinki

Einige Jahre nachdem Finnland autonomes russisches Großfürstentum wurde, trat Helsinki als Hauptstadt an die Stelle des alten Turku: Das politische und kulturelle Zentrum verschob sich in Richtung Rußlands und seiner Metropole Petersburg. Nach dem Brand Helsinkis im Jahre 1808 ging man nach veränderten und erweiterten Plänen an den Wiederaufbau. Der Politiker und Diplomat Johann Albrecht Ehrenström, einer der großen Bürger dieser Stadt und ein Mann von visionärer Weitsicht, überwachte als Vorsitzender eines Planungskomitees die Arbeiten. Er schlug eine Stadt mit geraden Straßen und offenen Plätzen vor. Sein Verdienst war es auch, daß man Carl Ludwig Engel, einen Studienkollegen Schinkels, nach Helsinki rief. 1824 wurde Engel als Nachfolger von Charles Bassi zum Generalintendanten des Landesbauwesens ernannt und übernahm die Verantwortung für den weiteren Ausbau der Hauptstadt. Innerhalb eines Vierteljahrhunderts realisierte er den größten, nach einer einheitlichen Vorstellung entwickelten architektonischen Komplex der nordischen Länder: den Senatsplatz (Bild 17) mit seinen großartigen Empirebauwerken. Der leicht nach Süden abfallende Platz wird im Westen von der Universität (Bild 15) und im Osten vom Senatsgebäude begrenzt. Die erhöht stehende Domkirche (Bild 18) mit dem hohen Säulenportal bildet den Abschluß nach Norden. Die bedeutendste Schöpfung Engels ist die neben der Universität errichtete Bibliothek (Bild 16) mit ihrem hohen Kuppelsaal, an die sich das ehemalige Militärhospital anschließt. Nur ein Teil des Lebenswerkes dieses großen Architekten steht in Helsinki; weitere Bauten wie Kirchen, Herrenhöfe, Residenzen und Wohnhäuser finden sich im ganzen Land.

15. C. L. Engel. Helsinki university, 1832.
16. C. L. Engel. University library, Helsinki, 1844.
17. Senate Square, Helsinki, site plan.
18. C. L. Engel. Helsinki cathedral, 1830-52.

15. C. L. Engel. Universität Helsinki, 1832.
16. C. L. Engel. Universitätsbibliothek Helsinki, 1844.
17. Senatsplatz Helsinki, Lageplan.
18. C. L. Engel. Dom in Helsinki, 1830-52.

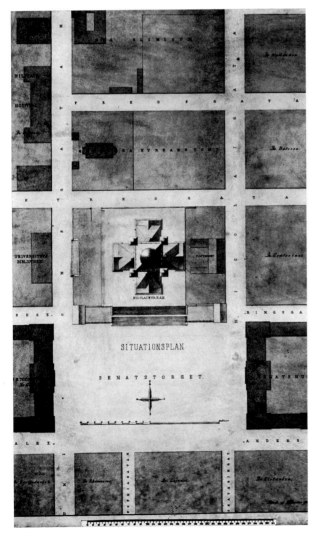

Historicism

After Carl Ludwig Engel's death in 1840 building activity declined and the Empire style lost its inspiration. Elements adopted from mediaeval and Renaissance architecture were introduced. The leading architects came from Sweden or had at least been trained at the Stockholm Academy. Their neo-Renaissance buildings, however, suffered less from the exaggerated tendencies noticeable in other European countries (ill. 21). In addition to such historical plagiarism, industrialization was leading to new forms, which were seen for the first time at the industrial exhibition of 1876. Carl Theodor Höijer, who designed the exhibition buildings, was among the most typical representatives of this movement (ill. 19, 20). Exuberant plaster decorations were an essential factor in the general conception of his buildings. Although the industrial exhibition showed no fundamental architectural change, it was a first indication that new ideas were brewing.

Historizismus

Nach Carl Ludwig Engels Tod (1840) flaute die Bautätigkeit ab. Das Empire verlor seine Kraft. Stilelemente, die aus der Baukunst des Mittelalters und der Renaissance übernommen wurden, setzten sich durch. Die führenden Architekten kamen aus Schweden oder waren wenigstens an der Stockholmer Akademie ausgebildet. Ihre Neo-Renaissancebauten neigten indessen viel weniger zu Übertreibungen, wie sie in anderen europäischen Ländern zu beobachten sind (Bild 21). Neben diesen Imitationen historischer Stile entwickelten sich durch die Industrialisierung des Landes neue Formen, die zum erstenmal in der Industrieausstellung von 1876 in Erscheinung traten. Carl Theodor Höijer, der die Ausstellungsbauten entwarf, war einer der repräsentativsten Vertreter dieser Richtung (Bild 19, 20). Ihm gelang es auch, die üppigen Gipsornamente in die Gesamtkonzeption seiner Bauten einzuordnen. Obwohl die Industrieausstellung keine wesentliche Änderung der Architektur zeigte, war sie doch ein erstes Zeichen des sich anbahnenden Stilwandels.

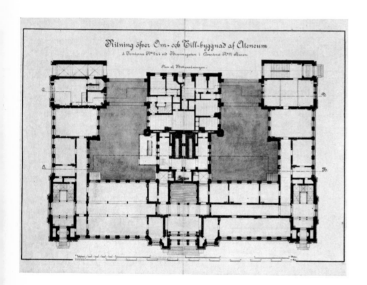

19, 20. C. Th. Höijer. Ateneum art gallery, Helsinki, 1887.
21. A. H. Dalström. Students' residence, Helsinki, 1870.

19, 20. C. Th. Höijer. Kunstakademie Ateneum in Helsinki, 1887.
21. A. H. Dalström. Studentenhaus in Helsinki, 1870.

Precursors of Modern Architecture

Eclectic, neo-Renaissance, elements conflicting with Finnish tradition were as unsuited to Finland's national awakening, already proclaimed in literature, music and applied arts, as the Gothic pretensions of the new cathedral. Looking for a path of her own, she turned to the vernacular tradition and its clear and simple forms. Herman Gesellius, Armas Lindgren and Eliel Saarinen went into partnership, even before the completion of their studies, and, by so doing, began a new era in Finnish architecture.

The Finnish pavilion at the 1900 International Exhibition in Paris, adorned with frescoes by Akseli Gallén-Kallela, was their first joint effort. In 1902 they built close to Helsinki the Hvitträsk house as a combined home and studio-office (ill. 22-24). Both buildings show clearly the national romantic influence as a Finnish variant of Jugendstil. The intervention of the young architects Gesellius, Lindgren, Jung, Neovius and Sonck into the debate over the building of the Finnish national museum reflects the wide enthusiasm at the turn of the century. They forced a competition, which was won by Gesellius, Lindgren and Saarinen. The national museum (ill. 25) was built between 1906 and 1912. It was the principal work of these architects in their first national romantic period.

In 1902 Armas Lindgren became director of the Helsinki School of Arts and Design while Gesellius and Saarinen built Viipuri station in 1909-13, in which the functionalist tendency is already discernible, first clearly defined in Saarinen's main station (1910-14) at Helsinki (ill. 26). After Ehrensvärd and Ehrenström, the creator of classical Helsinki, Saarinen was Finland's third great town-designer. His general plans for Greater Helsinki and Munkkiniemi-Haaga have lost none of their validity today. Eliel Saarinen emigrated to the United States in 1923 and thus became one of the first protagonists of Finnish architecture abroad.

Wegbereiter einer modernen Baukunst

Dem nationalen Erwachen des finnischen Volkes, das sich in Literatur, Musik und bildender Kunst schon lange angekündigt hatte, wurden die eklektizistischen, der finnischen Tradition widersprechenden Stilelemente der Neo-Renaissance ebensowenig gerecht wie die gotischen Formimitationen den neuen Kathedralen. Auf der Suche nach eigenen Wegen orientierte man sich an der bodenständigen Bautradition und ihren einfachen, klaren Formen. Herman Gesellius, Armas Lindgren und Eliel Saarinen gründeten 1896, noch vor Abschluß ihrer Studien, ein gemeinsames Büro und leiteten damit eine neue Epoche der finnischen Architektur ein.

Der finnische Pavillon auf der Weltausstellung 1900 in Paris, ausgeschmückt mit Fresken von Akseli Gallén-Kallela, ist ihre erste gemeinsame Arbeit. 1902 bauen sie in der Nähe von Helsinki das Haus Hvitträsk als gemeinsame Wohn- und Arbeitsstätte (Bild 22-24). Beide Gebäude zeigen deutlich den nationalromantischen Einfluß als finnische Variante des Jugendstils. Das Eingreifen der jungen Architekten Gesellius, Lindgren, Jung, Neovius und Sonck in die Auseinandersetzung um den Bau des finnischen Nationalmuseums spricht für den um die Jahrhundertwende verbreiteten Enthusiasmus. Sie erzwingen einen Wettbewerb, den Gesellius, Lindgren und Saarinen gewinnen. Das Nationalmuseum (Bild 25) wird von 1906-12 realisiert. Es ist das Hauptwerk dieser Architekten in ihrer ersten, nationalromantischen Schaffensperiode.

1902 wurde Armas Lindgren Leiter der Kunstgewerbeschule Helsinki. Gesellius und Saarinen bauten 1909-13 den Bahnhof von Viipuri. In ihm läßt sich bereits die Hinwendung zum Funktionalismus erkennen, der dann in Saarinens Hauptbahnhof (Bild 26) von Helsinki (erbaut 1910-14) seine erste eindeutige Formulierung erlebt. Saarinen war nach Ehrensvärd und Ehrenström, dem Schöpfer des klassizistischen Helsinki, der dritte große Städtebauer Finnlands. Seine Generalpläne für Groß-Helsinki und Munkkiniemi-Haaga haben bis heute nichts von ihrer Aktualität verloren. 1923 siedelte Eliel Saarinen in die Vereinigten Staaten über und wurde so zu einem der ersten Vermittler finnischer Baukunst im Ausland.

22. H. Gesellius, A. Lindgren and E. Saarinen. Hvitträsk, the architects' house at Kirkkonummi, 1902.

22. H. Gesellius, A. Lindgren und E. Saarinen. Hvitträsk, Haus der Architekten in Kirkkonummi, 1902.

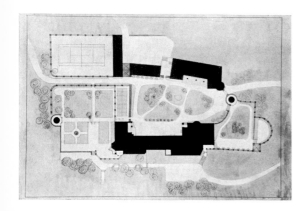

Lars Sonck

Lars Sonck was the most powerful personality in the new movement. Like Eliel Saarinen, he belonged to the generation of architects who were the first to graduate from the Helsinki Polytechnic
founded in 1890. As early as 1894 he had built a log-house villa
on the Åland isles, and was to become the outstanding represen-
tative of national romanticism, the Finnish version of Jugendstil.
In the town-planning field he won back for architects the influence
lost to engineers since Engel's death. Soon after 1900 Sonck sub-
mitted plans for the cathedral at Tampere, which was built in
1902-07 (ill. 28-30). If Tampere Cathedral can be regarded as the
zenith of Sonck's national romantic period, in the villa of the spring
park (ill. 27) and the Kallio church in Helsinki (1909-12) signs of a
rationalistic formality may be detected, which was most conspicuous in the stock exchange (ill. 31, 32) of 1911.

Lars Sonck

Lars Sonck ist die kraftvollste Persönlichkeit in der Periode der
Neuorientierung. Er gehört wie Eliel Saarinen zu der Architekten-
generation, die als erste das 1890 in Helsinki gegründete Polytech-
nikum absolvierte. Schon 1894 baute er auf Åland seine erste
Blockhausvilla. Sonck wird zum ausgeprägtesten Vertreter der
Nationalromantik, der finnischen Version des Jugendstils. Auf dem
Gebiet der Stadtplanung gewinnt er den Architekten ihren seit
Engels Tod an die Ingenieure verlorengegangenen Einfluß wieder
zurück. Bald nach 1900 legte Sonck die Pläne für die Domkirche in
Tampere vor, die in den Jahren 1902-07 gebaut wurde (Bild 28-30).
Kann der Dom von Tampere als Höhepunkt der nationalroman-
tischen Periode Soncks angesehen werden, so ist an der Villa im
Brunnenpark (Bild 27) und der Kallio-Kirche in Helsinki (1909-12)
bereits eine Hinwendung zu rationalistischer Strenge zu beobachten, die sich dann beim Haus der Börse (Bild 31, 32) von 1911 voll
durchsetzt.

23, 24. H. Gesellius, A. Lindgren and E. Saarinen. Hvitträsk, the architects' house at Kirkkonummi, 1902.
25. H. Gesellius, A. Lindgren and E. Saarinen. National museum, Helsinki,
1906-12.
26. E. Saarinen. Main station, Helsinki, 1910-14.
27. L. Sonck. House in the Kaivopuisto park, Helsinki, 1911.

23, 24. H. Gesellius, A. Lindgren und E. Saarinen. Hvitträsk, Haus der
Architekten in Kirkkonummi, 1902.
25. H. Gesellius, A. Lindgren und E. Saarinen. Nationalmuseum in Helsinki, 1906-12.
26. E. Saarinen. Hauptbahnhof Helsinki, 1910-14.
27. L. Sonck. Wohnhaus im Brunnenpark, Helsinki, 1911.

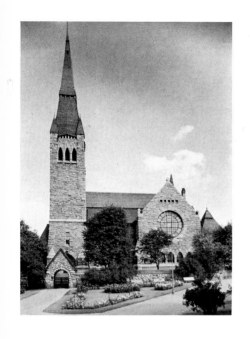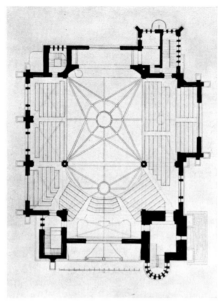

Sigurd Frosterus and Johan Siegfried Sirén

Unaffected by national romanticism, the art theorist and architect Sigurd Frosterus, who had worked for a short time with Henry van de Velde, went his own way. He had early become an adherent of international functionalism and a compelling generator of ideas on the new European architecture. Frosterus, whose design for Helsinki railway station (ill. 35) won second prize, demanded of the architecture of the future the most economical use of materials, minimal display and confinement to structural needs. His largest building (1924-31), the Stockmann department store (ill. 33, 34), is still one of the best of its kind in the North.

The neoclassicism, which spread through the Northern countries after 1920, is especially well demonstrated by the Finnish parliament building (ill. 37), built by J. S. Sirén in 1927-31. Parliament House and the (1935) office building of the firm of Lassila and Tikanoja (ill. 36), also in Helsinki, are the only two major buildings of this development.

Sigurd Frosterus und Johan Siegfried Sirén

Unbeeinflußt von der Nationalromantik ging der Kunstphilosoph und Architekt Sigurd Frosterus, der kurze Zeit Mitarbeiter Henry van de Veldes war, seinen eigenen Weg. Er wurde schon früh zum Anhänger des internationalen Funktionalismus und einflußreichen Vermittler in der Auseinandersetzung um eine neue europäische Architektur. Frosterus, dessen Entwurf für den Hauptbahnhof Helsinki (Bild 35) den 2. Preis erhielt, forderte von der Architektur der Zukunft rationellste Materialverwendung, geringsten Aufwand und Beschränkung auf das konstruktiv Notwendige. Sein größter, 1924-31 erstellter Bau, das Warenhaus Stockmann (Bild 33, 34), gilt heute noch als eines der besten Kaufhäuser des Nordens.

Der Neoklassizismus, der sich nach 1920 in den nordischen Staaten ausbreitete, zeigt sich besonders am finnischen Reichstagsgebäude (Bild 37), das 1927-31 von J. S. Sirén erbaut wurde. Der Reichstag und das 1935 entstandene Verwaltungsgebäude der Firma Lassila & Tikanoja (Bild 36), gleichfalls in Helsinki, sind die beiden einzigen Großbauten dieser Richtung.

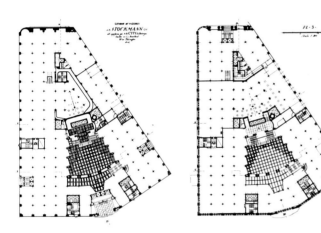

28-30. L. Sonck. Cathedral at Tampere, 1902-07.
31, 32. L. Sonck. Stock exchange, Helsinki, 1911.
33, 34. S. Frosterus. Stockmann department store, Helsinki, 1924-31.

28-30. L. Sonck. Domkirche in Tampere, 1902-07.
31, 32. L. Sonck. Börse in Helsinki, 1911.
33, 34. S. Frosterus: Warenhaus Stockmann in Helsinki, 1924-31.

35. S. Frosterus. Competition design for Helsinki railway station. 1904.
36. J. S. Sirén. Lassila & Tikanoja office building, Helsinki, 1935.
37. J. S. Sirén. Parliament House, Helsinki, 1927-31.

35. S. Frosterus. Wettbewerbsentwurf für den Bahnhof Helsinki, 1904.
36. J. S. Sirén. Verwaltungsgebäude Lassila & Tikanoja in Helsinki, 1935.
37. J. S. Sirén. Parlamentsgebäude in Helsinki, 1927-31.

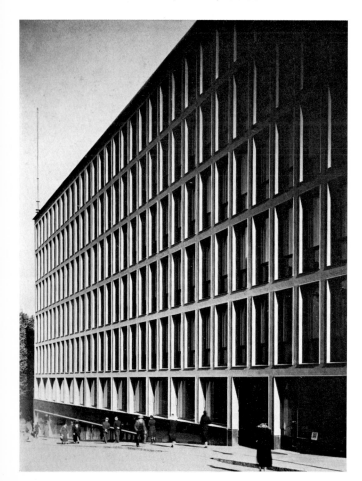

Erik Bryggman

For a short time at the end of the twenties and in the thirties Turku became, when Aalto and Bryggman were working there together, the centre of architectural events. In 1929 they designed Turku's seven-hundreth anniversary exhibition. Both architects had started as neoclassicists, inspired by the Swedish architect Erik Gunnar Asplund, the strongest personality among the neoclassicists of the 1920s. Asplund's later conversion to functionalism influenced architectural development in Finland at least as much as Le Corbusier's work and the Bauhaus. These exciting years saw Bryggman's sports institute (ill. 38) of Vierumäki (1933-36) and his cemetery chapel (ill. 39, 40) at Turku (1938-41) — both in a very pure, rational style, enhanced in the chapel by the lyrical use of light as an architectural component.

Erik Bryggman

Für kurze Zeit wird Turku Ende der zwanziger und in den dreißiger Jahren, als Aalto und Bryggman gemeinsam dort arbeiten, zum Zentrum des architektonischen Geschehens. 1929 gestalten Aalto und Bryggman die Ausstellung zur Siebenhundertjahrfeier von Turku. Beide Architekten hatten als Neoklassizisten begonnen und Anregungen von dem schwedischen Architekten Erik Gunnar Asplund aufgenommen, der stärksten Persönlichkeit unter den Neoklassizisten der zwanziger Jahre. Asplunds späterer Übergang zum Funktionalismus beeinflußte die architektonische Entwicklung in Finnland mindestens ebenso wie das Werk Le Corbusiers und die Bauhauslehre. In diesem Spannungsfeld entsteht in den Jahren 1933-36 Bryggmans Sportinstitut von Vierumäki (Bild 38) und die Friedhofskapelle (Bild 39, 40) in Turku (1938-41) — beide in einem sehr reinen, rationalen Stil, der bei der Kapelle durch die Führung des Lichts eine lyrische Komponente erhält.

38. E. Bryggman. Sports institute at Vierumäki, 1933-36.
39, 40. E. Bryggman. Cemetery chapel, Turku, 1938-41.

38. E. Bryggman. Sportinstitut in Vierumäki, 1933-36.
39, 40. E. Bryggman. Friedhofskapelle in Turku, 1938-41.

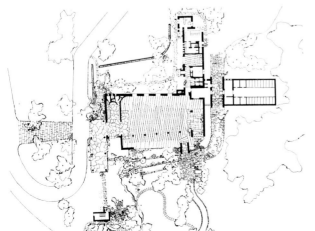

Alvar Aalto

Aalto's early work shows fundamental grasp of the functionalism of the international style, to which he made a masterly contribution with his sanatorium (ill. 41, 42) at Paimio (1929-33). To this, his "white" period, also belongs his own house (ill. 44), the pavilions for the international exhibitions in Paris (1937) and New York (1939), and the villa Mairea (1938-39).

All these works demonstrate the characteristic features of his maturity: a loosening of the strict formal plan; the lavish, but always sure, handling of materials; sculptural modelling of masses, of which the lecture hall of the library (ill. 43) at Viipuri (1927-35) is one of the best examples.

Owing to the war and its aftermath Aalto paid increasing attention during the forties to problems of regional and urban planning. The buildings of these years are distinguished by unrendered brick and thus have affinities with the picturesque and romantic tendencies dominating the international architectural scene after World War II. In addition to the national pensions institute in Helsinki (ill. 48), the town hall scheme (ill. 45, 46) of Säynätsalo (1950-52) is especially memorable because of its masterly spatial coherence.

In recent years the pattern of geometrical relationships in Aalto's architecture has developed in complexity, culminating in a consummate blending of space and mass. Aalto's own office building (ill. 47), the Maison Carré at Bazoches (ill. 49) near Paris (1956-58), the community centres at Wolfsburg and Helsinki and the opera house scheme at Essen (see page 140) illustrate the richness of this evolution.

Alvar Aalto

Aaltos Frühwerk ist im wesentlichen eine Auseinandersetzung mit dem Funktionalismus des internationalen Stils, zu dem er mit dem Sanatorium in Paimio (1929-33) (Bild 41, 42) einen meisterlichen Beitrag leistet. Zu dieser, seiner »weißen« Epoche gehören auch sein eigenes Haus (Bild 44), die Pavillons für die internationalen Ausstellungen in Paris (1937) und New York (1939) und die Villa Mairea (1938-39).

In all diesen Werken kündigen sich schon die charakteristischen Züge seines reifen Werkes an: das Durchbrechen einer strengen Grundrißgestaltung, die reiche, aber immer sichere Anwendung der Materialien und die plastische Durchformung des Raumgefüges, für die der Vortragssaal der Bibliothek in Viipuri (1927-35) (Bild 43) eines der besten Beispiele ist.

Wegen des Krieges und seinen Folgen befaßte sich Aalto in den vierziger Jahren stärker mit Aufgaben der Regional- und Stadtplanung. Die Bauten dieser Jahre zeichnen sich durch Verwendung von unverputztem Backstein aus und stehen dadurch auch im Zusammenhang mit den pittoresken und regionalistischen Tendenzen, die nach dem zweiten Weltkrieg die internationale Architekturszene beherrschten. Aus dieser Periode ist neben der Volkspensionsanstalt in Helsinki (Bild 48) das Rathaus von Säynätsalo (1950-52) (Bild 45, 46) wegen seiner meisterhaften räumlichen Gliederung besonders hervorzuheben.

In den letzten Jahren hat sich das Beziehungsspiel in Aaltos Architektur zu einer Vielschichtigkeit entwickelt, die zu einer vollendeten räumlich-plastischen Durchformung seiner Bauten führte.

Aaltos eigenes Bürogebäude (Bild 47), die Maison Carré in Bazoches bei Paris (1956-58) (Bild 49), die Kulturzentren in Wolfsburg und Helsinki und der Entwurf des Opernhauses in Essen (siehe Seite 140) illustrieren den Reichtum dieser Entwicklung.

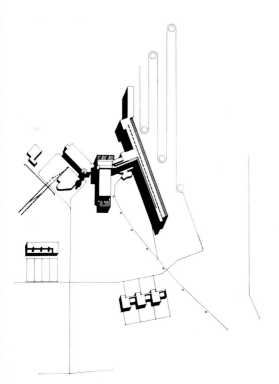

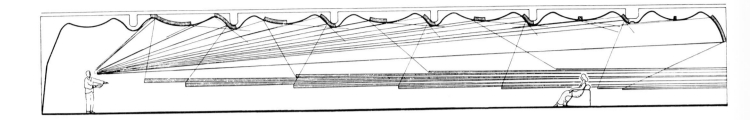

41. 42. A. Aalto. Tuberculosis sanatorium, Paimio, 1929-33.
43. A. Aalto. Library at Viipuri, 1927-35. Section through lecture hall.
44. A. Aalto. Own House, Helsinki-Munkkiniemi, 1935-36.
45, 46. A. Aalto. Town hall, Säynätsalo, 1950-52.

41, 42. A. Aalto. Tuberkulose-Sanatorium in Paimio, 1929-33.
43. A. Aalto. Bibliothek in Viipuri, 1927-35. Schnitt durch den Vortragssaal.
44. A. Aalto. Eigenes Haus in Helsinki-Munkkiniemi, 1935-36.
45, 46. A. Aalto. Rathaus von Säynätsalo, 1950-52.

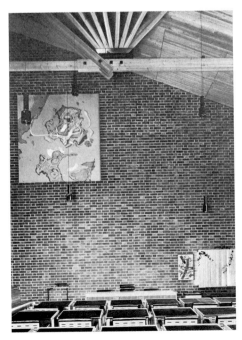

47. A. Aalto. Own office, Helsinki-Munkkiniemi, 1956.
48. A. Aalto. National Pensions Institute, Helsinki, 1952-56.
49. A. Aalto. Maison Carré, Bazoches, near Paris, 1956-58.

47. A. Aalto. Eigenes Büro in Helsinki-Munkkiniemi, 1956.
48. A. Aalto. Volkspensionsanstalt in Helsinki 1952-56.
49. A. Aalto. Maison Carré in Bazoches bei Paris, 1956-58.

24

Functionalism and the Thirties

The powerful upswing of building activity in the thirties produced a whole series of important schemes, as well as Aalto's works. One of the big projects of this time was the Olympic stadium in Helsinki (ill. 51), by Yrjö Lindegren and Toivo Jäntti, begun in 1936, but only completed in 1952. In the housing field the Olympic village by Hilding Ekelund and Martti Välikangas represented the first such development of entirely modern design. In 1938 Märta Blomstedt and Matti Lampén built near Hämeenlinna, amid the typical inland lakescape, Finland's largest tourist hotel (ill. 52). In church building, too, the clear conceptions of the international style were applied in the projects of Erkki Huttunen at Nakkila (1937) and P. E. Blomstedt at Kannonkoski (1938) (ill. 50). The increasing industrial character of the economy was reflected in a number of good buildings like the customs warehouse at Helsinki (1937) by the city architect Gunnar Taucher and the storage and office building of the state alcohol monopoly (1937-40), also in Helsinki, by Vainö Vähäkallio.

The war interrupted all building operations, and Finland, which had been preparing for the friendly rivalry of the 1940 Olympic Games, once again found her national existence threatened as a frontier state between East and West.

Funktionalismus der dreißiger Jahre

Der kräftige Aufschwung der Bautätigkeit in den dreißiger Jahren bringt neben Aaltos Werken eine ganze Reihe bedeutender Bauten hervor. Eines der großen Projekte dieser Zeit ist das 1936 begonnene, jedoch erst nach dem Krieg (1952) vollendete Olympiastadion in Helsinki (Bild 51) von Yrjö Lindegren und Toivo Jäntti. Auf dem Gebiet des Siedlungsbaues entsteht mit dem Olympischen Dorf die erste einheitlich modern geplante Anlage von Hilding Ekelund und Martti Välikangas. Märta Blomstedt und Matti Lampén bauen 1938 bei Hämeenlinna, inmitten einer typischen Binnenseelandschaft, das größte Touristenhotel Finnlands (Bild 52). Auch im Sakralbau setzen sich die klaren Vorstellungen des »internationalen Stils« durch. Bezeichnend dafür sind die Projekte von Erkki Huttunen in Nakkila (1937) und von P. E. Blomstedt in Kannonkoski (1938) (Bild 50). Vom neuerlichen Aufschwung des Wirtschaftslebens zeugen eine Reihe guter Industriebauten wie das Zollmagazin in Helsinki (1937) des Stadtarchitekten Gunnar Taucher und das Lager- und Bürogebäude des staatlichen Alkoholmonopols in Helsinki (1937-40) von Vainö Vähäkallio.

In den folgenden Jahren wurde alle Bautätigkeit durch den Krieg unterbrochen. Finnland, das sich auf den friedlichen Wettbewerb der Olympischen Spiele 1940 vorbereitet hatte, sah als Grenzland einmal mehr seine nationale Existenz in Frage gestellt.

50. P. E. Blomstedt. Church at Kannonkoski, 1938.
51. Y. Lindegren and T. Jäntti. Olympia stadium, Helsinki, 1936-52.
52. M. Blomstedt and M. Lampén. Aulanko hotel, near Hämeelinna, 1938.

50. P. E. Blomstedt. Kirche in Kannonkoski, 1938.
51. Y. Lindegren und T. Jäntti. Olympiastadion in Helsinki, 1936-52.
52. M. Blomstedt und M. Lampén. Hotel Aulanko bei Hämeenlinna, 1938.

The Post-World War II Period

The post-war years brought an intense impetus to building, with a compelling emphasis on housing, since some half a million refugees from the truncated Eastern regions had to be accommodated. In 1949 the State Building Commission (ARAVA) was therefore founded and this stimulated home construction by the offer of favourable loans. As a result quality was sacrificed to quantity, although some admirable individual schemes were carried out, among which the garden city of Tapiola is the most important.

The pressing demands of industrialization produced many new factories, but none quite reach the level of Aalto's cellulose plant at Sunila of 1936-39. Good examples of work in this field are the power stations on the Oulu river, to which the Pyhäkoski hydro-electric installation (ill. 58) erected by Aarne Ervi in 1949 belongs. While in the early years after the war a bias towards romanticism is distinguishable, from 1950 onwards there appeared a renewed interest in the functionalism of the thirties. Typical of the picturesque realisations of the former are the serpentine flats (1951) of Yrjö Lindegren (ill. 53). The House of Industry in Helsinki (ill. 55) by Viljo Revell and Keijo Petäjä (1950-53) shows the return to rationalism. Besides Aalto, Ervi and Revell (who died in 1964), the most noteworthy representatives of present-day Finnish architecture are Jorma Järvi, who carried out the swimming stadium in Helsinki in 1952, Kaija and Heikki Siren and Aulis Blomstedt. The Sirens came to the fore with "the little house" for the national theatre (ill. 56, 57). In the same year Aulis Blomstedt built his row houses at Tapiola (ill. 54).

With these examples we have reached the stage recorded by the picture section which follows. This is an attempt to examine and present a broad conspectus of present-day Finnish architecture and to establish why, with its idiosyncratic qualities, it commands such wide international acclaim.

Die Jahre nach dem zweiten Weltkrieg

Die Nachkriegszeit stand im Zeichen einer gesteigerten Bautätigkeit. Als vordringlich erwies sich vor allem der Wohnungsbau, da etwa eine halbe Million Umsiedler aus den abgetrennten Ostgebieten des Landes unterzubringen waren. So wurde 1949 die staatliche Wohnungsbaukommission ARAVA gegründet, die vor allem durch das Angebot günstiger Baudarlehen die Bautätigkeit aktivierte. Das hatte allerdings zur Folge, daß die Qualität weit hinter der Quantität zurückblieb. Es entstanden aber auch vorbildliche, geschlossene Baukomplexe und Siedlungen, unter denen die Gartenstadt Tapiola die bedeutendste ist.

Erneute Anstrengungen zur Industrialisierung ließen zahlreiche Fabriken entstehen, von denen jedoch keine ganz an Aaltos Zellulosefabrik in Sunila (1936-39) heranreicht. Ein gutes Beispiel für die Aktivität auf diesem Gebiet sind die Kraftwerke am Oulu-Fluß, zu denen auch das von Aarne Ervi 1949 errichtete Elektrizitätswerk Pyhäkoski (Bild 58) gehört.

Während in den ersten Jahren nach dem Krieg wieder ein gewisser Hang zur Romantik feststellbar ist, zeichnet sich ab 1950 eine erneute Hinwendung zum Funktionalismus der dreißiger Jahre ab. Typisch für die pittoresken Vorstellungen der ersten Nachkriegszeit ist etwa das Schlangenhaus (1951) von Yrjö Lindegren (Bild 53). Das Haus der Industrie in Helsinki (Bild 55) von Viljo Revell und Keijo Petäjä (1950-53) zeigt den Umschlag in einen neuen Rationalismus. Neben Aalto, Ervi und dem 1964 verstorbenen Revell sind die markantesten Vertreter finnischer Gegenwartsarchitektur Jorma Järvi, der 1952 das Schwimmstadion in Helsinki vollendete, das Ehepaar Siren und Aulis Blomstedt. Kaija und Heikki Siren treten 1954 mit der Kleinen Bühne des Finnischen Nationaltheaters (Bild 56, 57) hervor. Im gleichen Jahr baut Aulis Blomstedt seine Kettenhäuser in Tapiola (Bild 54).

Mit diesen Beispielen ist der Zeitabschnitt erreicht, den der folgende Bildteil dokumentiert. Er versucht das breit gestreute Spektrum der heutigen finnischen Architektur zu erfassen und darzulegen, warum die moderne finnische Baukunst mit ihren unverwechselbaren Zügen in aller Welt höchste Anerkennung findet.

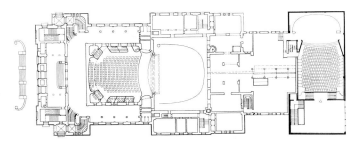

53. Y. Lindegren. Serpentine housing, Helsinki, 1951.
54. A. Blomstedt. Ketju terrace houses, Tapiola, 1954.
55. V. Revell and K. Petäjä. House of Industry, Helsinki, 1950-53.
56, 57. K. and H. Siren. "Little house" of the Finnish National Theatre, Helsinki, 1954.
58. A. Ervi. Pyhäkoski electricity plant, 1949.

53. Y. Lindegren. Schlangenhaus in Helsinki, 1951.
54. A. Blomstedt. Kettenhäuser Ketju in Tapiola, 1954.
55. V. Revell und K. Petäjä. Haus der Industrie in Helsinki, 1950-53.
56, 57. K. und H. Siren. Kleines Haus, Nationaltheater Helsinki, 1954.
58. A. Ervi. Elektrizitätswerk Pyhäkoski, 1949.

Examples · Beispiele

The house lies on a gently undulating promontory of the Gulf of Finland, sited away from the shore among pine trees and separated from adjacent plots by a meadow behind it. The building is carried on stilts to give the owners a view of the sea, while also providing covered outside space and a car port. The under-storey accommodates the entrance, sauna, and toilet and dressing rooms. More than half the floor above is occupied by a large living-room incorporating kitchen and eating and work places. A parents' room, two children's rooms, and one for guests completes the programme. The house is constructed of wood, the supporting stilts standing in steel shoes.

Das Sommerhaus liegt auf einer leicht welligen Landzunge des Finnischen Meerbusens. Es ist vom Strand in ein tannenbewachsenes Waldstück zurückgenommen. Eine dahinterliegende Wiese isoliert es gegen die Nachbargrundstücke. Das Gebäude wurde auf Stützen gestellt, um den Bewohnern einen Ausblick auf das Meer zu ermöglichen. Damit ergaben sich zugleich überdachte Außenräume und ein Einstellplatz für das Auto. Im Untergeschoß befinden sich Eingang, Sauna, Wasch- und Umkleideräume. Mehr als die Hälfte des Obergeschosses wird vom großen Wohnraum mit der innenliegenden Küche und dem Eß- und Arbeitsplatz eingenommen. Elternschlafraum, zwei Kinder- und ein Gastzimmer vervollständigen das Raumprogramm. Das Haus ist eine reine Holzkonstruktion. Die Stützen stehen in Stahlschuhen.

1. View from the South. Left, living area with window extending entire width; right, parents' room.

1. Ansicht von Süden. Links der Wohnteil mit dem über seine ganze Breite gehenden Fenster, rechts der Elternschlafraum.

2. The house is largely closed to the North, except for two small bedroom windows and a large window close to the internally-placed stairs.
3. Floor plans (ground level left). Key: 1 dressing room, 2 shower, 3 sauna, 4 open sitting space, 5 entrance hall, 6 car port, 7 chimney unit, 8 living-room, 9 work space, 10 eating space, 11 kitchen, 12 children's rooms, 13 parents' room, 14 guest room.
4. Living-room with glimpse of eating space. Storey-high windows marry the house to the landscape.

2. Nach Norden ist das Haus weitgehend geschlossen, mit Ausnahme der beiden kleinen Schlafraumfenster und des großen Fensters im Bereich der Innentreppe.
3. Grundrisse von Erdgeschoß (links) und Obergeschoß. Legende: 1 Umkleideraum, 2 Dusche, 3 Sauna, 4 Freisitzplatz, 5 Eingangshalle, 6 Autoeinstellplatz, 7 Kaminblock, 8 Wohnraum, 9 Arbeitsplatz, 10 Eßplatz, 11 Küche, 12 Kinderzimmer, 13 Elternschlafraum, 14 Gastzimmer.
4. Wohnraum mit Eßplatz. Geschoßhohe Fenster.

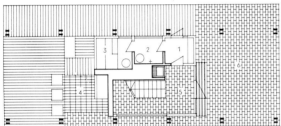

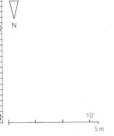

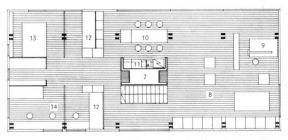

Summer house at Puumala. 1962
Architects: Marjatta and Martti Jaatinen

Sommerhaus in Puumala. 1962
Architekten: Marjatta und Martti Jaatinen

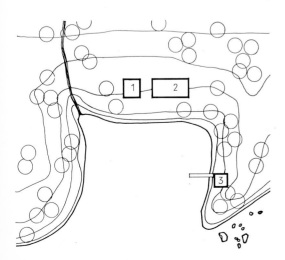

The site is flat woodland bordering a small bay. The house and garage are close together, while the sauna is placed some distance away. A holiday home, intended for the summer months only, the house is slightly raised on a concrete base and is approached from the lakeside by way of a terrace (with open fireplace) which penetrates deep into the house. The living-room with kitchen and eating space connects with this terrace. Sliding partitions separate the living area from the bedrooms, which open on to another veranda. The house has a continuous band of natural light below roof-level. All glazed walls can be screened by wood sliding doors running on steel rails. Floors, ceilings and walls are wood.

Das Grundstück ist Teil eines ebenen Waldgeländes am Finnischen Meerbusen. Das Wohngebäude und die Garage liegen dicht beieinander, während die Sauna etwas abseits angeordnet ist. Das Ferienhaus ist nur für Aufenthalte in den Sommermonaten gedacht. Es steht etwas erhöht auf einem Betonfundament. Der Zugang erfolgt von der Seeseite über eine in das Haus einbezogene Terrasse mit offenem Kamin, die auch als Freisitzplatz dient. An diese Terrasse schließen sich der Wohnraum mit Küche und der Eßplatz an. Schiebetüren trennen den Wohnbereich von den Schlafräumen, die sich auf eine zweite Terrasse öffnen. Das Haus hat ein rundum laufendes Oberlichtband. Alle Glaswände sind mit in Stahlschienen laufenden Holzschiebetüren verschließbar. Böden, Decken und Wände des Gebäudes bestehen aus Holz.

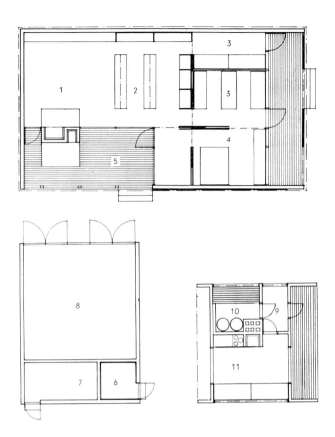

1. View from lake side. Left, garage; right, house with terrace open towards the lake.
2. Site plan: 1 garage, 2 house, 3 sauna.
3. Floor plans: house (above), garage (below) and sauna. Key: 1 living-room, 2 kitchen, 3 bedrooms, 4 parents' rooms, 5 veranda, 6 cellar, 7 storeroom, 8 double garage, 9 lobby, 10 sauna, cloaks and heating.
4. The veranda in front of the bedrooms is partly enclosed by wood panels of rough fir boards. Two steps lead straight into the open.
5. View of terrace in front of living-room with red brick open fireplace (providing heat on two sides), the only masonry construction in the whole house.
6. Sauna with bathing and boat pier.

1. Ansicht von der Seeseite. Links die Garage, rechts das Wohngebäude mit der zum Wasser offenen Terrasse.
2. Lageplan. Legende: 1 Garage, 2 Wohngebäude, 3 Sauna.
3. Grundrisse von Wohngebäude (oben), Garage (unten links) und Sauna. Legende: 1 Wohnraum, 2 Küche, 3 Schlafraum, 4 Elternschlafraum, 5 Veranda, 6 Keller, 7 Vorratsraum, 8 Doppelgarage, 9 Vorraum, 10 Sauna, 11 Umkleide- und Heizraum.
4. Die Terrasse vor den Schlafräumen ist teilweise durch Wandscheiben aus rohen Fichtenriemen geschlossen. Über zwei Stufen gelangt man direkt ins Freie.
5. Blick auf die Terrasse vor dem Wohnraum mit dem von beiden Seiten beheizbaren offenen Kamin in roten Klinkern, der das einzige gemauerte Element im ganzen Haus ist.
6. Die Sauna mit dem Bade- und Bootssteg.

Holiday house at Teisko. 1962
Architects: Mirja and Heikki Castrén

Ferienhaus in Teisko. 1962
Architekten: Mirja und Heikki Castrén

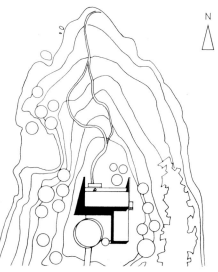

N

The house lies on a hill top in the central highlands, with a view to the South across fields and Northward of lake country. The plan is L-shaped. The pitched roof over the living area forms triangular gable surfaces, which extend beyond the façade and thus protect the terrace on the North side. The entrance is in the East gable wall. In the sitting-room, which has an open fireplace on the North side, the ceiling rises Southward to an equivalent height of two storeys. The lower (bedroom) wing comprises two single-bed and one two-bed rooms. Kitchen and eating space are provided where the two wings intersect. Warm-air heating and complete electrical and plumbing installations make the house suitable for winter use. Wood is the principal building material.

Das Haus liegt auf einer Bergkuppe im hügeligen Mittelfinnland. Die Aussicht geht im Süden über die Felder von Teisko, nach Norden blickt man auf die Seenlandschaft. Der Grundriß des Gebäudes ist L-förmig angelegt. Das Pultdach des Wohntraktes läßt drei-eckige Giebelflächen entstehen, die über die Fassade hinausgeführt sind und so die Ter-rasse auf der Nordseite schützen. Der Eingang liegt in der östlichen Giebelwand. Im Wohn-raum, an dessen Nordseite sich der offene Kamin befindet, steigt die Decke nach Süden bis zur doppelten Geschoßhöhe an. Der niedrigere Schlaftrakt besteht aus zwei Einbett- und einem Zweibettzimmer. Im Schnittpunkt der beiden Flügel liegen Küche und Eßplatz. Warm-luftheizung und volle elektrische und sanitäre Ausstattung machen das Haus auch während der Wintermonate bewohnbar. Als Baumaterial wurde vorwiegend Holz verwendet.

34

1. View into the living-room with open fireplace on North side. The exposed roof construction and exploitation of height gives the room its particular charm.
2. Site plan.
3. Windows on two sides make the room transparent. Left foreground, top of fireplace unit. Behind eating space and way through to kitchen.
4. South view of house. Right, bedroom wing.
5. Plan and section: 1 entrance, 2 living-room, 3 fireplace, 4 eating space, 5 kitchen, 6 parents' bedroom, 7 bedrooms, 8 terrace.
6. From the North the house seems to nestle into the ground.

1. Blick in den Wohnraum mit dem offenen Kamin in der Nordfassade. Die sichtbar belassene Dachkonstruktion und die voll ausgenützte Höhe geben dem Raum seinen besonderen Reiz.
2. Lageplan.
3. Durch die Öffnung nach zwei Seiten wird der Raum transparent. Links im Vordergrund die Abdeckung des Kaminblocks. Im Hintergrund der Eßplatz mit dem Durchgang zur Küche.
4. Ansicht des Hauses von Süden. Rechts der Schlaftrakt.
5. Grundriß und Schnitt. Legende: 1 Eingang, 2 Wohnraum, 3 Kamin, 4 Eßplatz, 5 Küche, 6 Elternschlafraum, 7 Schlafraum, 8 Terrasse.
6. Von Norden gesehen scheint sich das Haus in die Erde zu schmiegen.

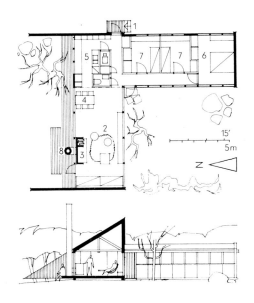

Summer house at Tvärminne near Hanko. 1965
Architect: Clas-Olof Lindqvist

Sommerhaus in Tvärminne bei Hanko. 1965
Architekt: Clas-Olof Lindqvist

1. South view, with the veranda in front of the parents'
bedroom adjoining the living-room.
2. East side.

1. Ansicht von Süden mit der Terrasse vor dem Elternschlafraum im Anschluß an den Wohnraum.
2. Ansicht von Osten.

The exposed site on the Gulf of Finland made wind protection especially necessary. Open-air spaces are therefore contrived inside the house. The South veranda is shielded from the West wind by the protecting living-room and the second open area forms an internal corridor-like patio. This patio, separating the house into two, is partly roofed over and enclosed on the outer sides by glass partitions. The result is a completely protected room, largely open to the sunlight, from which the whole living area is accessible. The sitting room faces the sea, and from the recessed fireside the view stretches above the unseen coastline far out over the water. The kitchen and dining area (which can be transferred to the patio) occupy the middle of this part of the house, the adjacent parents' bedroom being divided from the eating space by a storage wall. The other smaller wing on the North side contains the children's rooms, sauna, etc. Stanchions and cross-beams are solid wood, ceiling joists are laminated timber.

Die ungeschützte Lage des Grundstücks am Finnischen Meerbusen machte vor allem Wind-schutz erforderlich. Deshalb wurden die Freiflächen in das Haus einbezogen: die Südter-rasse ist durch den vorspringenden Wohnraum gegen die Westwinde geschützt, und die zweite Freifläche liegt als flurartiges Atrium im Hausinnern. Dieses Atrium teilt das Haus in zwei Raumgruppen. Es ist zum Teil überdacht und an den Außenseiten durch Glaswände abgeschlossen. Es entsteht so ein vollkommen geschützter aber trotzdem der Sonne weit-gehend zugänglicher Raum, über den die gesamte Wohnfläche erschlossen wird. Der Wohn-raum ist zum Meer hin orientiert. Vom vertieften Kaminplatz aus wandert der Blick, ohne die Uferlinie zu berühren, weit über die See. Küche und Eßplatz, den man in das Atrium verlegen kann, nehmen den Mittelteil dieses Hausflügels ein. Daran schließt sich der Eltern-schlafraum an, der durch eine Schrankwand vom Eßplatz getrennt ist. Im kleineren, zweiten Flügel auf der Nordseite sind die Kinderzimmer, Nebenräume und die Sauna untergebracht. Stützen und Längsgurte bestehen aus Massivholz, die Deckenunterzüge sind Schichtholz-balken.

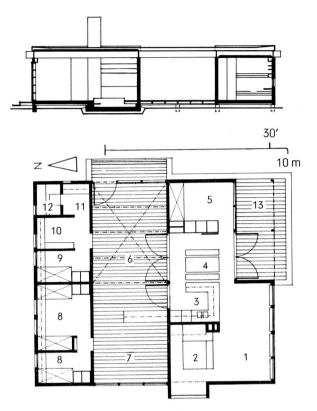

3. Section and floor plan: 1 living-room, 2 fireside sitting area, 3 kitchen, 4 eating space, 5 parents' bedroom, 6 patio, 7 covered part of patio, 8 children's room, 9 maid's room, 10 dressing-room, 11 toilet, 12 sauna, 13 veranda.

3. Schnitt und Grundriß. Legende: 1 Wohnraum, 2 Kaminsitzplatz, 3 Küche, 4 Eßplatz, 5 Elternschlafraum, 6 Atrium, 7 Überdachter Teil des Atriums, 8 Kinderzimmer, 9 Mädchenzimmer, 10 Umkleideraum, 11 Waschraum, 12 Sauna, 13 Terrasse.

4. From the patio, the sea can be seen through the dining area.
5. The large glass expanse of the living-room South front is mitigated by a system of wood shelves.
6. A service hatch links the kitchen with the dining area.

4. Vom Atrium sieht man über den Eßplatz auf das Meer.
5. Die große Glasfront des Wohnraumes geht nach Süden und wird optisch durch ein Holzregal gegliedert.
6. Blick vom Eßplatz über die Küche in den Wohnraum.

Ulfves house at Westend near Helsinki. 1963
Architect: Kristian Gullichsen

Haus Ulfves in Westend bei Helsinki. 1963
Architekt: Kristian Gullichsen

The house stands on a corner lot, which rises slightly from South to North. It is placed on the far end of the site, away from the main road passing to the South, to shield the owners from traffic noise. Trees and shrubs along the boundaries provide added protection. The architect divided the accommodation into three clearly defined parts, ranged in a U-shape about an inner court. Living-rooms and parents' bedroom face South on to the garden and open on to a terrace, extending the whole width of the house and widening in front of the dressing room and study. The children's rooms form the linking unit with the third wing facing North, which contains service and utility rooms and lies parallel to the living-room block. Wood and lime-washed brick characterize the house.

Das Haus steht auf einem Eckgrundstück, das von Süden nach Norden leicht ansteigt. Es ist in die Tiefe des Grundstückes, weit von der im Süden vorbeiführenden Hauptverkehrsstraße zurückgenommen, um den Verkehrslärm von den Bewohnern fernzuhalten. Für eine zusätzliche Abschirmung sorgen Bäume und Sträucher. Der Architekt verteilte alle Räume auf drei deutlich voneinander abgesetzte Gebäudeflügel, die U-förmig um einen Innenhof gelegt sind. Wohntrakt und Elternschlafraum sind nach Süden, zum Garten hin orientiert. Sie öffnen sich auf eine über die ganze Hausbreite reichende Terrasse, die sich im Bereich des Arbeitszimmers und der Ankleide erweitert. Die Kinderzimmer bilden das Verbindungsglied zu dem nach Norden orientierten dritten Gebäudeflügel, der die Nebenräume enthält. Holz und weißgeschlämmte Mauern bestimmen das Gesicht des Hauses.

1. View into inner court. Main entrance, left.
2. Living-room with door to terrace.
3. East aspect. The brick wall in the foreground shields the study from the road.
4. Floor plan: 1 internal court with pool, 2 entrance hall, 3 living-room, 4 study, 5 terrace, 6 dining-room, 7 kitchen, 8 linen room, 9 parents' bedroom, 10 dressing-room, 11 WC and shower, 12 children's bedrooms, 13 play area, 14 maid's room, 15 store, 16 heating, 17 WC, 18 sauna, 19 bath, 20 hobbies, 21 garage, 22 cold store.
5. View from the South. The terrace is slightly raised.

1. Blick in den Innenhof. Links der Haupteingang.
2. Der Wohnraum mit der Tür zur Terrasse.
3. Ostansicht. Die Backsteinmauer im Vordergrund schirmt das Arbeitszimmer gegen die Straße ab.
4. Grundriß. Legende: 1 Innenhof mit Wasserbecken, 2 Eingang und Diele, 3 Wohnraum, 4 Arbeitszimmer, 5 Terrasse, 6 Eßzimmer, 7 Küche, 8 Hauswirtschaftsraum, 9 Elternschlafraum, 10 Ankleide, 11 WC und Dusche, 12 Kinderzimmer, 13 Spielflur, 14 Mädchenzimmer, 15 Abstellraum, 16 Heizraum, 17 WC, 18 Sauna, 19 Bad, 20 Hobbyraum, 21 Garage, 22 Kühlraum.
5. Ansicht von Süden. Die Terrasse ist leicht angehoben.

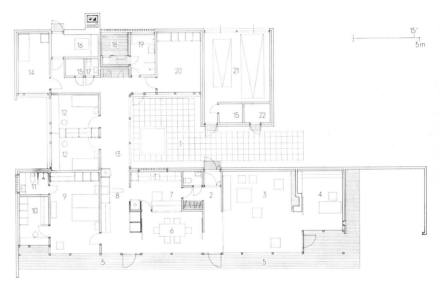

Architect's house at Helsinki-Lauttasaari. 1960
Architect: Toivo Korhonen

Architektenhaus in Helsinki-Lauttasaari. 1960
Architekt: Toivo Korhonen

Lauttasaari, part of Helsinki, lies on one of the many smaller islands bordering the Gulf of Finland, not very far from the city centre. The desire for seclusion and the comparatively small site led the architect to choose a patio-type of house almost completely closed on the outside. The two-storey building stands on gently sloping ground, fenced in by high precast concrete elements. All living-rooms are on the upper floor, with service and utility accommodation below, and also a swimming pool. The central feature of the house is the gaily planted courtyard garden, with its own small pool, on the same level as the upper floor. All rooms open through storey-high glass partitions on to this inner court, which extends South to the outside wall (glass, in this instance). This U-shaped group of rooms ranged about the courtyard receives additional daylight from a continuous ribbon window. The entrance is on the North side of the top storey.

Lauttasaari, ein Stadtteil Helsinkis, liegt auf einer der zahlreichen kleineren Inseln am Rande des Finnischen Meerbusens, nicht sehr weit vom Stadtzentrum entfernt. Der Wunsch nach Zurückgezogenheit und das verhältnismäßig kleine Grundstück ließen den Architekten den Typ des nach außen fast völlig abgeschlossenen Atriumhauses wählen. Das zweigeschossige Gebäude steht auf einem leicht abfallenden Gelände, das von hohen vorgefertigten Betonelementen umfriedet wird. Alle Wohnräume befinden sich im Obergeschoß, während im Erdgeschoß die Nebenräume und die Zimmer der Dienstboten untergebracht sind. Auch das Schwimmbecken fand hier seinen Platz. Mittelpunkt des Hauses ist das geschickt bepflanzte Atrium mit seinem kleinen Wasserbecken. Es liegt auf dem Niveau des Obergeschosses. Alle Räume öffnen sich über raumhohe Glaswände auf diesen Innenhof, der nach Süden bis an die hier in Glas aufgelöste Außenfassade reicht. Die U-förmig um das Atrium gruppierten Räume erhalten über ein außen rundumlaufendes Fensterband zusätzliches Tageslicht. Der Eingang befindet sich auf der Nordseite im Obergeschoß.

1. North view. The concrete baulk in front of the entrance ensures privacy and shelter from wind. Left, the opening in the garden-wall leads to the garage on the lower floor.
2. View into the garden on the South side with free-standing staircase leading to the cantilevered floor above.
3, 4. The house is only open on the South side. A concrete slab fence protects the garden from intrusion, but the view from the living-room is not impeded.

1. Nordansicht. Die Betonblende vor dem Eingang gibt Sicht- und Windschutz. Links in der Öffnung der Gartenmauer die Einfahrt zur Garage im Erdgeschoß.
2. Blick in den Garten auf der Südseite mit der frei stehenden Treppe, die in das auskragende Obergeschoß führt.
3, 4. Nur auf der Südseite öffnet sich das Haus nach außen. Betonplatten schützen den Garten gegen Einblick. Die Aussicht wird dagegen nicht behindert.

5. View of sitting space in living-room. Behind the cross-wall is the library. Left, one of the two doors to the courtyard.
6. Library. The large South windows have blinds in place of curtains.

5. Blick auf die Sitzgruppe im Wohnraum. Hinter der querstehenden Wandscheibe liegt der Bibliotheksbereich. Links eine der beiden Türen zum Atrium.
6. Die Sitzgruppe in der Bibliothek. Die großen Südfenster haben Jalousien statt Vorhängen.

7, 8. All rooms face the courtyard, which can be seen from anywhere inside the house.
9. Section and plans of lower (left) and upper floors. Key: 1 entrance, 2 studio, 3 dining-space, 4 living-room, 5 library, 6 second eating-space, 7 kitchen, 8 guest room, 9 children's bedrooms, 10 parents' bedroom, 11 courtyard, 12 hobby room, 13 swimming pool, 14 sauna, 15 toilet, 16 dressing-room, 17 maid's room, 18 housekeeper, 19 garage.

7, 8. Alle Räume sind zum Atrium hin orientiert, das von jedem Punkt im Innern des Hauses sichtbar ist.
9. Schnitt und Grundrisse von Untergeschoß (links) und Obergeschoß. Legende: 1 Eingang und Diele, 2 Studio, 3 Eßplatz, 4 Wohnraum, 5 Bibliothek, 6 Zweiter Eßplatz, 7 Küche, 8 Gastzimmer, 9 Kinderzimmer, 10 Elternschlafraum, 11 Atrium, 12 Hobbyraum, 13 Schwimmbecken, 14 Sauna, 15 Waschraum, 16 Umkleidezimmer, 17 Mädchenzimmer, 18 Hausmeister, 19 Garage.

30'

10 m

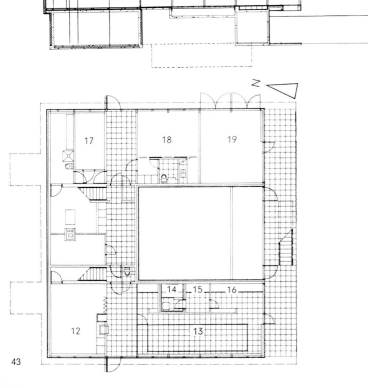
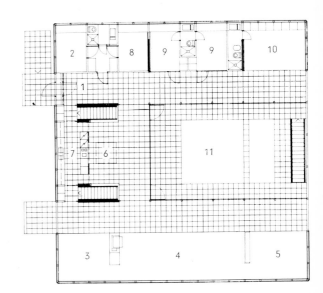

The house clings to a steep South slope. The living accommodation is raised above the uneven site by an almost completely closed understorey to the level of the adjoining ground on the North side, where the main entrance is located. The living-rooms and bedrooms open on to a balcony extending almost the entire length of the South and East fronts. The kitchen, and dependent service and maid's rooms, face North. The central feature of the house is a large room with dining space, from which an internal stairway leads to the lower storey and cellars. The narrow terrace in front of this lower storey is connected to a light well open above. The understorey concrete is left boardmarked. Above, the house is fair-faced inside and out.

Das Haus steht auf einem steil abfallenden Südhang. Das Wohngeschoß wird durch ein fast völlig geschlossenes Untergeschoß über das bewegte Gelände auf das Niveau des nach Norden anschließenden Terrains angehoben, wo sich auch der Haupteingang befindet. Die Wohn- und Schlafräume öffnen sich auf einen fast über die ganze Süd- und Ostfront geführten Balkon. Küche, Wirtschaftshof und Mädchenzimmer wenden sich nach Norden. Das Zentrum des Hauses bildet die innenliegende Diele mit dem Eßplatz, von der aus eine interne Treppe zum Untergeschoß mit den Kellerräumen führt. An die kleine Terrasse vor dem Untergeschoß schließt sich ein nach oben offener Lichthof an, in dem eine zweite Treppe die beiden Geschosse miteinander verbindet. Der Beton des Untergeschosses ist schalungsroh belassen. Das Wohngeschoß wurde außen und innen verputzt.

1. View from the South-West. The East balcony (right) connects with the garden.

1. Ansicht von Südwesten. Der Ostbalkon (rechts) schließt an das Gelände an.

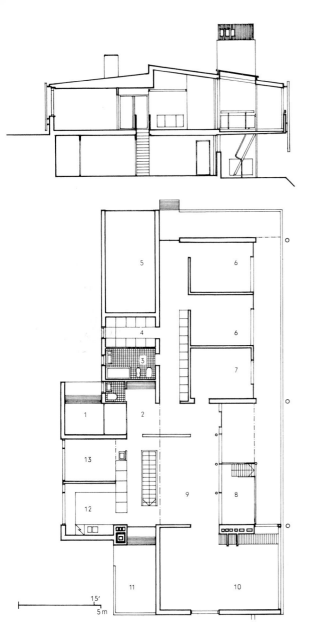

2. Section and floor plan: 1 entrance, 2 hall and cloaks, 3 bath and WC, 4 storage, 5 garage, 6 bedrooms, 7 workroom, 8 two-storey-high well, 9 large central room with dining space, 10 living room, 11 tools and garden room, 12 kitchen, 13 maid's room.
3. The balcony on the South side widens in front of the large central room, which is lit from above at this point.
4. View of the stair well, linking the two floors.
5. Rain gutters hang clear of the façade. The deep-projecting roof shields the balcony from sun and rain.

2. Schnitt und Grundriß. Legende: 1 Eingang, 2 Diele mit Garderobe, 3 Bad und WC, 4 Schrankraum, 5 Garage, 6 Schlafraum, 7 Arbeitszimmer, 8 Zweigeschossiger Lichthof, 9 Diele mit Eßplatz, 10 Wohnraum, 11 Wirtschaftshof, 12 Küche, 13 Mädchenzimmer.
3. Der Balkon der Südseite verbreitert sich vor der Diele.
4. Blick auf die Treppe im Lichthof.
5. Die Regenfallrohre hängen frei vor der Fassade. Das weit vorgezogene Dach gibt Sonnenschutz.

House and offices for Aarne Ervi at Helsinki-Kuusisaari. 1950 and 1962
Architect: Aarne Ervi

Wohnhaus und Architekturbüro Ervi in Helsinki-Kuusisaari. 1950 und 1962
Architekt: Aarne Ervi

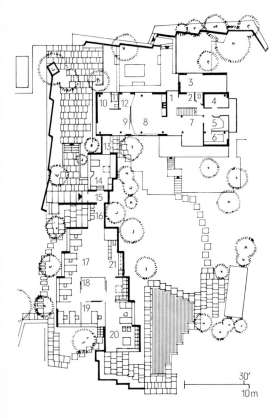

The house lies at the Eastern edge of Kuusisaari island (opposite Munkkiniemi), a part of Helsinki on the South-East perimeter of the Gulf of Finland. Garden walls and dense vegetation protect the building from the road along the West side. Cars approach the house by the North front, but the main entrance lies on the West side and is reached direct from the road by a dog-legged path. The parents' bedroom, sitting-room and dining space are on the ground floor facing the garden, which extends to the sea. The kitchen and dependent rooms, and breakfast alcove, occupy the adjoining North part of the house. Children's and guest rooms are on the floor above. In 1962 the architect added to the house (which itself remained unaltered) a single-storey office wing. This spreads out to the East, reaching down to the sea, to which it is linked by a system of walled banks and terraces. A small mooring bay brings the water right up to the South East corner of the building. Work space in the middle of the building is lit from above.

Das Haus liegt am Ostrand der Insel Kuusisaari, gegenüber Munkkiniemi, einem Stadtteil Helsinkis am Südostufer des Finnischen Meerbusens. Gartenmauern und dichte Randbepflanzung schirmen das Gebäude gegen die im Westen vorbeiführende Straße ab. Die Zufahrt führt vor die Nordfront des Wohnhauses. Der Haupteingang dagegen liegt in der Westfassade und ist über einen rechtwinklig abgeknickten Zugang direkt von der Straße erreichbar. Elternschlafraum, Wohnraum und Eßplatz sind im Erdgeschoß zusammengefaßt und wenden sich zum Garten, der bis ans Meer reicht. Hauswirtschaftsraum und Küche mit Frühstücksplatz belegen den anschließenden Nordteil des Hauses. Im Obergeschoß befinden sich Kinder- und Gastzimmer. — 1962 fügte der Architekt an das Wohngebäude, das unverändert blieb, einen eingeschossigen Bürotrakt an. Dieser verbreitert sich nach Osten und greift bis zum Meer aus, an das er mit klar gegliederten Ufermauern und Terrassen angeschlossen ist. Eine kleine Anlegebucht führt das Wasser dicht an die Südostecke des Gebäudes. Oberlichter erhellen die Arbeitsbereiche in der Gebäudemitte.

1. View from the house over the garden to the office wing.
2. Entrance-floor plan. Key: 1 entrance, 2 cloaks, 3 garage, 4 utility room, 5 breakfast alcove, 6 kitchen, 7 dining room, 8 sitting room, 9 bedroom, 10 dressing room, 11 shower bath, 12 study, 13 communicating way from office to ground floor of house, 14 secretary, 15 office entrance, 16 waiting room, 17 office, 18 records, 19 principal's room, 20 Ervi's office and conference room, 21 cloaks.
3. Conference room and Ervi's office open on to the garden.
4. Architects' office. Entrance at back.
5. View of swimming pool with sauna behind, almost completely embowered.
6. Sitting-room and bedroom (in background) are separated by a sliding door. The bedroom is two steps above the level of the sitting-room.

1. Blick vom Wohnhaus über den Garten auf den Büroflügel.
2. Grundriß des Eingangsgeschosses. Legende: 1 Eingang, 2 Garderobe, 3 Garage, 4 Hauswirtschaftsraum, 5 Frühstücksplatz, 6 Küche, 7 Eßzimmer, 8 Wohnraum, 9 Schlafraum, 10 Ankleide, 11 Dusche, 12 Arbeitsraum, 13 Verbindungsgang vom Büro zum Untergeschoß des Wohnhauses, 14 Sekretärin, 15 Büroeingang, 16 Warteraum, 17 Büro, 18 Archiv, 19 Bürochef, 20 Ervis Büro und Konferenzraum, 21 Garderobe.
3. Das Konferenz- und Chefzimmer öffnet sich zum Wohngarten. Links der Durchgang zum Büro.
4. Das Architekturbüro. Im Hintergrund der Büroeingang.
5. Blick auf das Schwimmbecken mit der dahinterliegenden, fast völlig eingewachsenen Sauna.
6. Wohn- und Schlafraum (im Hintergrund) sind durch eine Schiebetür voneinander getrennt. Der Schlafraum liegt zwei Stufen über dem Niveau des Wohnraums.

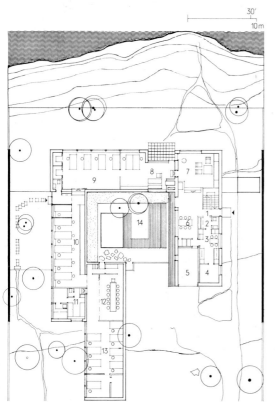

The group stands on gently falling ground on the Gulf of Finland, only a few steps away from the Korhonen house. The two-storey home was built in 1951, together with an adjoining range of offices, containing the principal's room and accommodation for four assistants. In 1956 a wing was added at right angles to the first range with space for five assistants, and a secretary's room next to the newly completed separate office entrance. The other end of this annexe is occupied by the sauna with toilet and rest room. Finally in 1960 the office built a further extension, forming a third wing parallel to the second, to accommodate eight assistants. The last stage also included a conference room (with a small kitchen attached and light from above), which can be isolated from the passage area by a folding door. The building therefore comprises four parts, forming the three sides of a courtyard opening on to the drive. The sitting-room faces the sea, the dining area looks on to the courtyard; bedrooms, bath and WC are upstairs. Wood and rendered brick are the materials used.

Der Gebäudekomplex steht auf einem schwach fallenden Gelände am Finnischen Meerbusen, nicht sehr weit von T. Korhonens Haus entfernt. Zunächst wurde im Jahre 1951 das zweigeschossige Wohnhaus mit dem ersten, anschließenden Büroteil errichtet, in dem das Chefzimmer und vier weitere Arbeitsplätze untergebracht waren. 1956 bekam das Büro einen im rechten Winkel dazu geführten Anbau mit Plätzen für fünf Mitarbeiter und einem eigenen Raum für den Sekretär neben dem neugeschaffenen, separaten Büroeingang. Den Abschluß dieses Anbaues bildet die Sauna mit Wasch- und Ruheraum. Schließlich erfuhr das Büro eine letzte, im Sommer 1960 fertiggestellte Erweiterung durch einen dritten Flügel, der parallel zum zweiten liegt und Platz für acht Mitarbeiter bietet. In dieser Bauphase entstand auch der Konferenzraum mit der anschließenden kleinen Küche, der durch Oberlicht ausgeleuchtet ist und mit einer Faltwand von der Durchgangszone abgetrennt werden kann. Es ergaben sich so vier Baukörper, die die drei Seiten eines zur Zufahrt hin offenen Innenhofes bilden. Der Wohnraum ist zum Meer hin orientiert, der Eßplatz zum Innenhof. Schlafräume, Bad und WC befinden sich im Obergeschoß. Als Baumaterial fanden Holz und verputztes Mauerwerk Verwendung.

1. The house is the dominant feature. The offices, their windowless back walls turned towards it, stand half a storey lower on the sloping ground.
2. Groundfloor plan: 1 entrance, 2 cloaks, 3 kitchen, 4 maid's room, 5 garage, 6 dining space, 7 sitting-room, 8 principal's room, 9 office, 10 office 2, 11 sauna, 12 conference room, 13 office 3, 14 courtyard with pool.
3. The entrance-forecourt of the offices is shielded from the road by a storey-high wall.
4. View into office 2, with secretary's room and office entrance behind. In background, way into office 1.
5. View into conference room with roof lights. In background, office 3.

1. Das Wohnhaus ist das dominierende Gebäude. Die Büros wenden ihm ihre fensterlose Rückseite zu. Sie sind um ein halbes Geschoß versenkt.
2. Grundriß Erdgeschoß. Legende: 1 Eingang, 2 Garderobe, 3 Küche, 4 Mädchenzimmer, 5 Garage, 6 Eßplatz, 7 Wohnraum, 8 Chefzimmer, 9 Büro 1, 10 Büro 2, 11 Sauna, 12 Konferenzraum, 13 Büro 3, 14 Innenhof mit Wasserbecken.
3. Der Eingangshof vor den Büros ist gegen die Straße mit einer geschoßhohen Mauer abgeschlossen.
4. Blick in das Büro 2 mit der Kabine für die Sekretärin und dem dahinterliegenden Büroeingang. Im Hintergrund der Aufgang zum Büro 1.
5. Blick in den Konferenzraum mit den Oberlichtern. Im Hintergrund Büro 3.

Flats at Helsinki-Munkkiniemi. 1961-62
Architect: Viljo Revell

Mehrfamilienhaus in Helsinki-Munkkiniemi. 1961-62
Architekt: Viljo Revell

1. View across the shore boulevard of the South front of the house with the walled front-garden, to which both the ground-floor flats have direct access.

1. Blick über den Strandboulevard auf die Südfront des Hauses mit dem ummauerten Vorgarten, zu dem die beiden Erdgeschoßwohnungen direkten Zugang haben.

This apartment-house stands on a corner site on the shore boulevard, for which a two-storey building was stipulated. The plan is arranged so that four dwellings have a view of the Gulf of Finland. The fifth, a two-room flat, is in an annexe on the side away from the sea and is raised half a storey above garden level. It opens on to a balcony facing East. The flats on the sea side are square in plan, with the living-room in the middle and the other rooms grouped about it. Each of these six-room homes has a South-facing balcony or veranda. The partition-walls are glazed above door-height. Thus, despite the relatively cramped living-space, the impression of a continuously extending ceiling gives a sense of roominess. The front garden is shielded from street-gazers by walls and vegetation.

Das Haus steht auf einem Eckgrundstück am Strandboulevard, für das eine zweigeschossige Bebauung vorgeschrieben war. Der Grundriß des Gebäudes ist so angelegt, daß vier Wohnungen Aussicht auf den Finnischen Meerbusen haben. Die fünfte Wohnung im Haus, ein kleines Zweizimmer-Apartment, liegt in einem Anbau auf der seeabgewandten Seite und ist um ein halbes Geschoß über das Niveau des Gartens angehoben. Diese Wohnung öffnet sich über einen Balkon nach Osten. Die Wohnungen auf der Seeseite haben einen quadratischen Grundriß. Im Mittelpunkt liegt jeweils der Wohnraum, um den sich die anderen Räume gruppieren. Zu jeder der Sechszimmerwohnungen gehört ein Südbalkon oder eine Südterrasse. Die Raumtrennwände sind über Türhöhe verglast. Bei durchlaufender Decke entsteht so trotz der relativ knapp bemessenen Wohnfläche der Eindruck von Geräumigkeit. Der Vorgarten des Hauses ist durch Mauern und Bepflanzung gegen Einblick von der Straße geschützt.

2. One of the South-front ground-floor verandas in front of the living-room. The balcony above provides sun-protection.
3. Section and floor plan: 1 living-room, 2 eating space, 3 kitchen, 4 study, 5 parents' bedroom, 6 children's bedrooms.
4. East view of the apartment-house. The entrance and communal staircase are placed at the angle of the two wings.

2. Eine der südseitigen Erdgeschoßterrassen vor dem Wohnraum. Der darüberliegende Balkon gibt Sonnen-schutz.
3. Schnitt und Grundriß. Legende: 1 Wohnraum, 2 Eß-platz, 3 Küche, 4 Arbeitsraum, 5 Elternschlafraum, 6 Kin-derzimmer.
4. Ostansicht der Apartmentwohnung. Im Winkel der beiden Gebäudeflügel liegen Eingang und gemeinsames Treppenhaus.

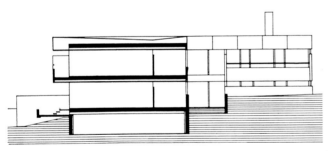

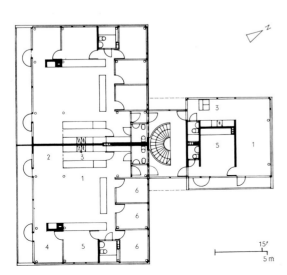

Flats at Kaivopuisto, Helsinki. 1961-62
Architect: Aarne Ervi

Mehrfamilienhaus im Kaivopuisto, Helsinki. 1961-62
Architekt: Aarne Ervi

The spring park (Kaivopuisto), thanks to its very delightful natural setting close to the city centre, is a favourite Helsinki residential area. Planning regulations therefore require that the many projected buildings shall be planned with the landscape, as the dominant element, suffering the least possible detriment. To avoid intrusive bulk, the architect separated the scheme into two masses which, owing to the sloping site, stand at different levels. Both structures have their own entrance and staircase. The flat plans, while differing for each building, are identical for all floors. Every storey comprises two dwellings which face in various directions according to their position. To the East lies a view of the harbour, to the North one looks across the shore boulevard to the market square, with the government quarter close by, or over the Senate square to Engel's imposing cathedral, while to the South stretches the sea. All flats have balconies. The sauna for all twelve families is on the ground-floor.

Die Gegend um den Brunnenpark (Kaivopuisto) gehört durch ihre landschaftlich sehr schöne Lage nahe dem Stadtzentrum zu den bevorzugtesten Wohngebieten Helsinkis. Deshalb sind auch die nach dem Bebauungsplan vorgesehenen zahlreichen Bauten so zu planen, daß die Landschaft als dominierendes Element erhalten bleibt und möglichst wenig Beeinträchtigung erfährt. Um eine allzustarke Massierung zu vermeiden, gliederte der Architekt den Komplex in zwei verschiedene Volumen, die infolge des fallenden Geländes auf unterschiedlichem Niveau stehen. Beide Baukörper haben einen eigenen Eingang und ein separates Treppenhaus. Die für jedes Haus verschiedenen Grundrisse sind für alle Geschosse gleich. Ein Geschoß enthält jeweils zwei Wohnungen, die sich ihrer Lage entsprechend nach verschiedenen Seiten öffnen. Nach Osten hat man die Aussicht zum Hafen. Nach Norden blickt man über den Strandboulevard zum Marktplatz mit dem anschließenden Regierungsviertel und über den Senatsplatz auf Engels mächtigen Dom; im Süden erstreckt sich das Meer. Alle Wohnungen haben Balkone. Die Sauna für alle zwölf Familien befindet sich im Erdgeschoß.

1. View from the East. The stepped plan was adopted to preserve the existing vegetation. Small marble slabs provide external cladding.
2. The view from the South-West clearly illustrates the contrasting levels of the two structures.
3. Plan and section. Key: section A-A, 1 entrance hall, 2 parents' bedroom, 3 children's bedrooms, 4 bath, 5 kitchen, 6 eating space, 7 living-room, 8 WC, 9 maid's room, 10 utility room.

1. Ansicht von Osten. Durch die Staffelung der Baukörper konnte zugleich Rücksicht auf die bestehende Bepflanzung genommen werden. Die Fassaden sind mit Marmorplättchen verkleidet.
2. Der Blick von Südwesten läßt deutlich die Niveauversetzung der beiden Baukörper erkennen.
3. Grundriß und Schnitt. Legende: A-A Schnittebene, 1 Eingang und Diele, 2 Elternschlafraum, 3 Kinderzimmer, 4 Bad, 5 Küche, 6 Eßplatz, 7 Wohnraum, 8 WC, 9 Mädchenzimmer, 10 Hauswirtschaftsraum.

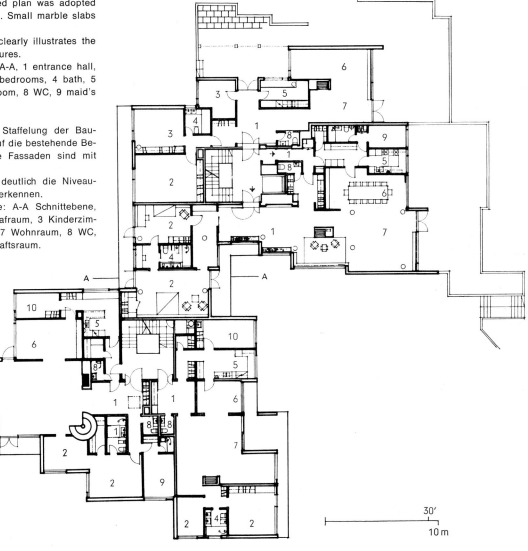

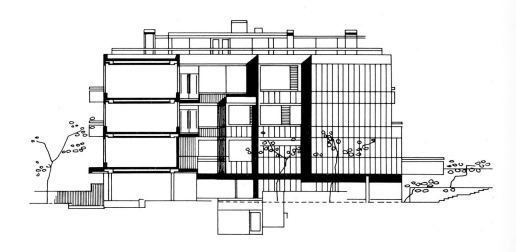

4. Recessed entrance with canopy.
5. The staircase is placed in the large, transparent, entrance hall, which opens on two sides.

4. Der zurückgesetzte Haupteingang mit dem Windfang.
5. Das Treppenhaus liegt in der großen, transparent gestalteten Eingangshalle, die sich nach zwei Seiten öffnet.

6. View into the communal sauna on the entrance floor. The materials used, wood lining for walls and ceilings, dark ceramic tiles for the washroom walls and red brick and tile floors blend well.
7. View of the sauna front room with sunk basin and terrace. Natural wood was used for seats and furniture.
8. The partly two-storeyed living-room of a top-floor flat, with roof light above the staircase to the gallery.

6. Blick in die gemeinsame Sauna im Eingangsgeschoß. Die verwendeten Materialien, Holzriemen für Wände und Decken, dunkle Keramikfliesen für die Wände des Waschraumes und der rohe Klinkerboden sind gut aufeinander abgestimmt.
7. Blick in den Vorraum zur Sauna mit Bassin und Terrasse. Für die Sitzgruppe wurde naturbelassenes Holz verwendet.
8. Der teilweise zweigeschossige Wohnraum einer Wohnung im Dachgeschoß mit Oberlicht über der Treppe zur Galerie.

Housing block, Niittykumpu, 3A, Espoo. 1964
Architect: Osmo Lappo, in collaboration with Erkki Kairamo

Wohnblock Niittykumpu 3A in Espoo. 1964
Architekt: Osmo Lappo. Mitarbeiter: Erkki Kairamo

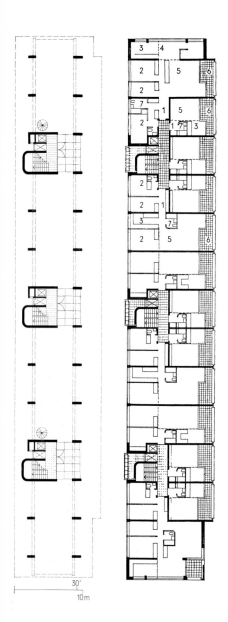

1. Plan of ground floor (left) and typical floor plan (2nd to 5th storeys): 1 entrance, 2 bedroom, 3 kitchen, 4 eating space, 5 living-room, 6 loggia, 7 bath.
2. Detailed view of South front, which is given a coherent form by the loggias and prominent party-walls.

1. Grundriß des Erdgeschosses (links) und eines Normalgeschosses (2.–5. Obergeschoß). Legende: 1 Eingang, 2 Schlafraum, 3 Küche, 4 Eßplatz, 5 Wohnraum, 6 Loggia, 7 Bad.
2. Detailansicht der Südfassade, die durch die Loggien mit den vorgezogenen Trennwänden eine klare Gliederung erhält.

Pile foundations and stilt construction for this eight-storey building without basement were dictated by ground water under the site. The ground floor was also left open for the same reason, apart from the three entrances and staircases. The narrow first floor placed between the roofs of supports accommodates saunas, store rooms and service installations. In this way the floors with flats are raised high enough to provide all tenants with an unobstructed view over the low surrounding buildings. From the second to fifth floors there are spacious loggias on the South side. The dwellings on the sixth floor are linked by spiral stairs to a roof terrace and sauna. The block, containing in all 65 homes of various sizes, is a reinforced concrete structure.

Pfahlgründung und Stützenkonstruktion des achtgeschossigen, nicht unterkellerten Gebäudes sind durch den wasserreichen Untergrund des Bauplatzes bedingt. So bleibt auch das Erdgeschoß bis auf die drei Eingänge und Treppenhäuser frei. Das schmale, zwischen den beiden Stützenreihen liegende erste Obergeschoß nimmt Saunas, Vorrats- und andere Nebenräume und die Versorgungsleitungen auf. Damit werden zugleich die Wohnetagen soweit angehoben, daß alle Bewohner ungehinderten Ausblick über die niedrige Bebauung der Umgebung haben. Im zweiten bis fünften Obergeschoß liegen geräumige Loggien auf der Südseite. Die Wohnungen des sechsten Obergeschosses sind durch Wendeltreppen mit Dachterrassen und Sauna verbunden. Der Wohnblock, der insgesamt 65 Wohnungen unterschiedlicher Größe enthält, ist eine Betonkonstruktion.

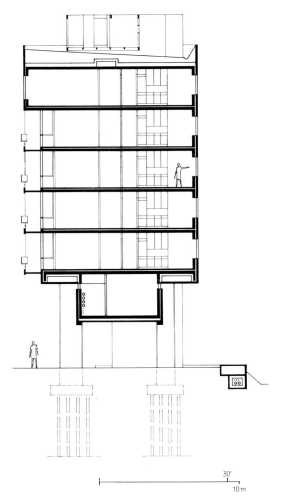

3. Section.
4. South view. The powerful substructure lifts the dwelling floors away from the ground. Ribbon windows in the end walls serve as additional sources of light to flats on the floor extremities and accentuate the horizontal character of the building. The two-storey housing (at right of picture) has the same elevational treatment as the high block.
5. View into a flat living-room.
6. The high block provides a focal point amid the low built environment.

3. Querschnitt.
4. Südostansicht. Der kräftige Unterbau hebt die Wohngeschosse von der Erde ab. Fensterbänder in den Giebelfronten dienen als zusätzliche Lichtquelle für die Eckwohnungen und betonen die horizontale Gliederung des Gebäudes. Bei den zweigeschossigen Wohnbauten, rechts im Bild, finden wir die gleiche Fassadengliederung wie am Wohnblock.
5. Blick in den Wohnraum einer Apartmentwohnung.
6. Das Hochhaus bildet innerhalb der umliegenden flachen Bebauung einen Schwerpunkt.

Sato housing scheme at Pihlajamäki near Helsinki. 1962-65
Town planning consultant: Olli Kivinen. Architect: Lauri Silvennoinen

Siedlung SATO in Pihlajamäki bei Helsinki. 1962-65
Städtebauliche Planung: Olli Kivinen. Architekt: Lauri Silvennoinen

The scheme comprises 1152 dwellings, accommodated in four-storey terraces and eight-storey point-blocks. The whole project derives from the programme of a competition, which stipulated industrialized building methods. Accordingly all the buildings were erected to a unit system of construction from standardized r. c. components manufactured on the site. The scheme represents the first instance in the Finnish housing field of method-building with r. c. elements. The flats in the tall blocks have one to three rooms. With an average area of more than 60 m² to each, they are relatively large. There are four rooms to a floor, grouped about a central staircase and lift. Store-rooms and communal sauna are at the top of the buliding.

Die Siedlung umfaßt 1152 Wohnungen, die auf viergeschossige Wohnblocks und achtgeschossige Punkthäuser verteilt sind. Das Gesamtprojekt geht auf einen Wettbewerb zurück, dessen Programm industrialisierte Baumethoden zur Bedingung machte. Dementsprechend wurden in relativ kurzer Zeit alle Bauten in Elementbauweise aus standardisierten, am Bauplatz hergestellten Betonteilen errichtet. Es ist dies der erste Fall einer Anwendung der Baumethode mit Betonelementen auf dem Gebiet des Wohnbaues in Finnland. Die Wohnungen in den Hochhäusern haben ein bis drei Zimmer. Mit durchschnittlich mehr als sechzig Quadratmetern je Wohnung sind sie relativ groß. Auf jedem Geschoß liegen vier Wohnungen, gruppiert um das zentrale Treppenhaus mit Aufzug. Die Abstellräume und die gemeinsame Sauna befinden sich im Dachaufbau.

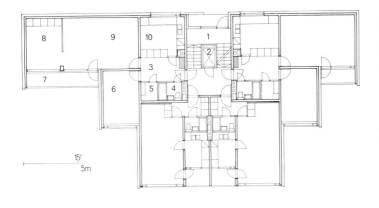

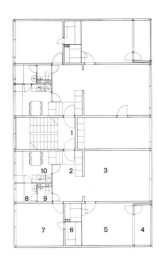

15'
5m

1. View of point blocks from South-West. The stepped plan reflects the position of the circulation core and concern for favourable lighting.
2. Point blocks from South-East. The blind surfaces of the end walls accentuate the verticality of the building in contrast to the horizontal emphasis of the South front.
3. Typical floor plan of point block. Key: 1 staircase, 2 lift, 3 hall, 4 bath and WC, 5 store-room, 6 children's room, 7 balcony, 8 parents' bedroom, 9 living-room, 10 kitchen.
4. Floor plans of four-storey blocks. Key: 1 staircase, 2 hall and sitting-room 3 living-room, 4 balcony, 5 parents' bedroom, 6 clothes closet, 7 children's room, 8 bath, 9 WC, 10 kitchen.
5. North-East view. The buildings are almost windowless at the back.
6. Aerial view from South-East. The basic layout was the work of Olli Kivinen. The existing woods were carefully and skilfully exploited in the plan.

1. Ansicht der Turmhäuser von Südwesten. Die Staffelung der Hauskörper ergibt sich durch die Lage des Verkehrskernes und berücksichtigt zugleich Überlegungen für eine günstige Belichtung.
2. Die Turmhäuser von Südosten. Die geschlossenen Giebelflächen betonen die Vertikalität des Baues.
3. Normalgeschoßgrundriß eines Turmhauses. Legende: 1 Treppenhaus, 2 Aufzug, 3 Diele, 4 Bad und WC, 5 Abstellraum, 6 Kinderzimmer, 7 Balkon, 8 Elternschlafraum, 9 Wohnraum, 10 Küche.
4. Grundrisse der viergeschossigen Wohnblocks. Legende: 1 Treppenhaus, 2 Wohndiele, 3 Wohnraum, 4 Balkon, 5 Elternschlafraum, 6 Schrankraum, 7 Kinderzimmer, 8 Bad, 9 WC, 10 Küche.
5. Nordostansicht. Die Baukörper sind auf der Rückseite fast völlig geschlossen.
6. Luftaufnahme von Südosten. Der Bebauungsplan wurde von Olli Kivinen entworfen. Der vorhandene Wald wurde weitgehend geschont und geschickt in die Planung einbezogen. Er schließt die offene Seite der Siedlung und schützt gegen Lärm und Staub der Straße.

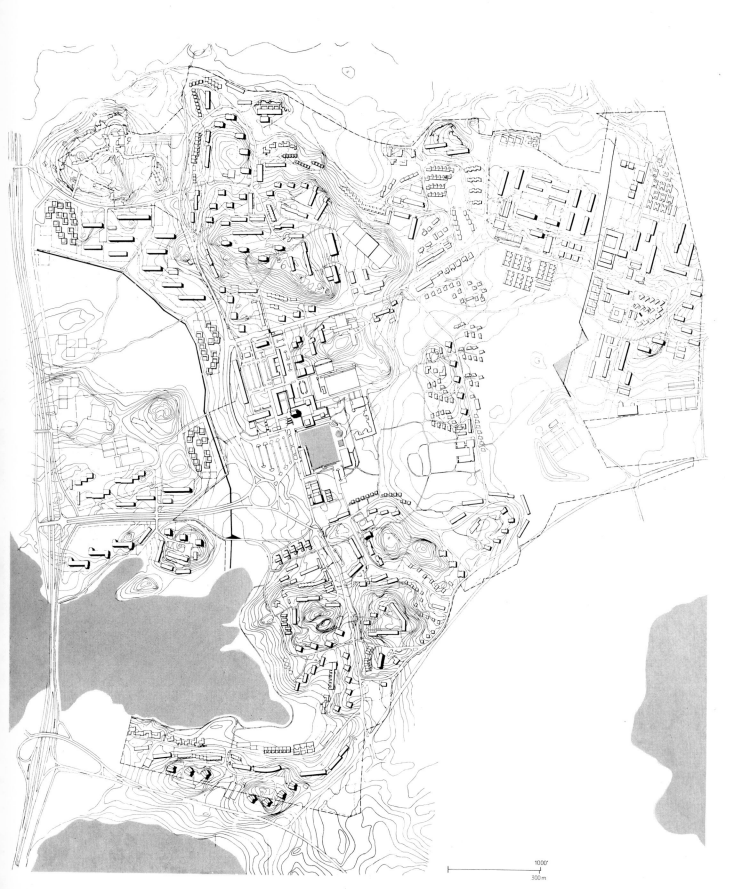

1000'
300 m

Tapiola garden city near Helsinki

Die Gartenstadt Tapiola bei Helsinki

1. General plan of the garden city.
2. Aerial view of the town from the North-East and its rugged setting.

1. Gesamtplan der Gartenstadt.
2. Luftaufnahme der Stadt von Nordosten mit Blick auf die Schärenlandschaft.

Because the steadily expanding capital is wholly unable to absorb the annual increase in inhabitants, new suburbs have had to be created, in which the aim has been to reflect the Finns' particular enthusiasm for living close to nature. In 1951, therefore, a housing association, founded by several civic organizations, purchased a 250-hectare site to the West of the city, and here the garden city of Tapiola subsequently came into being. Tapiola comprises three neighbourhood units grouped about a community centre. Each of these neighbourhoods, separated from one another by green zones, has its own schools and shopping centres. The residential areas are mixed developments of flats, terrace houses and detached one-family homes. The total population of about 16,000 is housed to a density of 65 to a hectare. The general layout is basically an adaptation of a plan by Otto-I. Meurman.

Da Helsinki schnell wächst, mußten neue Vorstädte geschaffen werden, bei deren Planung besonders das Streben des Finnen nach naturverbundenem Wohnen zu berücksichtigen war. So kaufte 1951 eine von mehreren Bürgerschaftsorganisationen gegründete Siedlungsgemeinschaft ein 250 Hektar umfassendes Gelände im Westen der Stadt, auf dem die Gartenstadt Tapiola entstand. Tapiola besteht aus drei Nachbarschaftsgebieten, die um ein gemeinsames Zentrum gruppiert sind. Jede dieser durch Grünzonen voneinander getrennten Nachbarschaften hat eigene Schulen und Einkaufszentren. In den Wohngebieten finden wir Mischbebauung mit Mehrfamilien-, Reihen- und Einfamilienhäusern. Bei einer Gesamteinwohnerzahl von rund 16000 entfallen auf den Hektar 65 Einwohner. Der Gesamtanlage liegt ein revidierter Bebauungsplan von Otto-I. Meurman zugrunde.

Landscape and garden design of the centre of Tapiola. 1960
Landscape architect: Jussi Jännes

Landscape and garden design of the centre of Tapiola. 1960
Landscape architect: Jussi Jännes

Landschafts- und Gartengestaltung des Zentrums von Tapiola. 1960
Gartenarchitekt: Jussi Jännes

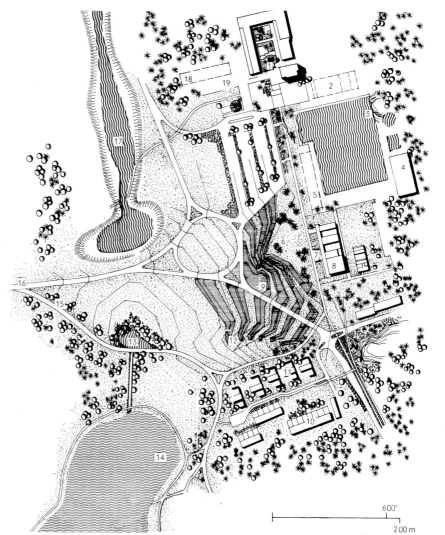

1. Site plan. Key: 1 shopping centre and administrative block, 2 theatre (planned), 3 large pool with fountains, 4 covered swimming stadium, 5 hotel (planned), 6 indigenous pine-trees, 7 main promenade, 8 church, 9 varying schemes with ornamental plants and shrubs designed for mass effects, 10 terrace houses with front gardens, 11 detached single-family homes, 12 mass-planted phlox, 13 water garden connected to a small inlet of the Gulf of Finland, 14 illuminated waterside promenade, 15 footpath, 16 road approach from Helsinki, 17 dam with pool (planned), 18 public building (planned), 19 Information centre for tourists.

1. Lageplan. Legende: 1 Einkaufszentrum und Verwaltungshochhaus, 2 Theater (geplant), 3 Großes Wasserbecken mit Fontänengruppen, 4 Hallenschwimmbad, 5 Hotel (geplant), 6 Alte Föhren, 7 Hauptpromenade, 8 Kirche, 9 Auf Massenwirkung abgestimmte wechselnde Anpflanzungen, Ziersträucher, 10 Reihenhäuser mit Vorgärten, 11 Einfamilienhäuser, 12 Phloxfelder, 13 Sumpfpflanzenanlage in Verbindung mit einer kleinen Bucht des Finnischen Meerbusens, 14 Illuminierte Strandpromenade, 15 Fußgängerweg, 16 Einfahrt aus Richtung Helsinki, 17 Damm mit Wasserbecken (geplant), 18 Öffentlicher Bau (geplant), 19 Informationszentrum für Touristen.

The landscape design of Tapiola derived from premises largely conditioned by geology and entirely different from those, for example, of the garden cities of the Continent and England. Characteristic of the Southern coastal area of Finland, and therefore of Tapiola, are outcrops of rocks and moraine, interspersed with beds of clay, which are used for grazing and crops. The firmer ground of rocky hills was chosen for building development, while the fields were landscaped and converted into parks. The centre of Tapiola, the Kontio "square", is also the town's traffic centre, where in- and out-going vehicles circulate, disperse and converge. The design of the "square" stresses the value of large, visually striking, surfaces, which can be quickly appreciated by car-users as they pass.

Für die Landschaftsgestaltung Tapiolas waren ganz andere, vor allem geologisch bedingte Voraussetzungen gegeben als beispielsweise für die Gartenstädte des Kontinents und Englands. Charakteristisch für die südlichen Küstengebiete Finnlands und damit auch für Tapiola sind Fels- und Moränenhügel, eingestreut in Lehmebenen, die als Wiesen und Ackerland genutzt werden. Für die Bebauung nahm man den festeren Boden der Felsen und Hügel, die Wiesen und Äcker verwandelte man in ausgedehnte Anlagen und Parks. Das Zentrum Tapiolas, der Kontioplatz, ist zugleich das Verkehrszentrum der Stadt, wo der ein- und ausfahrende Verkehr verteilt und zusammengeführt wird. Die Gestaltung des Platzes legt deshalb vor allem Wert auf große, optisch eindrucksvolle Flächen, die vom Autobenutzer im Vorbeifahren rasch erfaßt werden können.

2. Bird's eye view of shopping and administrative centre and central lake. In the background, Revell's high blocks.
3. Looking East from the centre office block. In foreground, larger detached homes; behind them, terrace houses by Siren.

2. Blick aus der Vogelschau auf das Einkaufs- und Verwaltungszentrum mit dem Zentrumsee. Im Hintergrund die Turmhäuser von Revell.
3. Blick vom Bürohaus des Zentrums nach Osten. Im Vordergrund größere Einfamilienhäuser, dahinter Reihenhäuser von Siren.

Administrative and shopping-centre at Tapiola. Begun in 1959
Architect: Aarne Ervi

Verwaltungs- und Geschäftszentrum von Tapiola. Im Bau seit 1959
Architekt: Aarne Ervi

In the 1955 competition for the design of Tapiola town centre, the scheme entered by Aarne Ervi was awarded first prize. The project envisaged an administrative, business and cultural centre for 50,000 people — Tapiola will ultimately have 20,000 and the surrounding area 30,000 — with the various buildings round a lake, originally used as a gravel pit. The shopping and administrative centre was completed in 1961. The two-storey buildings form a "U" about an inner court, towards which the shopfronts are turned. The tall block consists principally of offices, with a restaurant on the top floor and a cafeteria arranged under the roof superstructure. A hotel, and sports and cultural centres, are planned.

In dem 1955 ausgeschriebenen Wettbewerb für die Gestaltung des Stadtzentrums von Tapiola wurde der von Aarne Ervi eingereichte Vorschlag mit dem ersten Preis ausgezeichnet. Zu planen waren als »City« für 50 000 Menschen — Tapiola im Endausbau 20 000 und Umgebung rund 30 000 — Verwaltungs-, Geschäfts- und kulturelle Bauten, zusammen mit dem nötigen Parkraum für Kraftfahrzeuge. Ervi gruppiert die verschiedenen Bauten um einen zentralen, ursprünglich als Kiesgrube dienenden See. Das Einkaufs- und Verwaltungszentrum wurde 1961 fertiggestellt. Der zweigeschossige Gebäudekomplex ist in U-Form um einen Innenhof angelegt, dem sich die Ladenfronten zuwenden. Das Hochhaus enthält vor allem Büros. Im obersten Geschoß ist ein Restaurant und unter dem Dachaufbau eine Cafeteria untergebracht. Geplant sind ein Hotel, ein Sport- und ein Kulturzentrum.

1. The roof structure (over the office-building cafeteria), which is illuminated at night, can be seen a long way off and has become the symbol of Tapiola.

1. Der nachts beleuchtete Dachaufbau über der Cafeteria des Verwaltungsgebäudes ist weithin sichtbar und inzwischen zum Wahrzeichen Tapiolas geworden.

2. South-West view of office-building.
3. North-West view of office-building.
4. Typical floor plan of office-building. Key: 1 lobby,
2 lift, 3 office, 4 conference room.

2. Südwestansicht des Verwaltungsgebäudes.
3. Ansicht des Verwaltungsgebäudes von Nordwesten.
4. Normalgeschoßgrundriß des Verwaltungsgebäudes.
Legende: 1 Liftvorplatz mit anschließendem Empfangs-
und Wartebereich, 2 Aufzug, 3 Büro, 4 Konferenzraum.

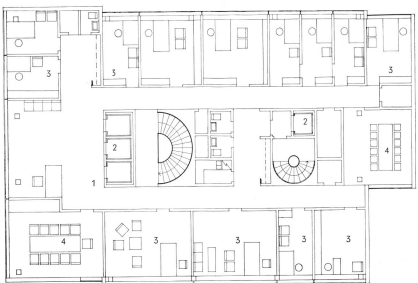

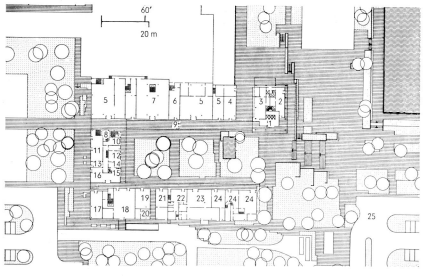

5. Ground floor plan of shopping centre and office-building. Key: 1 entrance hall of office block with lifts, 2 furniture, 3 bank, 4 stationery, 5 groceries, 6 chemist, 7 domestic stores, 8 photographer, 9 passage, 10 cosmetics, 11 clothes, 12 clocks and jewellery, 13 radios, 14 drug-store, 15 confectioner, 16 toys, 17 cleaners, 18 wines and spirits, 19 shoes, 20 children's clothes, 21 advertisement office of daily newspaper, 22 shoes, 23 post office, 24 bank, 25 parking.
6. View of shopping-centre from office-block. Pedestrian traffic passes in front of the shops. Islands of greenery and pools enliven a clearly co-ordinated scheme.
7. Section through the roof superstructure of the office-building, cafeteria and restaurant. Below, plan of cafeteria. Key: 1 terrace, 2 lift, 3 buffet, 4 kitchen, 5 cafeteria.
8. Roof terrace in front of cafeteria, with its fine view.
9. Office-block at night.

5. Erdgeschoßgrundriß des Einkaufszentrums und des Verwaltungsgebäudes. Legende: 1 Eingangshalle des Verwaltungsgebäudes mit den Aufzügen, 2 Möbel, 3 Bank, 4 Papierwaren, 5 Lebensmittel, 6 Apotheke, 7 Haushaltswaren, 8 Foto, 9 Passage, 10 Kosmetik, 11 Kleidung, 12 Uhren, Schmuck, 13 Radiogeräte, 14 Drogerie, 15 Konditorei, 16 Spielzeug, 17 Reinigung, 18 Alkohol, 19 Schuhe, 20 Kinderkleidung, 21 Anzeigenbüro einer Tageszeitung, 22 Schuhe, 23 Post, 24 Bank, 25 Parkplatz.
6. Blick vom Verwaltungsgebäude auf das Einkaufszentrum. Der Verkehr wird entlang der Ladenfronten geführt. Grüne Inseln und Wasserbecken tragen zur Belebung der klar gegliederten Anlage bei.
7. Schnitt durch den Dachaufbau des Verwaltungsgebäudes, die Cafeteria und das Restaurant. Darunter Grundriß der Cafeteria. Legende: 1 Terrasse, 2 Aufzug, 3 Buffet, 4 Küche, 5 Cafeteria.
8. Die Dachterrasse vor der Cafeteria.
9. Nachtaufnahme des Bürogebäudes.

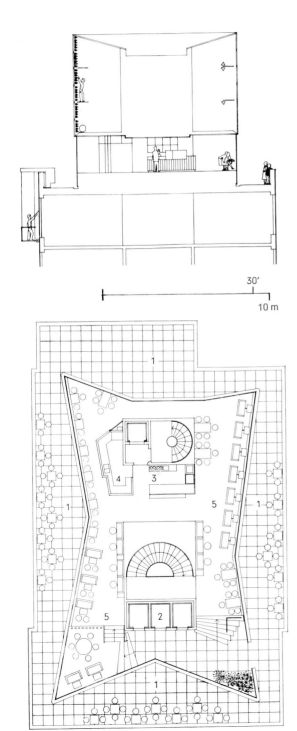

30'

10 m

Swimming stadium at Tapiola. 1964-65
Architect: Aarne Ervi

Schwimmhalle in Tapiola. 1964-65
Architekt: Aarne Ervi

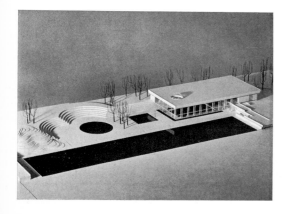

The covered swimming stadium lies on the North (long) side of the central lake, which was transformed out of a gravel pit. It will be supplemented by an open-air bath with two pools. So that both baths may be used together in summer, part of the glazed walls can be lowered on the South and West sides. In addition to the large bath with spring-board, the stadium contains a children's pool. As the hall is comparatively low, the architect has roofed over the spring-board area with a glass dome which provides the necessary height and at the same time supplies an additional light source. The building is adapted to a depression in the site, and is entered from the higher ground into a hall on the same level, from which one can overlook the stadium as from a gallery.

Die Schwimmhalle liegt an der nördlichen Längsseite des Zentrumsees, der durch die Umgestaltung einer Kiesgrube entstand. Sie soll durch ein Freibad mit zwei Becken entlang des Sees ergänzt werden. Damit man beide Badeanstalten im Sommer zusammen benutzen kann, ist ein Teil der Fensterfront der Halle auf der Süd- und Westseite versenkbar. Die Schwimmhalle enthält neben dem großen Becken mit dem Sprungturm auch ein Kinderbassin. Da sie verhältnismäßig niedrig ist, überwölbte der Architekt den Sprungturm mit einer großen Glaskuppel, die die nötige Höhe gibt und gleichzeitig als zusätzliche Lichtquelle dient. Das Gebäude ist in einen Geländesprung eingefügt. Der Zugang erfolgt von der Hangseite in die auf gleichem Niveau und damit über dem Becken liegende Eingangshalle. Unter dieser Eingangsempore befinden sich Umkleideräume.

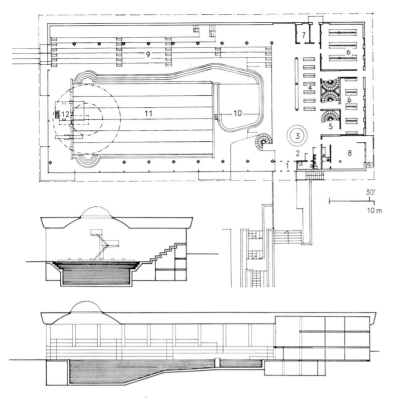

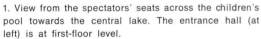

1. View from the spectators' seats across the children's pool towards the central lake. The entrance hall (at left) is at first-floor level.

2. The photo of the model shows how skilfully the architect has exploited the contours of the site in planning and designing the two baths.

3. Plan of entrance hall, cross and longitudinal sections. Key: 1 canopy, 2 entrance hall, 3 pay desk, 4 cloakroom, 5 stairs to showers, 6 changing rooms, 7 baths supervisor, 8 supervisor's flat, 9 spectators' seats, 10 children's pool, 11 swimming bath, 12 spring board.

4. Swimming stadium seen from central lake. Plants enliven the square-slabbed piazza.

5. View of main bath from entrance gallery.

6. The children's pool is separated from the main bath by a low wall. In the background the spring board with dome of light above.

1. Blick von den Zuschauerrängen über das Kinderbecken zum Zentrumsee. Die Eingangshalle (links) liegt im ersten Obergeschoß.

2. Das Modellfoto zeigt, wie geschickt der Architekt die Geländestufe in die Planung und Gestaltung der beiden Bäder einbezieht.

3. Grundriß des Eingangsgeschosses, Querschnitt und Längsschnitt. Legende: 1 Windfang, 2 Eingangshalle, 3 Kasse, 4 Garderobe, 5 Treppe zu den Duschräumen, 6 Umkleideräume, 7 Bademeister, 8 Wohnung des Bademeisters, 9 Zuschauerränge, 10 Kinderbecken, 11 Schwimmbecken, 12 Sprungturm.

4. Die Schwimmhalle vom Zentrumsee her gesehen. Der plattenbelegte Platz wird durch Pflanzenbecken aufgelockert.

5. Blick von der Eingangsgalerie in die Halle.

6. Das Kinderbecken ist vom Hauptbassin durch eine niedrige Mauer getrennt. Im Hintergrund der Sprungturm mit der darüberliegenden Lichtkuppel.

Church at Tapiola. 1964-65
Architect: Aarno Ruusuvuori

Kirche in Tapiola. 1964-65
Architekt: Aarno Ruusuvuori

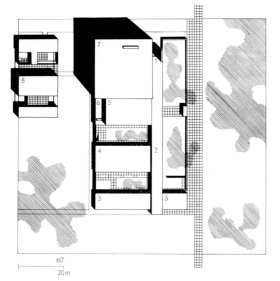

The church and related buildings adjoin the main traffic axis of the town centre. The dominant feature is the cubical church itself, which can be extended by incorporating an adjacent room. Serving principally as a parish hall, the church is lit by a large window in the West wall on the opposite side to the altar, and from this a grid-like screen of concrete elements projects into the interior to reduce the incidence of light. An internal passage, parallel to the main road, links the church to community rooms and offices, which are grouped about small inner courts. The low bell tower stands at the South front of the Church. Away from the church, on the Northern limits of the site, are three dwellings, which are partly two-storeyed and have a view of the lake. Also to the North, and adjoining the church site, there is a car park.

Kirche und Nebengebäude liegen an der Hauptverkehrsachse des Stadtzentrums. Dominierend ist der kubische Kirchensaal, der sich durch einen anschließenden Raum erweitern läßt. Er dient hauptsächlich als Gemeindesaal. Die Kirche wird nur durch das große Glasfenster in der dem Altar gegenüberliegenden Westwand belichtet. Tiefe Betonelemente auf der Innenseite, die in einem klaren Raster angeordnet sind, dämpfen den Lichteinfall. Ein interner, parallel zur Hauptstraße geführter Gang verbindet die Kirche mit den Gemeinschaftsräumen und den Büros, die sich um kleine Innenhöfe gruppieren. Der niedrige Glockenturm ist an die Südfassade der Kirche angebaut. An der Nordgrenze des Grundstücks, von der Kirche abgerückt, stehen drei Wohngebäude. Sie sind zum Teil zweigeschossig und haben Seeblick. Ebenfalls im Norden, anschließend an das Kirchengelände, befindet sich der Parkplatz.

1. South-East view. The church site is shielded from the main road (in the foreground) by a low concrete wall. At left, the main entrance. The façade is clad with precast r. c. elements strengthened by evenly spaced vertical ribs.
2. Site plan: 1 bell tower, 2 connecting passage, 3 offices, 4 community rooms, 5 parish hall, 6 vestry, 7 church, 8 dwellings.
3. View of South-West front with its large glazed wall. In foreground, the blind external wall of the offices.
4. View of the internal court in front of the parish hall (left).
5. Section and plan. Key: 1 anteroom, 2 church, 3 altar, 4 chapel, 5 organ, 6 choir gallery, 7 vestry, 8 parish hall, 9 kitchen, 10 passage, 11 office, 12 community rooms, 13 kitchen, 14 confirmation classrooms, 15 smaller parish hall, 16 office for Finnish-speaking parishioners, 17 office for Swedish-speaking parishioners, 18 inner court, 19 forecourt.

1. Südostansicht. Das Kirchengelände ist gegen die Hauptverkehrsstraße im Vordergrund durch eine niedrige Betonmauer abgeschlossen. Links der Haupteingang. Die Fassade wurde mit vorgefertigten Betonelementen verkleidet, deren vertikale Verstärkungsrippen die Wand gliedern.
2. Lageplan. Legende: 1 Glockenturm, 2 Verbindungsgang, 3 Büros, 4 Gemeinschaftsräume, 5 Gemeindesaal, 6 Sakristei, 7 Kirche, 8 Wohngebäude.
3. Blick auf die Südwestfassade mit der großen Glaswand. Im Vordergrund die geschlossene Außenwand des Büroteiles.
4. Blick in den Innenhof vor dem Gemeindesaal (links).
5. Schnitt und Grundriß. Legende: 1 Vorraum, 2 Kirche, 3 Altar, 4 Kapelle, 5 Orgel, 6 Chorempore, 7 Sakristei, 8 Gemeindesaal, 9 Küche, 10 Verbindungsgang, 11 Büro, 12 Gemeinschaftsraum, 13 Küche, 14 Konfirmandenraum, 15 Kleiner Gemeindesaal, 16 Büro für finnisch sprechende Gemeindemitglieder, 17 Büro für schwedisch sprechende Gemeindemitglieder, 18 Innenhof, 19 Vorhof.

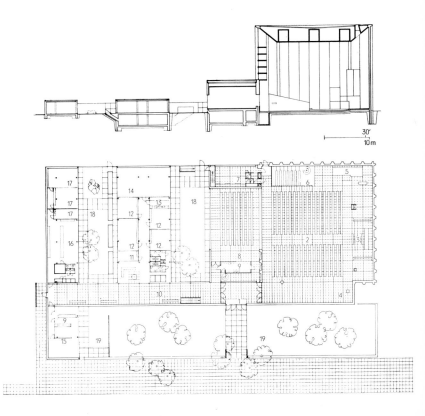

6. The incidence of light is controlled so that the brightest concentration falls on the altar area. The wall panels, which cover the opening into the adjoining parish room, can be removed.
7. View of altar and font (with light from above).

6. Das Licht wird so geführt, daß sich die Helligkeit auf den Altarbereich konzentriert. Die Wandfelder unter dem Fenster lassen sich entfernen. Sie verdecken die Öffnung zum anschließenden Gemeindesaal.
7. Blick auf Altar und Taufbecken mit Oberlicht.

The school is very close to the town centre in the middle of a small wood. A two-storey gymnasium and two single-storey classroom wings enclose at right angles to one another three sides of a spacious play area. With its curved roof composed of straight-edged hyperbolic paraboloids, the gymnasium and sports hall is the principal feature. It is separated by folding partitions from the adjoining long and narrow dining-hall, with which it can be made to form one room. The North and East classroom wings cater for general education. Science and vocational classes are held in the pavilion on the playground side. For these a hexagonal plan was chosen, answering the need in this type of teaching for a radial or lecture-room type of layout for seating and furniture.

Die Schule liegt in unmittelbarer Nähe des Zentrums, inmitten eines kleinen Wäldchens. Eine zweigeschossige Turnhalle und zwei eingeschossige Klassentrakte umschließen, rechtwinklig zueinander angeordnet, drei Seiten des geräumigen Schulhofes. Mit ihrem geschwungenen Dach, das sich aus gradlinig begrenzten hyperbolischen Paraboloiden zusammensetzt, ist die Turn- und Sporthalle das dominierende Gebäude. Sie ist von dem anschließenden, langgestreckten Speisesaal durch Faltwände getrennt und läßt sich mit diesem zu einem Raum vereinen. Nord- und Ostflügel der Anlage enthalten die Normalklassen. In den Pavillons auf der Hofseite sind die Fachklassen untergebracht. Für diese Pavillons wurde eine hexagonale Grundrißform gewählt, die der gewünschten radialen oder auditorienartigen Sitz- und Möbelanordnung in den Fachklassen entgegenkam.

1. View from the East across the play area to the gymnasium. The folds of the gymnasium roof reflect the roof pattern of the pavilions, and reduce the effect of the building's size.

1. Blick von Osten über den Pausenhof auf die Turnhalle. Die Faltung des Turnhallendaches nimmt das Motiv der Pavillondächer auf und reduziert optisch die Dimensionen des Gebäudes.

2. View of the gymnasium from West. The low building in front houses changing rooms and showers. The main entrance to the school is at the extreme left of the picture.

3. View into the school kitchen in one of the hexagonal pavilions which adjoins the dining-hall.

4. The general classrooms have lighting from two sides: by a glazed light band on the playground side and by windows on to the countryside.

2. Ansicht der Turnhalle von Westen. In dem vorgelagerten niedrigen Anbau befinden sich die Umkleide- und Duschräume. Am linken Bildrand der Haupteingang zur Schule.

3. Blick in die Schulküche in einem der sechseckigen Pavillons, der sich an den Speisesaal anschließt.

4. Die Normalklassen haben eine zweiseitige Belichtung: zum Schulhof ein hochliegendes Oberlichtband und zur Landschaft Fenster.

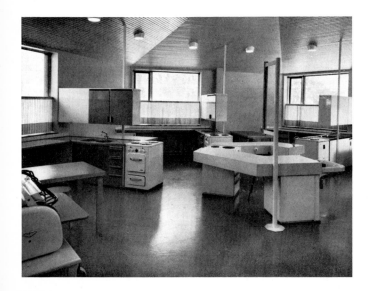

5. Floor plans (ground, below). Key: 1 general class-room, 2 art room, 3 library, 4 nature study, 5 laboratory, 6 equipment and teaching aids, 7 office, 8 principal, 9 work-room, 10 smoking-room, 11 kitchenette, 12 staff room, 13 hall, 14 geography classes, 15 natural history classes, 16 pupil's common room, 17 housekeeper's flat, 18 caretaker's flat, 19 entrance hall, 20 changing room, 21 and 22 showers, 23 stage, 24 assembly hall, 25 dining hall, 26 apparatus store, 27 kitchen, 28 school kitchen, 29 wash room, 30 drying room, 31 club room, 32 bowling rink, 33 spectators, 34 air raid shelter, 35 metalwork classes, 36 service room.
6. View of playground which is open on the South side.

5. Grundrisse von Ober- und Erdgeschoß (unten). Legende: 1 Normalklasse, 2 Zeichensaal, 3 Bücherei, 4 Naturkundeklasse, 5 Laboratorium, 6 Geräte und Lehrmittel, 7 Büro, 8 Rektor, 9 Werkraum, 10 Rauchzimmer, 11 Kochnische, 12 Lehrerzimmer, 13 Halle, 14 Geographieklasse, 15 Naturgeschichtsklasse, 16 Gemeinschaftsraum für Schüler, 17 Wohnung der Raumpflegerin, 18 Hausmeister-Wohnung, 19 Eingangshalle, 20 Umkleideraum, 21 und 22 Duschräume, 23 Bühne, 24 Fest- und Turnsaal, 25 Speisesaal, 26 Apparatelager, 27 Küche, 28 Schulküche, 29 Waschraum, 30 Trockenraum, 31 Klubraum, 32 Kegelbahn, 33 Zuschauer, 34 Luftschutzraum, 35 Metallarbeitsklasse, 36 Putzküche.
6. Blick in den Schulhof, der sich nach Süden öffnet.

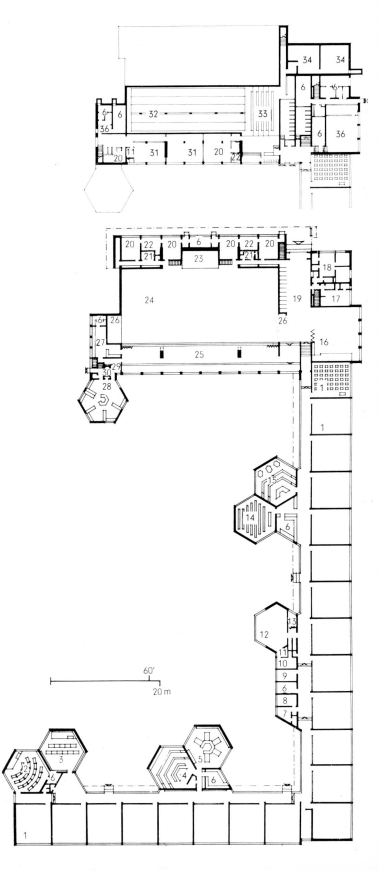

Tower blocks of flats at Tapiola. 1959-60
Architect: Viljo Revell

Turmhäuser in Tapiola. 1959-60
Architekt: Viljo Revell

1. General view from East. The path seen in the foreground provides a direct link with the town centre.
2. View from North-East.

1. Gesamtansicht von Osten. Der im Vordergrund sichtbare Weg stellt die direkte Verbindung zum Zentrum her.
2. Ansicht von Nordosten.

These four blocks, standing on high rocky ground, are conspicuous features of the garden city and are connected to the town centre by a paved footpath. On the East side a craggy tract of woodland extends up to the buildings, sited with their long axis North to South. To the West an elongated two-storey structure beyond the access road forms a link with adjacent development and defines the residential group as an architectural unit. Concave end-walls and a rhomboid plan give the effect of reducing mass. Undulating roofs make original coverings for the top-storeys. One of the latter houses the communal sauna for the whole scheme. The others comprise rooms for tenants' common use. The ground floor is recessed in every case and contains storage and service rooms. All dwellings are grouped around a central circulation core (of staircase and two lifts). The blocks are reinforced concrete structures. The continuous spandrels and blind end-walls are clad with Eternit panels.

Diese vier auf einem Felshügel stehenden Turmhäuser akzentuieren die Silhouette der Gartenstadt. Sie sind durch eine Fußgängerstraße mit dem Zentrum verbunden. Im Osten schließt sich an die mit ihrer Längsachse nordsüd-gerichteten Gebäude ein felsiges Waldgelände an. Im Westen bildet ein langgestreckter, zweigeschossiger Baukörper jenseits der Zufahrtstraße das Bindeglied zur benachbarten Bebauung und den Abschluß des Wohnquartiers als architektonische Einheit. Konkave Giebelscheiben und die rhombische Grundrißfigur der Häuser reduzieren optisch die Masse der Baukörper. Geschwungene Dächer geben einen originellen Abschluß. In einem dieser Dachgeschosse ist die Gemeinschaftssauna für das ganze Wohnquartier untergebracht, in den anderen befinden sich Räume zur allgemeinen Nutzung durch die Hausbewohner. Das Erdgeschoß ist in allen Fällen zurückgesetzt und enthält Abstell- und Vorratsräume. Alle Wohnungen gruppieren sich um den zentralen Verkehrskern aus Treppenhaus und zwei Aufzügen. Die Gebäude sind Stahlbetonkonstruktionen. Die Brüstungsbänder und Giebelfronten wurden mit Eternitplatten verkleidet.

3. Plans of ground floor (below) and typical floor of flats. Key: 1 cellar, 2 storage, 3 entrance hall, 4 laundry and drying room, 5 bicycles, 6 porter's rooms and cleaning equipment, 7 children's bedroom, 8 parents' bedroom, 9 living-room with eating space, 10 loggia, 11 kitchen, 12 breakfast space.
4. View from the road side. The continuous spandrels and bends in the façades counteract any impression of heaviness.
5. The four blocks are so placed that all tenants have an unobstructed view.

3. Grundrisse von Erdgeschoß (unten) und einem Normal-Wohngeschoß. Legende: 1 Keller, 2 Abstellraum, 3 Eingangsflur, 4 Waschküche, Trockenraum, 5 Fahrräder, 6 Putzgeräte, Hausmeister, 7 Kinderzimmer, 8 Elternschlafraum, 9 Wohnraum mit Eßplatz, 10 Loggia, 11 Küche, 12 Frühstücksplatz.
4. Blick auf die Straßenfront. Die durchgehenden Brüstungsbänder und die geknickten Fassaden reduzieren die Schwere der Baukörper.
5. Die vier Häuser sind gegeneinander versetzt. Alle Bewohner haben freie Aussicht.

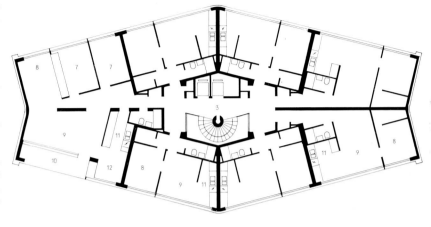

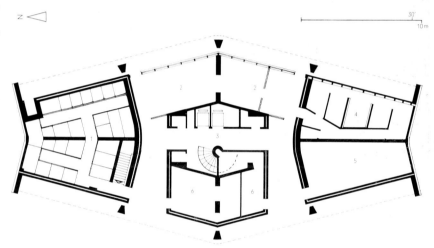

Terrace houses, Leppäkertuntie 4, Tapiola. 1964
Architect: Aulis Blomstedt

Reihenhäuser an der Leppäkertuntie 4 in Tapiola. 1964
Architekt: Aulis Blomstedt

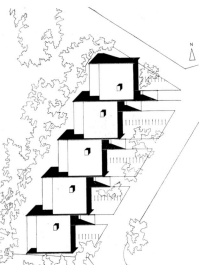

The five terrace houses are built into a slope, so that from the entrance side on the East they appear single-storeyed, and on the West (open-country side) two-storeyed. Access to the lower-floor garages is by means of a ramp. Next to the garage is a hobby (utility) room, which opens across a veranda on to the garden. A straight flight of steps links the two floors. A balcony, its privacy preserved by projecting side-walls, extends in front of the ground (upper) floor living-room. The kitchen is reached through the entrance hall, from which a passage branches to the bedrooms. The principal materials are concrete for the lower floor, lime-washed brick for the party-walls, and Eternit panels for external cladding.

Die fünf Einfamilienreihenhäuser sind so in den Hang hineingebaut, daß sie von der Eingangsseite im Osten eingeschossig und im Westen zur Landschaft hin zweigeschossig in Erscheinung treten. Der Zugang zu den Garagen im Untergeschoß erfolgt über eine Rampe. An die Garage schließt sich ein Hobbyraum an, der sich über eine Terrasse zum Garten hin öffnet. Eine gradläufige Treppe stellt die Verbindung von der Diele des Untergeschosses zum Erdgeschoß her. Dem Wohn-Eßraum des Erdgeschosses ist ein durch seitliche Mauerscheiben gegen Einblick geschützter Balkon vorgelagert. Der Zugang zur Küche erfolgt über die Eingangsdiele. Die Schlafräume werden über einen Stichflur erschlossen. Die vorherrschenden Materialien sind Beton für das Untergeschoß, weißgeschlämmte Backsteine für die Haustrennwände und Eternitplatten als Fassadenverkleidung.

1. General view from West. The wide balconies are carried on steel stanchions, to which the balcony rails are also fixed.
2. Site plan.
3. View of one of the house entrances, which are shielded by canopies.
4. Section and floor plans, lower storey (left). Plan and section are on a module of 2,25 m. Key: 1 dressing-room, 2 wardrobe space, 3 storage, 4 hall, 5 hobby room, 6 sauna, 7 garage, 8 bath, 9 entrance, 10 kitchen and breakfast space, 11 dining area, 12 living-room, 13 bedrooms.
5. View of East front of terrace houses from service road. Note the sunk garages.

1. Gesamtansicht von Westen. Die breiten Balkone werden von Stahlstützen getragen, an denen auch die Brüstungen befestigt sind.
2. Lageplan.
3. Blick auf einen der Hauseingänge, die durch ein Vordach geschützt sind.
4. Längsschnitt und Grundrisse von Untergeschoß (links) und Erdgeschoß. Grundriß und Aufriß folgen einem 2,25-m-Raster. Legende: 1 Ankleide, 2 Schrankraum, 3 Vorratsraum, 4 Diele, 5 Hobbyraum, 6 Sauna, 7 Garage, 8 Bad, 9 Eingang, 10 Küche mit Frühstücksplatz, 11 Eßplatz, 12 Wohnraum, 13 Schlafraum.
5. Blick von der Zufahrtsstraße auf die Ostfront der Reihenhäuser mit den angelegten Garageneinfahrten.

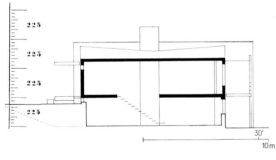

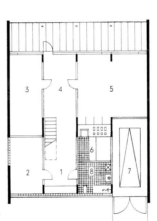

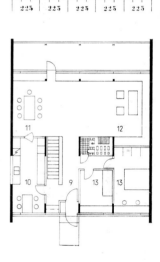

Patio houses at Tapiola. 1963-65
Architect: Pentti Ahola

Atriumhäuser in Tapiola. 1963-65
Architekt: Pentti Ahola

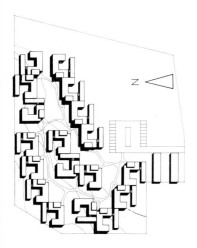

The scheme on gently undulating ground completes a residential area in the South-Western part of Tapiola, largely comprising multi-storey buildings. Four staggered rows of three and four patio houses form an uneven ring about a fifth row of three. Pedestrians only are allowed in this inner zone, but there is a communal garage and a parking place at the end of the service road. All rooms open on to the courtyard, which is laid out as a garden. The main entrance is set back. The open end of the courtyard can be shielded from the outside world by adjustable screens. The living and sleeping areas are separated by an intermediate section, containing dining space, kitchen and bath. A fourth section accommodates guest room, sauna, and utility and storage rooms.

Die Siedlung auf dem leicht bewegten Gelände bildet den Abschluß eines Wohngebietes im südwestlichen Teil Tapiolas, das vorwiegend aus mehrgeschossigen Gebäuden besteht. Vier gestaffelte Hauszeilen aus drei und vier Atriumhäusern gruppieren sich ringförmig um eine in der Mitte liegende fünfte Gruppe aus drei Gebäuden. Die Wege im Innenbereich sind reine Fußgängerwege. Eine Sammelgarage und ein Parkplatz befinden sich am Ende der Zufahrtsstraße. — Alle Räume des Hauses öffnen sich auf das Atrium, das als Wohngarten angelegt ist. Der Zugang erfolgt von außen über den zurückgenommenen Eingang. Die Öffnung des Atriums zum Außenbereich ist durch Sichtblenden abgeschirmt. Wohn- und Schlafbereich sind durch einen Zwischentrakt mit Eßzimmer, Küche und Bad getrennt. Ein vierter, separater Haustrakt nimmt Gästezimmer, Sauna, Hobby- und Abstellraum auf.

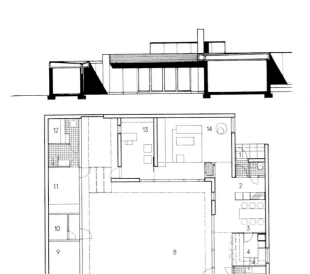

1. The houses present an almost windowless exterior to their surroundings. Existing trees were largely preserved.
2. Site plan.
3. Section and plan. Key: 1 entrance, 2 cloaks, 3 dining space, 4 kitchen, 5 bath, 6 children's room, 7 parents' room, 8 courtyard, 9 utility (hobby) room, 10 storage, 11 guest room, 12 sauna, 13 study, 14 living-room.
4. View of scheme from South-East.
5. View from the living-room towards the courtyard and sleeping wing.
6. Kitchen with breakfast and (left) dining areas.

1. Die Häuser wenden ihrer Umgebung eine fast fensterlose Außenfront zu. Es ist gelungen, den Baumbestand weitgehend zu erhalten.
2. Lageplan.
3. Schnitt und Grundriß. Legende: 1 Eingang, 2 Garderobe, 3 Eßplatz, 4 Küche, 5 Bad, 6 Kinderzimmer, 7 Elternschlafraum, 8 Atrium, 9 Hobbyraum, 10 Abstellraum, 11 Gästezimmer, 12 Sauna, 13 Arbeitszimmer, 14 Wohnraum.
4. Ansicht der Siedlung von Südosten.
5. Blick aus dem Wohnraum auf Atrium und den Schlafraumflügel.
6. Küche mit Frühstücksplatz und Eßplatz (links).

1. General view of the four houses from the street.
2. Site plan. Houses 1 and 3 are by Ervi, 2 Koskelo house, 4 Tavio house.

1. Gesamtansicht der vier Häuser von der Straße.
2. Lageplan. Legende: 1 und 3 Haus Ervi, 2 Haus Koskelo, 4 Haus Tavio.

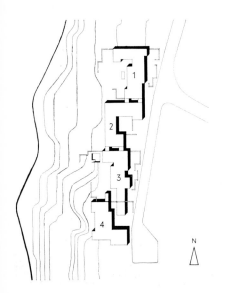

These four terrace houses near the sea are so alike in external form and materials that the particular contributions of individual architects are indistinguishable. Except for the architect Tavio's house, which has offices attached, all are purely residential. They are shielded from intrusive eyes on the road side by walls, behind which is a forecourt leading to the entrance hall, dining space, kitchen and other smaller rooms. Garages are placed at the extremities of the site. Living and sleeping areas face the shore side, which is also where, in each case, the sauna is found. The office wing of Tavio's house has its own separate entrance and a woodland setting. In contrast to the identical external design of the houses, with their yellow brick walls and painted aluminium-panel roofs, they have marked individuality as homes.

Diese vier Reihenhäuser in der Nähe des Meeres sind nach der äußeren Gestalt und im Materialcharakter so einheitlich, daß für den Betrachter die »Handschrift« der einzelnen Architekten nicht mehr erkennbar ist. Mit Ausnahme vom Haus des Architekten Tavio, dem ein Büroteil angeschlossen ist, handelt es sich um Wohnhäuser. Sie sind zur Straße durch Mauern gegen Einblick abgeschirmt. Hinter diesen Mauern liegt ein Vorhof, an den sich Eingangsdiele, Eßplatz, Küche und andere kleinere Räume anschließen. Die Garagen stehen an der Grundstücksgrenze. Wohn- und Schlafteil der Häuser öffnen sich zur Strandseite, auf der sich auch die Saunas der einzelnen Wohnungen befinden. Der Büroteil im Haus des Architekten Tavio hat einen separaten Eingang und liegt einem Waldstück gegenüber. Im Gegensatz zur einheitlichen äußeren Gestaltung der Gebäude mit ihren gelben Ziegelmauern und den Dächern aus emaillierten Aluminiumplatten, haben die verschiedenen Wohnungen einen individuellen Charakter.

3. House 1. View from garden side with swimming-pool in front of living-room.
4. Living-room of Ervi's house. Storey-height windows and similar treatment of internal and external walls achieve an impression of uninterrupted space.
5. Plan. Key: 1 entrance and hall, 2 living-room, 3 parents' bedroom, 4 household storeroom, 5 sauna, 6 garden tools, 7 garage, 8 maid's room, 9 kitchen, 10 dining space, 11 grandfather's bedroom, 12 library, 13 bedroom, 14 children's bedrooms, 15 swimming-pool.
6. View of dining space.

3. Haus 1, Ansicht von der Gartenseite mit dem vor dem Wohnraum liegenden Schwimmbecken.
4. Wohnraum im Haus des Architekten Ervi. Wandhohe Scheiben und die gleiche Behandlung von Innen- und Außenmauern schaffen ein nahtloses Raumkontinuum.
5. Grundriß. Legende: 1 Eingang und Diele, 2 Wohnraum, 3 Elternschlafraum, 4 Hauswirtschaftsraum, 5 Sauna, 6 Gartengeräte, 7 Garage, 8 Mädchenzimmer, 9 Küche, 10 Eßplatz, 11 Zimmer des Großvaters, 12 Bibliothek, 13 Schlafraum, 14 Kinderzimmer, 15 Schwimmbecken.
6. Blick auf den Eßplatz.

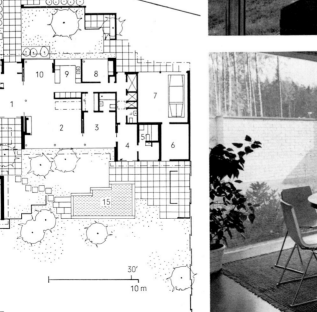

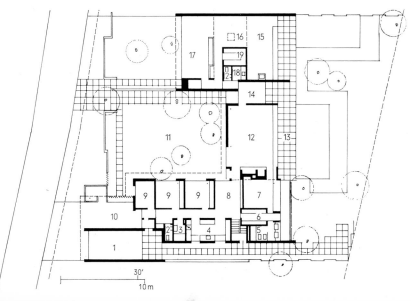

1. Koskelo house. View from garden of living-room side.
2. Open fireplace in living-room.
3. Living-room.
4. Plan. Key: 1 garage, 2 WC, 3 washroom, 4 kitchen, 5 bath, 6 cupboard space, 7 parents' bedroom, 8 dining space, 9 bedroom, 10 car port, 11 garden court, 12 living-room, 13 veranda, 14 main entrance, 15 drawing-office, 16 conference room, 17 studio, 18 dark room, 19 workshop.
5. The garden in front of the living-room extends down to the sea and is largely left in its natural state.

1. Haus des Architekten Koskelo. Blick vom Garten auf die Wohnraumfront.
2. Der offene Kamin im Wohnraum.
3. Blick in den Wohnraum.
4. Grundriß. Legende: 1 Garage, 2 WC, 3 Waschraum, 4 Küche, 5 Bad, 6 Schrankraum, 7 Elternschlafraum, 8 Eßplatz, 9 Schlafraum, 10 Autoeinstellplatz, 11 Gartenhof, 12 Wohnraum, 13 Terrasse, 14 Haupteingang, 15 Atelier, 16 Konferenzraum, 17 Studio, 18 Dunkelkammer, 19 Werkstatt.
5. Vor dem Wohnraum breitet sich ein Garten aus, der bis zum Meer reicht und weitgehend in seinem natürlichen Zustand belassen wurde.

1. Tavio house. View from the road. In the middle, the office wing with its continuous ribbon of top-lighting. Right, the courtyard in front of the living-rooms; next to it, the garage.
2. The veranda in front of the dining area, projecting across a socle, is lower than the living-room floor.

1. Haus des Architekten Tavio. Ansicht von der Straße. In der Mitte der Büroflügel mit dem Oberlichtband. Rechts der Hof vor dem Wohnteil, im Anschluß daran die Garage.
2. Die Terrasse vor dem Eßplatz ist über einen Sockel frei ausgekragt. Sie liegt tiefer als das Wohngeschoß.

3. View of the house from sea side.
4. View of entrance courtyard from living-room. In back-ground, the office-wing.
5. Living-room with glimpse of dining-room beyond.
6. Section and plan of ground floor (left) and basement. Key: 1 garage, 2 kitchen yard, 3 kitchen, 4 study, 5 dining-room, 6 living-room, 7 bedroom, 8 drawing office, 9 cupboard space, 10 storeroom, 11 television room, 12 sauna.

3. Ansicht des Hauses von der Seeseite.
4. Blick vom Wohnraum zum Innenhof auf der Eingangs-seite. Im Hintergrund der Büroflügel.
5. Wohnraum mit Durchblick zum Eßzimmer.
6. Schnitt und Grundrisse von Erdgeschoß (links) und Untergeschoß. Legende: 1 Garage, 2 Küchenhof, 3 Küche, 4 Arbeitszimmer, 5 Eßplatz, 6 Wohnraum, 7 Schlafraum, 8 Atelier, 9 Schrankraum, 10 Vorratsraum, 11 Fernseh-zimmer, 12 Sauna.

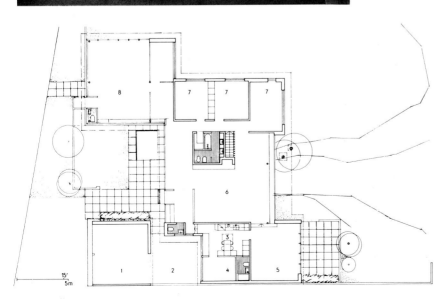

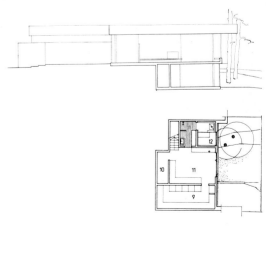

15'
5m

Terrace houses, Otsonpesä, Tapiola. 1959
Architects: Kaija and Heikki Siren

Reihenhäuser Otsonpesä in Tapiola. 1959
Architekten: Kaija und Heikki Siren

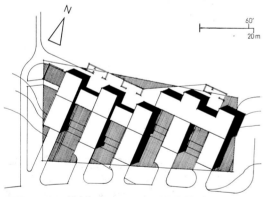

The five terrace houses stand on a South slope, and represent the concluding stage of a residential scheme consisting mostly of high-rise development. The entrance storey contains the garage and utility room, as well as other accommodation. A service yard adjoins the main storey which is at ground level on the hill side. All this floor is arranged as a single continuous space of sitting, eating, working and sleeping areas, although the latter can be isolated by movable partitions. Next to the kitchen is a small maid's room, which may also be used as a pantry, and between the kitchen and dining area cupboard space is provided. The sauna is on the roof storey, with wash and shower room, and a large rest room connected with the roof terrace over the main floor. The load-bearing walls of the house are built from calcareous sandstone and lime-washed. Balcony and roof-edge parapets have timber cladding.

Die fünf Reihenhäuser stehen auf einem Südhang. Sie bilden den Abschluß eines vorwiegend aus mehrgeschossigen Häusern bestehenden Wohngebietes. Das Eingangsgeschoß enthält unter anderem jeweils die Garage und einen Hobbyraum. An das darüberliegende Wohngeschoß schließt sich ebenerdig, zur Bergseite hin, ein Wirtschaftshof an. Die ganze Wohnfläche ist als ein einziger, offener Raum angelegt: Wohn-, Eß-, Arbeits- und Schlafbereich gehen ineinander über. Man hat jedoch die Möglichkeit, die Schlafräume mittels Schiebewänden abzutrennen. Neben der Küche liegt ein kleines Mädchenzimmer, das auch als Anrichte benützt werden kann. Daran schließt sich ein Schrankraum an. Im Dachgeschoß befindet sich die Sauna mit Wasch- und Duschraum und ein großer Ruheraum, der mit der Dachterrasse über dem Wohnteil in Verbindung steht. Die tragenden Wände der Häuser sind aus Kalksandsteinen gemauert und weiß geschlämmt. Brüstungen und Dachkanten haben eine Holzverkleidung.

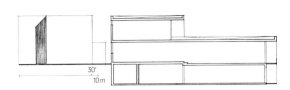

1. General view of terrace houses from South. The steps lead to a terrace, set in the angle between the living-room area and the bedroom wing.
2. Site plan.
3. Looking into the service yard on the North side. Left, storage sheds; right, the back entrance.
4. Section.
5. Plans of entrance floor (below), main floor (middle) and roof storey. Key: 1 entrance, 2 garage, 3 utility room, 4 laundry, 5 study, 6 living-room, 7 dining space, 8 household storeroom, 9 kitchen, 10 maid's room, 11 bedrooms, 12 storage sheds, 13 sauna, 14 wash and shower room, 15 dressing and rest room, 16 roof terrace.
6. A straight staircase leads from the entrance to the living-room, which is only separated from the open stair-well by a built-in sideboard.
7. Night view from South.

1. Gesamtansicht der Reihenhäuser von Süden. Die Treppen führen zur Terrasse, die im Winkel zwischen Wohn- und Schlafteil liegt.
2. Lageplan.
3. Blick in den Wirtschaftshof auf der Nordseite. Links die Abstellschuppen, rechts der Kücheneingang.
4. Längsschnitt.
5. Grundrisse von Eingangsgeschoß (unten), Wohnge-schoß (Mitte) und Dachgeschoß. Legende: 1 Eingang, 2 Garage, 3 Hobbyraum, 4 Waschküche, 5 Arbeitsraum, 6 Wohnraum, 7 Eßzimmer, 8 Hauswirtschaftsraum, 9 Küche, 10 Mädchenzimmer, 11 Schlafraum, 12 Abstellschuppen, 13 Sauna, 14 Wasch- und Duschraum, 15 Umkleide- und Ruheraum, 16 Dachterrasse.
6. Vom Eingang gelangt man über eine gradläufige Treppe in den Wohnraum, der nur durch ein eingebautes Sideboard gegen den Treppenschacht abgegrenzt ist.
7. Nachtaufnahme von Süden.

Group of detached row houses at Tapiola
Architect: Heikki Koskelo

Reihenhaussiedlung in Tapiola. 1965-66
Architekt: Heikki Koskelo

1. South view of scheme. Left, type A houses; right,
type B. Access is only by footpaths.
2. Site plan.

1. Südansicht der Siedlung. Links Häuser vom Typ A,
rechts Typ B. Die Siedlung wird über reine Fußgängerwege erschlossen.
2. Lageplan.

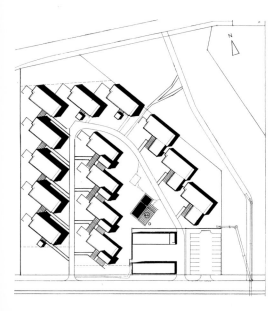

The group comprises fourteen detached dwellings, linked by outhouses and wood fences.
They are placed in an approximate semicircle round a straight row of four houses in the
middle and a small swimming-pool in front of two communal garages at the Southern
extremity of the site. The three types of home differ from one another only in the number
and position of subsidiary rooms. The main floor area is always 120 m² super. In type A,
the subsidiary rooms occupy in all 89 m² of the groundfloor. In type B, they use 31 m²
on the ground and first floors, while in type C 67 m² of the groundfloor and basement
are applied to this purpose. Wood is the main building material, with an insulating layer
of mineral wool. The limewashed North walls are brick. All houses are stepped on plan
in relation to each other on gently falling ground. The group reflects practical research
into possible variations for row houses and their effect on user values.

Die Hausgruppe umfaßt vierzehn frei stehende Gebäude, die durch Schuppen und Holz-
zäune miteinander verbunden sind. Sie gruppieren sich in annähernder Halbkreisform um
eine in der Mitte liegende gerade Zeile aus vier Häusern und ein kleines Schwimmbecken
vor den beiden Gemeinschaftsgaragen am Südrand des Grundstücks. Die drei Wohntypen
der Siedlung unterscheiden sich voneinander nur durch die Zahl und Lage der Nebenräume;
die Wohnfläche beträgt einheitlich 120 qm. Bei Typ A sind die Nebenräume mit insgesamt
89 qm im Erdgeschoß zusammengefaßt. Typ B hat 31 qm Nebenräume im Erdgeschoß und
im ersten Obergeschoß, und bei Typ C sind die 67 qm Nebenräume auf Erd- und Untergeschoß verteilt. Als Baumaterial fand in der Hauptsache Holz mit einer Isolierschicht aus
Mineralwolle Verwendung, die gekalkten Nordwände sind aus Backsteinen gemauert. Alle
Häuser sind auf dem schwach fallenden Gelände gegeneinander gestaffelt. — Mit dieser
Hausgruppe sollte ein Typ auf seine Variationsmöglichkeiten im Reihenhausbau und ihr Einfluß auf den Wohnwert untersucht werden.

3. View of living-room front of a type B house. Projecting roof and wall slab make a well-protected open-air retreat.

4. View of type C from South-East.

5. Plans of the three house types. Above, type C; left below, type A. Key: 1 entrance hall, 2 storage, 3 bath, shower, 4 WC, 5 washroom, 6 sauna, 7 utility room, 8 rest room, 9 veranda, 10 shed, 11 library and dining space, 12 kitchen, 13 bedrooms, 14 service yard, 15 living-room.

3. Blick auf die Wohnraumfront eines Hauses vom Typ B. Auskragendes Dach und vorgezogene Mauerscheibe schaffen einen geschützten Freisitzplatz.

4. Ansicht des Typs C von Südosten.

5. Grundrisse der drei Haustypen. Oben Typ C, links unten Typ A. Legende: 1 Eingangsdiele, 2 Vorratsraum, 3 Bad, Dusche, 4 WC, 5 Waschraum, 6 Sauna, 7 Hobbyraum, 8 Ruheraum, 9 Terrasse, 10 Schuppen, 11 Bibliothek und Eßzimmer, 12 Küche, 13 Schlafraum, 14 Wirtschaftshof, 15 Wohnraum.

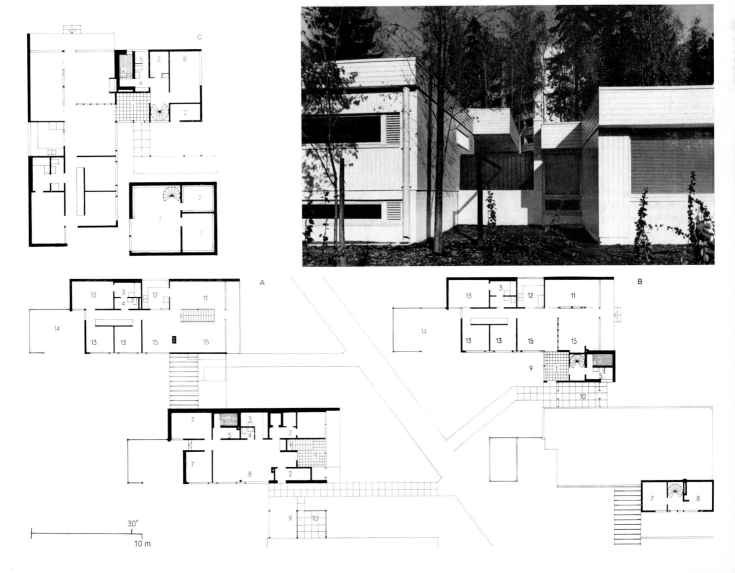

30'

10 m

1. The little tiered balconies protrude slightly like drawers from the West façade contributing a sculptural quality. The balcony parapets present an unbroken concrete surface in front, but the sides have shutterlike wood screens.
2. Site plan.

1. Die übereinanderliegenden Freisitzplätze der West-front sind als plastisch belebendes Element wie Schub-laden ein Stück aus der Fassade herausgezogen. Die Balkonbrüstungen bestehen auf der Stirnseite aus einer geschlossenen Betonfläche, während die seitliche Be-grenzung aus Holz lamellenartig aufgelöst ist.
2. Lageplan.

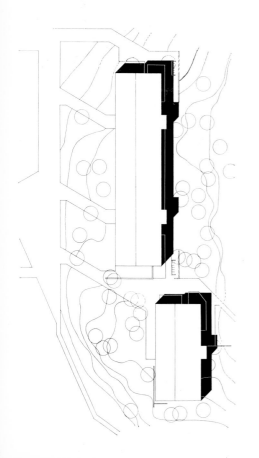

This group of two blocks of flats, placed roughly end to end, stands on a gently sloping site. The architect uses a uniform three-unit floor plan, with the larger block accommodating two. Each unit has a projecting, but centrally placed, staircase. The entrance floor, which is set back on the West side in relation to the dwelling floors above, contains communal facilities. Flats on the first to third storeys have West-facing balconies. The kitchen and bedrooms are orientated to the entrance front, while plumbing services are in the middle of the flats. The roof-storey (also setback) contains smaller three-room dwellings. All external walls, window-breasts and partition walls are of masonry construction and lime-washed, but balcony parapets are concrete.

Diese Hausgruppe aus zwei gegeneinander versetzten Mehrfamilienhäusern steht auf einem schwach fallenden Westhang. Der Architekt entwickelte für die drei Wohneinheiten einen einheitlichen Grundriß. Im Zentrum jeder Wohneinheit liegen die vorgezogenen Treppen-häuser. Das Eingangsgeschoß, das auf der Westseite gegenüber den Wohngeschossen zu-rückgesetzt ist, enthält die gemeinsam genutzten Wirtschaftsräume. Die Wohnungen des ersten bis dritten Obergeschosses haben nach Westen Balkone. Küche und Schlafräume sind zur Zugangsseite hin orientiert. Die Sanitärräume liegen im Zentrum der Wohnungen. Das zurückgesetzte Dachgeschoß enthält kleinere Dreizimmerwohnungen. Giebelscheiben, Treppenhaus, Wände und Brüstungsbänder sind gemauert und weiß geschlämmt. Für die Balkonbrüstungen wurde Beton verwendet.

3. West view of the larger twin-unit block of flats. The juxtaposition of the two units creates a double balcony in the middle. The restful horizontal emphasis of the building contrasts charmingly with the slender silhouettes of pine trees.

4. The prominent staircase tower accentuates the horizontality of the East elevation.

5. Section.

6. Plans of ground floor (above), and of typical main floor and roof storey (half in each case). Key: 1 kitchen, 2 bedroom, 3 living-room, 4 sports room, 5 utility room, 6 dressing room, 7 sauna, 8 washroom and shower, 9 storage, 10 air raid shelter, 11 electricity substation, 12 drying room, 13 laundry, 14 ironing room.

3. Blick von Westen auf die Wohnfront des großen Hauses, das aus zwei zusammengebauten kleinen Häusern besteht. Durch diese Aneinanderreihung entstehen in der Mitte Doppelbalkone. Die ruhigen horizontalen Schichtungen des Hauses stehen in reizvollem Kontrast zu dem dünnen Kiefernbestand.

4. Die vorgezogenen Treppenhäuser setzen einen vertikalen Akzent in die horizontale Gliederung der Ostfront.

5. Schnitt.

6. Grundrisse von Erdgeschoß (unten) und Normal- und Dachgeschoß (je zur Hälfte). Legende: 1 Küche, 2 Schlafraum, 3 Wohnraum, 4 Sportraum, 5 Hobbyraum, 6 Ankleide, 7 Sauna, 8 Wasch- und Duschraum, 9 Vorratsraum, 10 Luftschutzkeller, 11 Elt-Zentrale, 12 Trockenraum, 13 Waschküche, 14 Bügelzimmer.

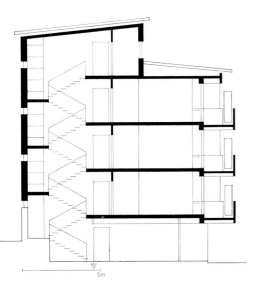

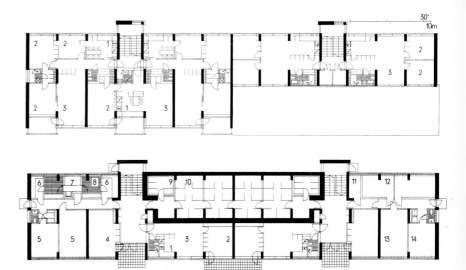

Weilin and Göös printing works at Tapiola. 1963-64
Architect: Aarno Ruusuvuori

Druckerei Weilin und Göös in Tapiola. 1963-64
Architekt: Aarno Ruusuvuori

1. View from South-East.
2. Aerial view of the light industry zone.

1. Ansicht von Südosten.
2. Luftaufnahme des Kleinindustriegebietes.

The two-storey printing works stands in the light industry zone of Tapiola on a site which falls gently towards the South. The entrance hall on the ground floor has direct access to the offices ranged along the North front. The North-West corner of the ground floor accommodates the canteen, which is brought into close contact with the woodland surroundings by storey-high glazed walls. The big loading ramp in the South-East side of the building enables delivery vehicles to drive inside. The upper floor is also directly accessible by a ramp. The large printing-shop on the upper storey has only four supports, one per 729 m². They have a diameter of 3 m and, serve as ventilation shafts. The roof is suspended from them, but the ground floor roof rests on columns spaced to a 9 m grid.

Das zweigeschossige Druckereigebäude liegt auf einem ebenen, stark bewaldeten Gelände im Kleinindustriegebiet Tapiolas. An die Eingangshalle im Erdgeschoß schließen sich die Büros an, die längs der Außenfront angeordnet sind. Die Nordwestecke des Grundrisses nimmt die Kantine ein. Ihre geschoßhoch verglasten Außenwände geben engen Kontakt zur Natur. Die große Laderampe auf der Südostseite des Gebäudes ist so angelegt, daß die Lieferwagen in das Gebäude hineinfahren können. Auch das Obergeschoß ist über eine Rampe direkt zugänglich. Der große Druckereisaal im Obergeschoß hat nur vier Stützen, das heißt eine für je 729 qm. Sie haben einen Durchmesser von drei Metern und dienen auch als Ventilationsschächte. An diesen Stützen ist das Dach aufgehängt. Die Decke des Erdgeschosses ruht auf Stützen, die in einem Neunmeterraster stehen.

94

3. The back of the building. The printing-shop on the upper floor is entirely glazed.

4. By retracting the ground floor, a covered way is created round the building.

5. Section and ground floor plan. Key: section B-B; 1 entrance hall, 2 reception, 3 office, 4 canteen, 5 kitchen, 6 staff locker room, 7 store, 8 workshop, 9 ventilation shaft, 10 paper store, 11 freight lift, 12 drive-in, 13 foremen, 14 dispatch, 15 emergency stairs.

6. The printing shop on the upper floor has a completely glazed North-West front. The other three sides have a continuous band of top lighting. The roof edge slopes inwards to provide additional light. The slope indicates the height of the hanging-roof structure.

3. Die Rückfront des Gebäudes. Der Druckereisaal im Obergeschoß ist ganz verglast.

4. Durch die Zurücknahme des Erdgeschosses entsteht ein überdachter Weg rings um das Gebäude.

5. Schnitt und Erdgeschoßgrundriß. Legende: B-B Schnittebene; 1 Eingangshalle, 2 Rezeption, 3 Büro, 4 Kantine, 5 Küche, 6 Garderobe, 7 Lager, 8 Werkstatt, 9 Ventilationsschacht, 10 Papierlager, 11 Lastenaufzug, 12 Einfahrt, 13 Vorarbeiter, 14 Versand, 15 Feuertreppe.

6. Der Druckereisaal im Obergeschoß hat nach Nordwesten eine voll verglaste Außenfront; die anderen drei Fassaden haben nur Oberlichtbänder. Die Dachkante ist nach innen abgeschrägt, um zusätzlichen Lichteinfall zu erreichen. Die Schräge zeigt die Konstruktionshöhe des Hängedaches.

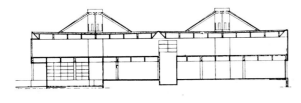

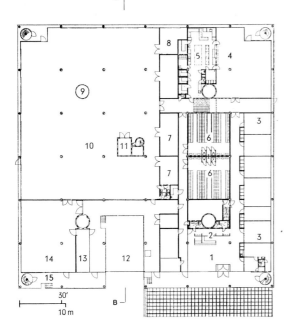

Central hospital at Tampere. 1958-62
Architects: Erkki Helamaa and Veijo Martikainen

Zentralkrankenhaus in Tampere. 1958-62
Architekten: Erkki Helamaa und Veijo Martikainen

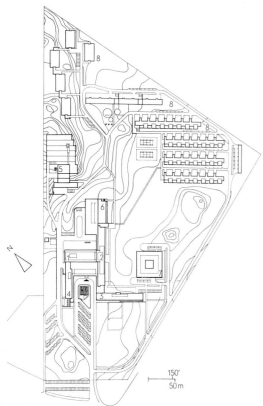

The hospital stands outside the town on the edge of a large wooded area. As the ground rises to the North-West, the main building was erected on the South-East part of the site. The centre of the group is formed by a twelve-storey ward block. The six-storey polyclinic is connected to the North-West side. At the point where the two buildings intersect are passenger (and patients') lifts. The three-storey administration wing is joined to the polyclinic and extends South-East, parallel to the ward block. The second floor contains patients' rooms. The children's clinic, like the polyclinic, is linked to the ward block by a common entrance hall and the first floor. From the North end of the ward block stretches the single-storey service wing with laundry, kitchen and restaurant for hospital staff. The hospital has 1000 beds. The various floors house individual departments. The accident department is on the ground floor, the central polyclinic is on the first floor, and, above, from the second to the sixth floors follow X-ray, central laboratory, obstetrics, operations, and throat-nose-ear departments.

Der Bau steht außerhalb der Stadt, am Rande eines größeren Waldgebietes. Da das Gelände nach Nordwesten ansteigt, wurden die Hauptgebäude auf dem südöstlichen Teil des Grundstücks erstellt. Das Zentrum der Anlage bildet das in die Höhe entwickelte zwölfgeschossige Bettenhaus. Auf der Nordwestseite schließt sich die sechsstöckige Poliklinik an. Im Schnittpunkt der beiden Gebäude liegen Betten- und Personenaufzüge. Der dreigeschossige Verwaltungstrakt ist mit der Poliklinik verbunden und greift, parallel zum Bettenhaus geführt, nach Südosten aus. Im zweiten Obergeschoß sind Krankenzimmer untergebracht. Wie die Poliklinik steht auch die Kinderklinik mit dem Bettenhaus über eine gemeinsame Eingangshalle und das erste Obergeschoß in Verbindung. An das Nordende des Bettenhauses schließt sich der eingeschossige Wirtschaftsteil mit Wäscherei, Küche und dem Speisesaal für das Krankenhauspersonal an. Das Krankenhaus hat insgesamt etwa 1000 Betten. In der Poliklinik sind die verschiedenen Stationen auf die einzelnen Geschosse verteilt. Im Erdgeschoß liegt die Unfallstation, im 1. Obergeschoß die Zentralpoliklinik und darüber vom 2. bis zum 6. Obergeschoß Röntgenabteilung, Zentrallabor, Geburtshilfeabteilung, Operationsabteilung und die Hals-Nasen-Ohren-Abteilung.

1. General view, showing access road and car park. In the middle, the ward block.
2. Site plan. Key: 1 polyclinic, 2 ward block, 3 children's polyclinic, 4 administration, 5 power house, 6 laundry, 7 infectious diseases, 8 staff housing.
3. Plan of second floor. Key: 1 X-ray examination, 2 dark room, 3 radiology, 4 radiation treatment, 5 radio-therapy, 6 examination, 7 office, 8 patients' rooms, 9 waiting room, 10 smoking room, 11 conference room, 12 departmental kitchen, 13 stores, 14 examination, 15 wash room, 16 children's reception, 17 staff.
4. Plan of first floor. Key: 1 information, 2 hall, 3 reception, 4 waiting room, 5 examination and treatment, 6 laboratory, 7 operating theatre, 8 dressing station, 9 post-operation room, 10 office, 11 duty doctor, 12 conference room, 13 accounts, 14 X-ray room, 15 post office, 16 kiosk, 17 cafe, 18 restaurant.

1. Gesamtansicht mit Zufahrt und Parkplatz. In der Mitte das Bettenhaus.
2. Lageplan. Legende: 1 Poliklinik, 2 Bettenhaus, 3 Kinderpoliklinik, 4 Verwaltung, 5 Kraftzentrale, 6 Wäscherei, 7 Infektionsabteilung, 8 Personalwohnungen.
3. Grundriß des 2. Obergeschosses. Legende: 1 Röntgenuntersuchung, 2 Dunkelkammer, 3 Röntgenvorführung, 4 Röntgenbehandlung, 5 Bestrahlung, 6 Untersuchung, 7 Büro, 8 Krankenzimmer, 9 Aufenthaltsraum, 10 Rauchzimmer, 11 Konferenzraum, 12 Abteilungsküche, 13 Lagerraum, 14 Untersuchung, 15 Waschraum, 16 Kinderaufnahme, 17 Personal.
4. Grundriß des 1. Obergeschosses. Legende: 1 Auskunft, 2 Halle, 3 Anmeldung, 4 Warteraum, 5 Untersuchung und Behandlung, 6 Labor, 7 Operationssaal, 8 Verbandsraum, 9 Raum für Frischoperierte, 10 Büro, 11 Diensttuender Arzt, 12 Konferenzraum, 13 Buchhaltung, 14 Durchleuchtungsraum, 15 Postschalter, 16 Kiosk, 17 Café, 18 Speisesaal.

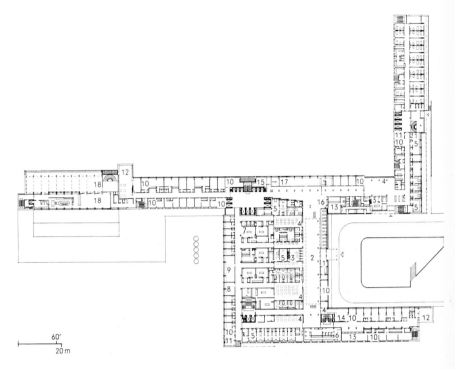

60'
20 m

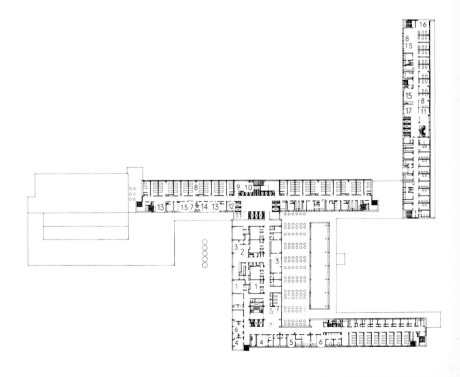

5. The children's clinic with its continuous lines of loggias. The play place is principally intended for visitors' children.
6. East view of power house.
7. The hall adjoining the main entrance is lit by a ribbon of light from above. Right, five separate ways to the reception counters.

5. Die Kinderklinik hat durchgehende Loggien. Der Spielplatz ist hauptsächlich für die Kinder der Besucher gedacht.
6. Ansicht der Kraftzentrale von Osten.
7. Die an den Haupteingang anschließende Halle wird über ein hochliegendes Fensterband belichtet. Rechts fünf getrennte Zugänge zu den Aufnahmeschaltern.

University central hospital at Helsinki. 1962-66
Architects: Reino Koivula and Jaakko Paatela

Universitäts-Zentralkrankenhaus in Helsinki. 1962-66
Architekten: Reino Koivula und Jaakko Paatela

1. North view.
2. Site plan.

1. Ansicht von Norden.
2. Lageplan.

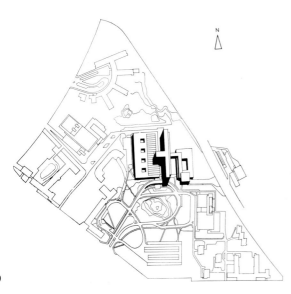

The group of buildings comprises three clinics for internal diseases, two for surgery and one each for tuberculosis and neurology. In all 990 beds are available. The hospital has three parts: a fifteen-storey ward block in the middle, which is connected on the East side with a treatment block, containing polyclinic, operating theatres, radiography, heart clinic, and physiological and outpatients departments; and, thirdly, a laboratory building, which also houses the lecture rooms, extending to the West. Because of the sloping site the main entrance is located on the third storey of the treatment building. The entire polyclinic area has North (shed) lighting. The restricted site and the desire for short circulation ways dictated the ward block's vertical layout, which at the same time provides patients with a wide view of the Gulf of Finland. The building has reinforced concrete construction with glass external cladding.

Der Gebäudekomplex enthält drei Kliniken für innere Krankheiten, zwei chirurgische Kliniken, eine Klinik für Lungenkrankheiten sowie eine neurologische Klinik. Zur Verfügung stehen insgesamt 990 Betten. Das Krankenhaus besteht aus drei Gebäudeteilen, aus dem in der Mitte liegenden, fünfzehngeschossigen Bettenhaus, dem nach Osten anschließenden Behandlungsbau mit Poliklinik, Operationsabteilung, Röntgenabteilung, Herzuntersuchungsabteilung, physiologischer Abteilung und Ambulanz. In dem nach Westen ausgreifenden Laborgebäude befinden sich auch die Vorlesungssäle. Der Haupteingang liegt auf Grund des ansteigenden Geländes im dritten Geschoß des Behandlungsbaues. Der gesamte Poliklinikbereich wird über Sheddächer belichtet. Der Wunsch nach kurzen Verkehrswegen und der knappe Baugrund waren die Ursache für die vertikale Anlage des Bettenhauses. Somit ergab sich zugleich für die Kranken ein weiter Ausblick auf den Finnischen Meerbusen. Das Gebäude ist eine Stahlbetonkonstruktion. Die Fassaden sind mit Glas verkleidet.

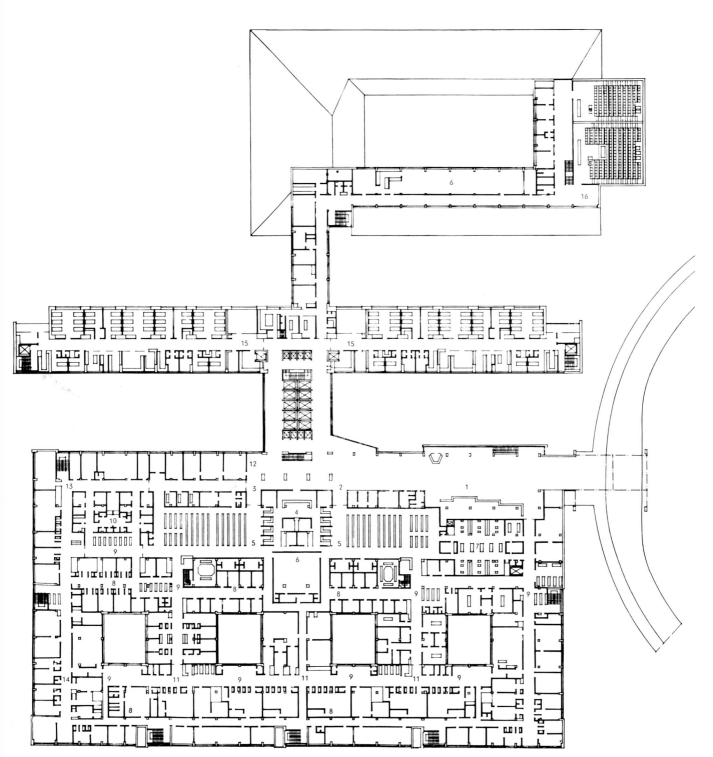

3. Plan of second floor. Key: 1 entrance hall, 2 surgical polyclinic, 3 clinic for internal diseases, 4 records, 5 waiting room, 6 cafeteria, 7 dressings, 8 examination, 9 waiting room, 10 test analysis, 11 X-ray department, 12 administrative office, 13 polyclinical laboratory, 14 gastro-enterological department, 15 wards, 16 lecture room.

3. Grundriß des zweiten Obergeschosses. Legende: 1 Eingangshalle, 2 Chirurgische Poliklinik, 3 Klinik für innere Krankheiten, 4 Kartei, 5 Wartesaal, 6 Cafeteria, 7 Verbandsraum, 8 Untersuchung, 9 Warteraum, 10 Probenentnahme, 11 Röntgenabteilung, 12 Verwaltungsbüros, 13 Poliklinisches Labor, 14 Gastroenterologische Abteilung, 15 Bettenabteilung, 16 Vorlesungssaal.

4. Main building from North.
5. Ward block with link building to laboratories. In foreground, parapet wall of curved ramp to main entrance.
6. View from ward block of the access road and main entrance on the top floor of the polyclinic. The lower-floor rooms are lit by a large well between the two buildings.
7. View into the entrance hall of the polyclinic. The suspended slatted ceiling gives an attractive vertical termination to the room and assures an even distribution of light.

4. Das Hauptgebäude von Norden.
5. Das Bettenhaus mit dem Verbindungsbau zum Laborgebäude. Im Vordergrund das Geländer der geschwungenen Rampe zum Haupteingang.
6. Blick vom Bettenhaus auf die Zufahrtsstraße und den Haupteingang in das Obergeschoß der Poliklinik. Die Räume des Untergeschosses werden über den zwischen den beiden Gebäuden liegenden Hof belichtet.
7. Blick in die Eingangshalle der Poliklinik. Die untergehängte Lamellendecke gibt dem Raum optisch einen Abschluß nach oben und sorgt für gleichmäßige Lichtstreuung.

Administration and communal services centre. University Hospital, Helsinki. 1963-65
Architect: Veli and Jaakko Paatela

Verwaltungs- und Wirtschaftszentrale des Universitätskrankenhauses in Helsinki. 1963-65
Architekten: Veli und Jaakko Paatela

The centre lies between the central hospital and the children's clinic. The administration section houses the managerial services of the central hospital directorate of the University of Helsinki, while the communal services section holds the central laundry and main kitchens. As the building rises over a depression in the site, the entrance to the loading ramp and adjacent cold-storage and store rooms was placed at ground level two storeys below the entrance floor of the administration building. The store and cold-storage rooms are underground, but the staff rooms on the South-East side have direct natural light. From the intermediate storey supply tunnels lead to the individual hospitals. This floor also contains the main kitchen, restaurant and laundry. A drive leads to the principal entrance on the ground floor of the administration building.

Das Verwaltungs- und Wirtschaftsgebäude liegt zwischen dem Zentralkrankenhaus und der Kinderklinik. Im Verwaltungsteil des Gebäudes ist die Verwaltung des Zentralkrankenhausverbandes der Universität Helsinki untergebracht, im Wirtschaftsteil die Zentralwäscherei und die Zentralküche für das Meilahti-Gebiet. Das Gebäude erhebt sich über einem Geländesprung. Die Einfahrt zur Verladerampe und den anschließenden Kühl- und Lagerräumen konnte so zwei Etagen unter dem Eingangsniveau des Verwaltungsgebäudes ebenerdig angelegt werden. Die Lager- und Kühlräume befinden sich im unterirdischen Teil des Gebäudes. Dagegen haben die Personalräume an der Südostseite Tageslicht. Vom Zwischengeschoß führen Versorgungstunnel zu den einzelnen Krankenhäusern. Dieses Geschoß nimmt auch die Hauptküche, das Restaurant und die Wäscherei auf. Zum Haupteingang im Erdgeschoß des dreigeschossigen Verwaltungsgebäudes führt eine Vorfahrt.

1. The administration block rises out of the broad mass of the communal services building placed in a depression of the ground. From the canteen in the understorey one looks on to the adjoining South-West garden.
2. Site plan.
3. View of communal services building from South-East.
4. Access side of communal services building. In background, entrances to supply tunnels.
5. Section and plans of intermediate floor, entrance floor and typical upper storeys of administration building. Key: 1 supply tunnel, 2 restaurant lobby, 3 WCs, 4 restaurant, 5 outside terrace, 6 kitchen of restaurant, 7 scullery, 8 kitchen staff dining room, 9 meal preparation, 10 main kitchen, 11 chef, 12 kitchen stores, 13 bakery, 14 bread issue, 15 scullery, 16 special diets chef, 17 special diets kitchen, 18 store for transportable containers, 19 vehicle park, 20 laundry store, 21 chemical cleaning, 22 laundry, 23 entrance hall, 24 information, 25 cloakrooms and WCs, 26 restaurant extension, 27 telephone exchange, 28 post.

1. Der dreigeschossige Verwaltungstrakt wächst aus dem breiten, in die Geländestufe eingefügten Wirtschaftstrakt des Gebäudes heraus. Aus der Kantine im Untergeschoß blickt man auf den anschließenden Garten.
2. Lageplan.
3. Ansicht des Wirtschaftsteiles von Südosten.
4. Die Zugangsseite des Wirtschaftstraktes. Im Hintergrund die Eingänge zu den Versorgungstunneln.
5. Schnitt und Grundrisse von Zwischengeschoß, Eingangsgeschoß und Normalgeschoß des Verwaltungstraktes. Legende: 1 Versorgungstunnel, 2 Vorhalle des Restaurants, 3 Toiletten, 4 Restaurant, 5 Außenterrasse, 6 Küche des Restaurants, 7 Spülküche, 8 Speisesaal des Küchenpersonals, 9 Vorbereitungsküche, 10 Hauptküche, 11 Küchenchef, 12 Vorratsraum, 13 Bäckerei, 14 Brotausgabe, 15 Spülküche, 16 Diät-Küchenchef, 17 Diätküche, 18 Lagerraum für die Transportgefäße, 19 Wagenhalle, 20 Wäschelager, 21 Chemische Reinigung, 22 Wäscherei, 23 Eingangshalle, 24 Auskunft, 25 Garderobe und Toiletten, 26 Nebenraum des Restaurants, 27 Telefonzentrale, 28 Post.

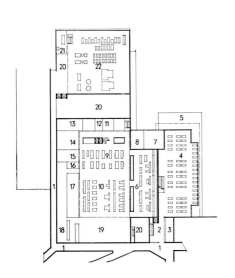

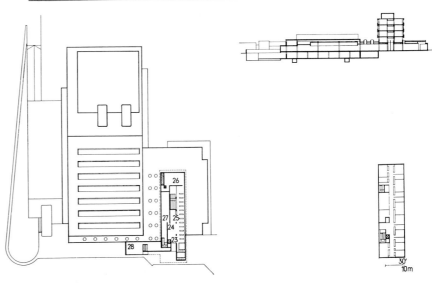

1. View of restaurant on first floor.
2. General view from street.

1. Blick in das Restaurant im ersten Obergeschoß.
2. Gesamtansicht von der Straße.

In developing this site at the city centre, the need was stressed for a multipurpose building. On the first basement floor there is a bar, and on the ground floor a bank and hotel reception lobby leading to public rooms. The restaurant with kitchen and subsidiary rooms is on the first floor. Stock rooms are accommodated on three storeys, and the choice of goods is so wide that almost any article can be bought as in a department store. The remaining space in the building is equipped as hotel rooms and offices, the latter being fairly easily convertible into the former. Reinforced concrete construction is used, with dark brown facing bricks as cladding.

Bei der Planung für das im Zentrum der Stadt liegende Grundstück wurde darauf Wert gelegt, ein vielseitig nutzbares Gebäude zu entwickeln. Im ersten Untergeschoß befindet sich eine Bar, im Erdgeschoß eine Bank und die Empfangshalle eines Hotels, an die sich die Gesellschaftsräume anschließen. Das Restaurant mit der Küche und weiteren Nebenräumen liegt im ersten Obergeschoß. Die Ladenräume sind auf drei Stockwerken untergebracht. Das Warenangebot ist so umfassend, daß man wie in einem Warenhaus fast jeden beliebigen Artikel kaufen kann. Die restlichen Räume des Hauses werden als Hotelzimmer und Büros verwendet. Die Büros lassen sich verhältnismäßig leicht in Hotelzimmer verwandeln. Das Gebäude ist eine Stahlbetonkonstruktion. Für die Fassadenverkleidung wurden dunkelbraune Klinker verwendet.

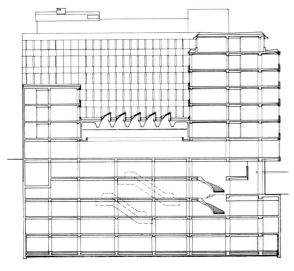

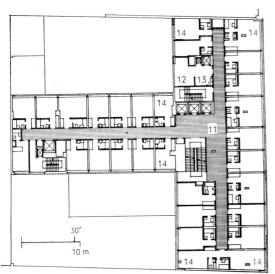

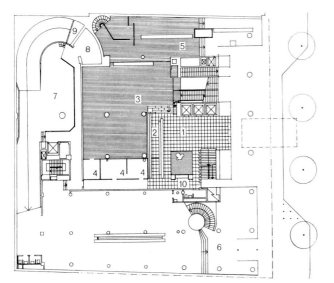

30'
10 m

3. Section and plans of typical hotel floor (middle) and entrance floor (below). Key: 1 hotel reception, 2 hall porter, 3 public room, 4 office, 5 bank, 6 stock room, 7 ramp to garage in lower basement, 8 refuse collection, 9 air conditioning plant, 10 left baggage, 11 hotel lobby, 12 pantry, 13 cleaning equipment, 14 hotel bedroom.
4. Hotel reception lobby on ground floor.
5. View into single-bed room.
6. Bar of cellar restaurant.

3. Schnitt und Grundrisse eines Hotelgeschosses (Mitte) und des Eingangsgeschosses (unten). Legende: 1 Hotelempfang, 2 Portier, 3 Gesellschaftsraum, 4 Büro, 5 Bank, 6 Laden, 7 Rampe zur Tiefgarage des zweiten Untergeschosses, 8 Müllsammelraum, 9 Klimaanlage, 10 Gepäckaufbewahrung, 11 Hotelflur, 12 Anrichte, 13 Putzgeräte, 14 Hotelzimmer.
4. Die Empfangshalle des Hotels im Erdgeschoß.
5. Blick in ein Einbettzimmer.
6. Die Bar des Kellerrestaurants.

Dance pavilion at Hanko. 1966
Architect: Clas-Olof Lindqvist

Tanzpavillon in Hanko. 1966
Architekt: Clas-Olof Lindqvist

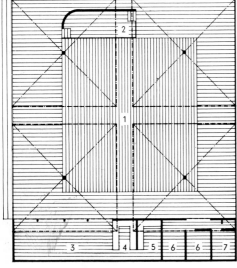

The dance pavilion stands in Hanko pleasure park and is only used during the summer months. A reinforced concrete foundation raises the dance floor a few steps above the ground. The orchestra is placed on a small podium shielded from the outside world by a curved wooden partition. All ancillary rooms are located in the low annex on the West side of the pavilion. The roof is composed of four separate square elements, each carried on a centrally placed stanchion. The wide gaps between these elements are glazed. The stanchions comprise four U-sections welded together. Roof joists and frames consist of laminated wood beams. The dance floor is faced with natural-coloured fir boards, the remaining floor surface, which slopes slightly outwards, with stained dark wood.

Der Tanzpavillon steht im Vergnügungspark von Hanko. Er wird nur während der Sommermonate benutzt. Ein Betonfundament hebt die Tanzfläche einige Stufen über den Boden. Auf einem kleinen, nach außen durch eine geschwungene Holzwand abgeschlossenen Podium findet das Orchester Platz. Alle Nebenräume sind in dem geschlossenen niedrigen Anbau auf der Westseite des Pavillons untergebracht. Das Dach setzt sich aus vier quadratischen, voneinander getrennten Elementen zusammen, die jeweils an einer zentralen Stütze aufgehängt sind. Die breiten Spalten zwischen diesen Elementen sind verglast. Die Stützen werden von vier zusammengeschweißten U-Profilen gebildet. Dachunterzüge und Rahmenkonstruktion bestehen aus Schichtholzbalken. Die Tanzfläche ist mit naturfarbig belassenen Kiefernriemen belegt, die übrige Bodenfläche mit imprägniertem dunklem Holz.

1. The reduction of the load-bearing frame to four stanchions and almost complete absence of walls create an impression of weightlessness.
2. Floor plan. Key: 1 dance floor, 2 orchestra, 3 cafe, 4 buffet, 5 kitchen, 6 artists' dressing rooms, 7 mech. control room.
3. The musicians' stand — its curved back wall serves to increase resonance — provides a lively feature for an impersonal structural exercise in straight lines.
4, 5. Views of the park from the pavilion.

1. Die Reduzierung des tragenden Gerüstes auf vier Stützen und der weitgehende Verzicht auf Wände verleihen dem Pavillon Schwerelosigkeit.
2. Grundriß. Legende: 1 Tanzfläche, 2 Orchester, 3 Café, 4 Buffet, 5 Küche, 6 Umkleideräume, 7 Elt-Zentrale.
3. Der Stand für die Musiker, dessen geschwungene Rückwand unter anderem die Funktion eines Resonanzbodens hat, wirkt als belebender Akzent.
4, 5. Blick aus dem Pavillon in den Park.

Finnish-Russian school at Helsinki. 1964
Architect: Osmo Sipari

Finnisch-russische Schule in Helsinki. 1964
Architekt: Osmo Sipari

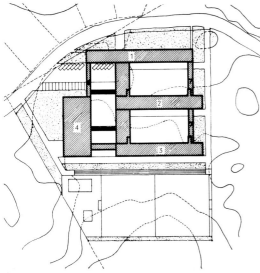

The school lies in the district of Etelä-Kaarela. Because of the terraced site, the class-room wings are sunk half a storey in relation to each other. The group comprises boarders' home, special subjects' classroom wing, standard (general) classroom wing and a gymnasium with assembly hall. The first three face South-East. Access to the school is by a service road on the North-East side. The ground floor of the boarding wing contains a kindergarten, sauna and offices. The teachers have small two-storey flats on the upper floor. The pupils' accommodation, also two-storeyed, has two working and two dormitory units per floor. The common rooms occupy the low buildings linking the wings. The playgrounds are on a different level.

Die Schule liegt in dem Stadtteil Etelä-Kaarela. Auf Grund des terrassierten Geländes sind die Klassentrakte um ein halbes Geschoß gegeneinander versetzt. Die Anlage besteht aus Internat, Spezialklassentrakt, Normalklassentrakt und Gymnastiksaal mit Aula. Internat, Spezial- und Normalklassen sind nach Südosten orientiert. Der Zugang zur Schule erfolgt von einer Nebenstraße im Nordosten. Im Erdgeschoß des Internatflügels befinden sich ein Kindergarten, Sauna und Büroräume. Die Lehrerwohnungen im Obergeschoß sind kleine zweigeschossige Apartments. Die ebenfalls zweigeschossigen Schülerwohnungen haben je Geschoß zwei Arbeits- und zwei Schlafplätze. In den niedrigen Verbindungsbauten zwischen den Trakten sind die Gemeinschaftsräume untergebracht. Die Pausenhöfe liegen auf verschiedenem Niveau.

1. Gymnasium (left), boarders' home, and classroom wings with linking buildings (right) form a spacious courtyard closed on the fourth side by the covered communicating way. The broad flight of steps and the differing heights of the buildings counteract the falling ground.
2. Site plan. Key: 1 boarders' home, 2 special classrooms, 3 standard classrooms, 4 gymnasium.
3. Quadrangle between special and standard classrooms.
4. View into assembly hall.
5. Plans of ground floor (left) and first floor. Key: 1 office, 2 sauna, 3 kindergarten, 4 cloakrooms, 5 administration, 6 kitchen, 7 large dining-room, 8 small dining-room, 9 principal, 10 hall, 11 records, 12 photography room, 13 workshop, 14 domestic science, 15 staff (teaching) room, 16 library, 17 standard (general) classrooms, 18 changing room and showers, 19 teachers' flats, 20 pupils' accommodation, 21 store, 22 special classrooms, 23 gymnasium, 24 assembly hall, 25 foyer.

1. Gymnastiksaal (links), Wohnflügel und die Klassentrakte mit den Verbindungsbauten (rechts) bilden einen tiefen Hof, dessen vierte Seite durch den überdachten Verbindungsgang geschlossen wird. Breite Treppen und die Höhenversetzung der Baukörper fangen den Geländeabfall auf.
2. Lageplan. Legende: 1 Internat, 2 Spezialklassen, 3 Normalklassen, 4 Gymnastiksaal.
3. Der Innenhof zwischen Spezial- und Normalklassen.
4. Blick in die Aula.
5. Grundrisse von Erdgeschoß (links) und erstem Obergeschoß. Legende: 1 Büro, 2 Sauna, 3 Kindergarten, 4 Garderobe, 5 Verwaltungs- und Wirtschaftsräume, 6 Küche, 7 Großer Speisesaal, 8 Kleiner Speisesaal, 9 Schulleitung, 10 Halle, 11 Archiv, 12 Fotolabor, 13 Werkstatt, 14 Haushaltsklasse, 15 Lehrerzimmer, 16 Bibliothek, 17 Normalklassen, 18 Umkleide und Dusche, 19 Lehrerwohnungen, 20 Schülerwohnungen, 21 Lager, 22 Spezialklassen, 23 Gymnastikhalle, 24 Aula, 25 Foyer.

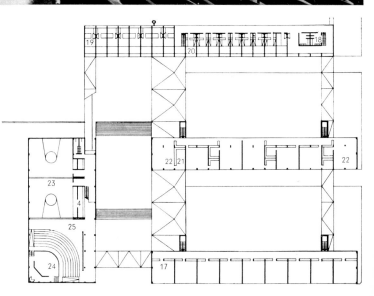

Secondary school at Hamina. 1961-62
Architects: Kaija and Heikki Siren

Mittelschule in Hamina. 1961-62
Architekten: Kaija und Heikki Siren

1. The school building seen from yard.
2. The covered way, extending the full width of the façade, but separated from it, serves as sheltered play space. The reinforced concrete walls af the school are faced with lime-washed bricks.

1. Das Schulgebäude vom Pausenhof aus gesehen.
2. Das über die ganze Frontbreite reichende, von der Fassade abgerückte Regenschutzdach dient als überdachter Pausenraum.

In this school all rooms are grouped about a central, square, gymnasium-cum-assembly hall (lit from above), from which an entrance foyer with demountable cloakroom space can be separated by folding partitions. The adjacent staff room, from which the school yard can be supervised, is placed between the two main entrances. By retracting folding partitions, the dining room on the ground floor can also open into the hall. Adjoining the dining hall are the school kitchen and the domestic science classroom with its own kitchen. Most of the classrooms are on the upper storey, which is linked to the ground floor by four staircases. A single-storey annex houses workshops for wood and metal work, and two dwellings. The link between the two buildings is the covered bicycle park.

Bei dieser Hallenschule gruppieren sich alle Räume um die zentrale, quadratische Turn- und Festhalle mit Oberlicht, von der sich durch Faltwände ein Eingangsbereich mit demontierbaren Garderoben abtrennen läßt. Das Lehrerzimmer auf der gegenüberliegenden Seite, von dem aus man den Schulhof überblicken kann, ist zwischen die beiden Haupteingänge geschoben. Auch der Speisesaal, der sich im Erdgeschoß befindet, kann durch Faltwände zur Halle geöffnet werden. An den Speisesaal schließen sich die Schulküche und die Haushaltsklasse mit der Lehrküche an. Die meisten Klassenräume befinden sich im Obergeschoß, das über vier Treppen mit dem Erdgeschoß verbunden ist. Ein eingeschossiges Nebengebäude nimmt die Werkstätten für Holz- und Metallbearbeitung sowie zwei Wohnungen auf. Das Bindeglied zwischen den beiden Gebäuden ist der überdachte Fahrradabstellplatz.

3. View of typical (standard) classroom.
4. Domestic science classroom and kitchen.
5. Section and plans of upper storey (middle) and ground floor (below). Key: A school, B covered bicycle park, C school yard, D workshops and dwellings. 1 gymnasium-cum-assembly hall, 2 cloakroom, 3 stage, 4 chair stack, 5 standard classroom, 6 special subjects classroom, 7 principal, 8 staff room, 9 dining room, 10 main kitchen, 11 domestic science room and kitchen, 12 workshop, 13 dwelling, 14 bicycles.

3. Blick in eine Normalklasse.
4. Die Haushaltsklasse mit Lehrküche.
5. Schnitt und Grundrisse von Obergeschoß (Mitte) und Erdgeschoß (unten). Legende: A Schule, B Überdachter Fahrradeinstellplatz, C Schulhof, D Werkstätten und Wohnungen. 1 Turn- und Festhalle, 2 Garderobe, 3 Bühne, 4 Stuhlmagazin, 5 Normalklasse, 6 Fachklasse, 7 Schulleitung, 8 Lehrerzimmer, 9 Speisesaal, 10 Hauptküche, 11 Haushaltsklasse mit Lehrküche, 12 Werkstatt, 13 Wohnung, 14 Fahrräder.

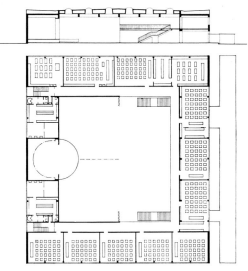

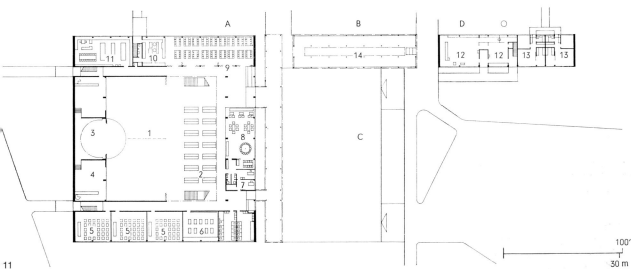

6, 7. View into gymnasium-cum-assembly hall, with cloakroom. The folding partition can isolate the entrance foyer from the main hall. The latter can also be used as an auditorium for plays.

6, 7. Blick in die Turn- und Festhalle mit den Garderoben. Mit der Faltwand kann der Eingangsbereich von der Turnhalle abgetrennt werden. Die Turnhalle dient auch als Zuschauerraum für Theatervorstellungen.

1. Street frontage with main entrance (right). The dining
room is behind the exposed concrete wall.
2. Photo of model.

1. Die Straßenseite des Gebäudes mit dem Haupteingang (rechts). Hinter der Mauer aus Sichtbeton liegt der
Speisesaal.
2. Modellfoto.

The school buildings have close links with the nearby park, into which the playground
opens. The concentrated several-storeyed complex, a departure from the common single-
storey school type, derives from the character of the "gymnasium" as the preliminary step
to a university. The focus of the school's life is the hall, which is also designed for out-
of-school activities without disturbance to the scholastic routine. The main entrance is in
the North front. The classrooms are principally located on the side facing the park. The
gymnasia are in the basement. A small observatory on the roof completes the up-to-date
facilities for special studies.

Das Schulgebäude ist in enge Beziehung zu dem benachbarten Park gesetzt, auf den sich
der Schulhof öffnet. Durch den besonderen Charakter des Gymnasiums als Vorstufe zur
Universität entstand ein vom verbreiteten eingeschossigen Schultyp abweichender mehrge-
schossiger und sehr konzentrierter Gebäudekomplex. Mittelpunkt, auch des Schulalltags,
ist der Festsaal, der so angelegt wurde, daß er auch für außerschulische Veranstaltungen
verwendet werden kann, ohne daß damit der Schulbetrieb gestört wird. Der Haupteingang
liegt in der Nordfront. Die Unterrichtsräume sind zum größten Teil auf der dem Park zu-
gewandten Seite zusammengefaßt. Die Gymnastikräume liegen im Kellergeschoß. Ein
kleines Observatorium auf dem Dach des Hauptgebäudes vervollständigt die moderne Ausstattung der Spezialklassen.

3. The East wall of the main building is completely blind.
4. Section and plans of basement (left) and ground floor.
Key: 1 store room, 2 teaching equipment, 3 workroom,
4 laboratory, 5 physics and chemistry classes, 6 preparation room for natural sciences, 7 biology, 8 cloakroom, 9 school shop, 10 bicycles, 11 play yard, 12 caretaker's flat, 13 art room, 14 music room, 15 library, 16 map room, 17 doctor, 18 principal, 19 staff room, 20 cloakroom, 21 assembly hall, 22 stage, 23 dining-room, 24 kitchen.

3. Der Ostgiebel des Hauptgebäudes ist völlig geschlossen.
4. Schnitt und Grundrisse von Untergeschoß (links) und
Erdgeschoß. Legende: 1 Abstellraum, 2 Materialraum,
3 Werkraum, 4 Labor, 5 Physik- und Chemieklasse, 6 Vorbereitungsraum für die naturwissenschaftlichen Fächer,
7 Biologieklasse, 8 Garderobe, 9 Verkauf von Schulbedarf, 10 Fahrräder, 11 Pausenhof, 12 Wohnung des Hausmeisters, 13 Zeichensaal, 14 Musikzimmer, 15 Bibliothek, 16 Kartenzimmer, 17 Arzt, 18 Schulleitung, 19 Lehrerzimmer, 20 Garderobe, 21 Aula, 22 Bühne, 23 Speisesaal, 24 Küche.

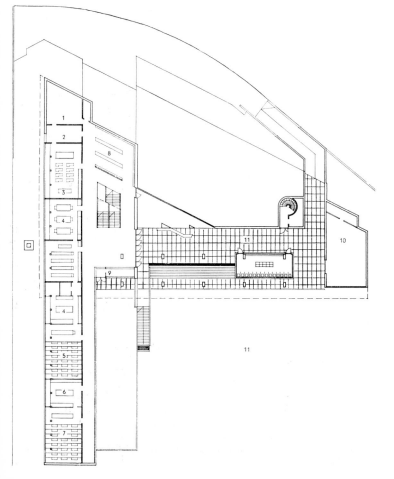

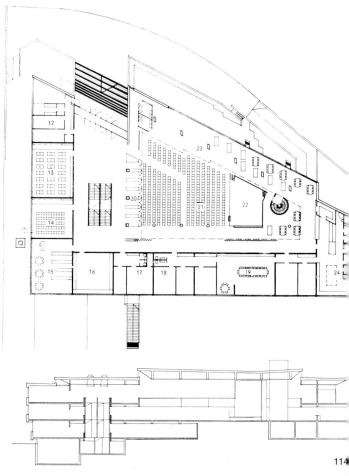

5. View of main entrance on ground floor, placed a few steps above street level.
6. The standard (general subjects) classrooms are lit from two sides, by windows and roof lights.
7. The internally placed assembly hall can be isolated from the surrounding circulation ways by folding partitions.

5. Blick auf den Haupteingang im Erdgeschoß, das einige Stufen über dem Straßenniveau liegt.
6. Die Normalklassen werden von zwei Seiten über Fenster und Oberlicht belichtet.
7. Die innenliegende Aula kann gegen die ringsum auf und unter der Empore verlaufenden Verkehrswege durch Faltwände abgetrennt werden.

The school of banking lies on the shore of the Gulf of Finland about twenty kilometres from Helsinki. It serves about 4000 staff for professional courses. The banking practice and lecture rooms are accommodated in two adjacent buildings, in which the administration is also located. A third building contains dining, sitting and reception rooms. The school includes a hotel for 80 guests. The hotel bedrooms are flexibly planned. Folding partitions enable the four-bed rooms to be converted into two (double-bed) rooms. Two buildings containing employees' flats adjoin the dining room on the North side. The teaching staff live in a separate house near the entrance drive. The buildings are in part skeleton-frame, and partly load-bearing masonry, structures.

1. View from West of the South façade of the three main buildings, which are separated from each other by courtyards. Left foreground, the storey-high glazed front of the dining-room, shaded by upper-floor balcony.

1. Blick von Westen auf die Südfassade der drei Hauptgebäude, die durch Höfe voneinander getrennt sind. Links im Vordergrund die geschoßhohe Glasfront des Speisesaales, die durch den Balkon des Obergeschosses beschattet wird.

Die Bankfachschule liegt am Strand des Finnischen Meerbusens, rund zwanzig Kilometer außerhalb Helsinkis und dient den etwa 4000 Angestellten der Bank für Lehrgänge und Fortbildungskurse. Die Banktübungsräume und Hörsäle verteilen sich auf zwei nebeneinanderliegende Gebäude, in denen auch die Verwaltung untergebracht ist. In einem dritten Gebäude sind Speisesaal, Aufenthalts- und Repräsentationsräume zusammengefaßt. Zur Schule gehört ein Hotel, das maximal 80 Gäste aufnehmen kann. Der Grundriß der Hotelzimmer ist flexibel gehalten: durch Faltwände lassen sich die Vierbettzimmer in Doppelzimmer verwandeln. Die beiden Angestellten-Wohnbauten liegen an kleinen Höfen. Das Schulpersonal wohnt in einem frei stehenden Haus neben der Einfahrt. Die Gebäude sind teilweise als Skelettkonstruktion, teilweise mit tragenden Wänden erstellt.

2. Ground floor plan. Key: A hotel, B administration and instruction, C lecture rooms, D restaurant, E-F employees' flats, G staff residence. 1 entrance hall, 2 administration, 3 lecture room, 4 sitting room, 5 dining-room, 6 main kitchen, 7 hotel entrance, 8 living-and-working accommodation for course participants, 9 club room, 10 guest rooms, 11 guest baths, 12 caretaker's flat, 13 housekeeper's flat, 14 director's dwelling, 15 staff accommodation.

2. Grundriß Erdgeschoß. Legende: A Hotel, B Verwaltungs- und Unterrichtsbau, C Hörsaalbau, D Restaurantgebäude, E, F Angestellten-Wohnbauten, G Personalwohnheim. 1 Eingangshalle, 2 Verwaltung, 3 Hörsaal, 4 Aufenthaltsraum, 5 Speisesaal, 6 Hauptküche, 7 Hoteleingang, 8 Wohn- und Arbeitsräume für die Kursteilnehmer, 9 Klubraum, 10 Gästezimmer, 11 Gästebad, 12 Wohnung des Hausmeisters, 13 Wohnung der Hostess, 14 Wohnung des Direktors, 15 Personalwohnungen.

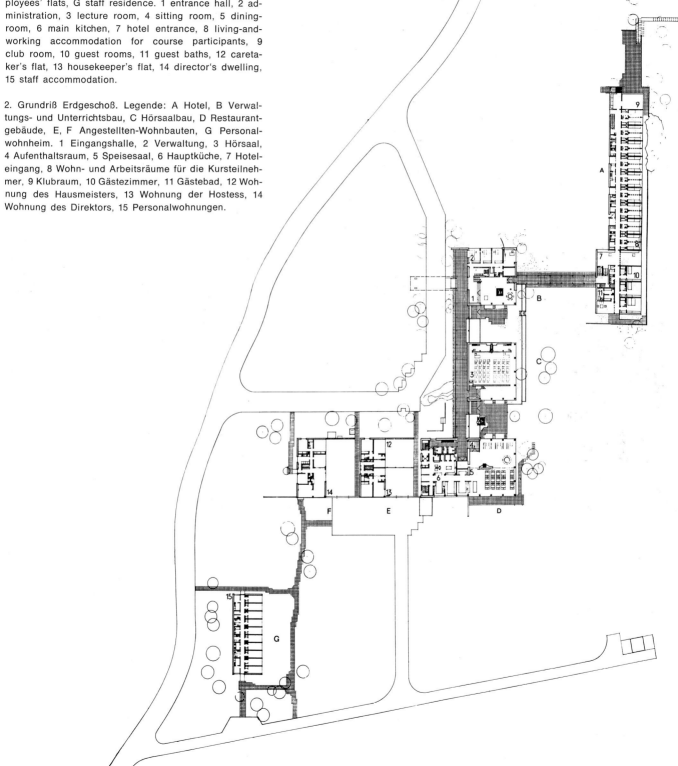

3. The hotel façade reflects the characteristic form and movement of the landscape.
4. A glazed covered way leads from the administration-and-instruction building to the hotel.
5. Foyer and sitting-room of restaurant block. The glazed façades convert the buildings, which are separated by spacious courtyards, into light and airy pavilions.
6. View of the corridor linking the three main buildings on the North side. The choice of materials — natural stone slabs for the floor, wood boards for the ceiling — and careful detailing make a coherent and satisfying room.

3. Die Hotelfassade nimmt in Struktur und Material motivisch Bewegung und Gestalt der Landschaft auf.
4. Vom Verwaltungs- und Unterrichtsbau (rechts) führt ein verglaster Gang zum Hotel.
5. Sitzgruppe im Aufenthaltsraum des Restaurantgebäudes. Die Auflösung der Fassaden in Glas macht die durch breite und tiefe Höfe getrennten Bauten zu leichten, luftigen Pavillons.
6. Blick in den Flur, der die drei Hauptgebäude auf der Nordseite verbindet. Materialwahl — Natursteinplatten für den Boden, Holzriemen für die Decke — und die sorgfältige Durcharbeitung aller Details schaffen einen klar gegliederten, ansprechenden Raum.

1. View of entrance hall (with staircase access to lecture ▷ room) rising through three storeys to roof.
2. Site plan. The green zones are indicated by hatched lines.

1. Blick in die Eingangshalle mit dem Treppenaufgang zum Hörsaal, die durch drei Geschosse bis zum Dach geht.
2. Lageplan. Die Grünflächen sind durch Parallelschraffur bezeichnet.

Sampola educational institute at Tampere. 1960-62
Architects: Timo Penttilä and Kari Virta

Volksbildungsinstitut Sampola in Tampere. 1960-62
Architekten: Timo Penttilä und Kari Virta

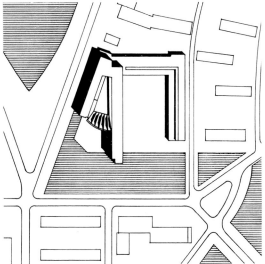

The site lies in a district of multi-storey housing at a heavily used crossroads. The architects succeeded in preserving part of the confined site as a connecting green zone between neighbouring parks. The institute functions throughout the day as a primary school and in the evening for adult education. Both for the most part use the same classrooms, while having their own rooms for special purposes: for the primary school, workshops, pupils' kitchen and gymnasia; for adults, library, art rooms and lecture hall (also used for social gatherings). The entrances to the two schools are separate. The building is a reinforced concrete structure erected with mobile shuttering.

Das Grundstück liegt in einem mit mehrgeschossigen Wohnhäusern überbauten Gebiet an einer stark befahrenen Straßenkreuzung. Es gelang den Architekten, einen Teil des knappen Baugrundes als verbindende Grünzone zwischen den Parkanlagen des Stadtteiles zu erhalten. In der Volksbildungsanstalt wird tagsüber von einer Volksschule und abends von einer Volkshochschule unterrichtet. Beide benutzen in der Hauptsache die gleichen Klassenräume. Nur für ihre besonderen Fachrichtungen haben beide Schulen ihre eigenen Spezialräume: Die Volksschule Werkstätten, Lehrküche und Turnräume, die Volkshochschule Bücherei, Räume für den Kunstunterricht und den Hörsaal, der auch als Festsaal dient. Die Eingänge zu den beiden Schulen sind getrennt. Das Gebäude ist eine Stahlbetonkonstruktion, erstellt im Gleitschalungsverfahren.

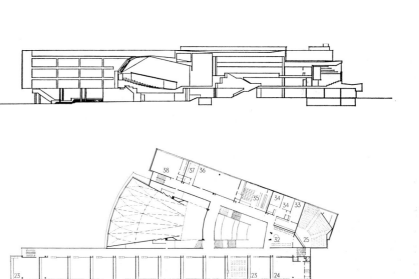

3. The large lecture-room — its functional design is apparent from outside — lies above the main entrance. The enclosed lattice girders extending above the roof give life and variety to an otherwise austere treatment of mass. The glazed staircase (to the right of the picture) leads to the primary school classrooms, which are also accessible via the main entrance.

4. The marked outward projection of the lecture-room provides shelter for the entrance forecourt, which is divided into sections by plastically moulded supports.

5. View into lecture-room with its raked and curving lines of seating. Restrained use of plastic features enhances the simple geometry of the room.

6. The dining-room lies next to the entrance hall on the ground floor. The obliquely rising ceiling near the windows accentuates the room's width and ensures additional light.

7. Section and plans of ground floor (below), first floor (middle) and second storey. Key: 1 cloakroom, 2 staff rooms, 3 principal, 4 office, 5 teaching aids, 6 caretaker, 7 library for adult school, 8 dining-room for adult school, 9 kitchen, 10 woodwork rooms, 11 woodwork machines, 12 metalwork classes, 13 forge, 14 domestic science supervision, 15 pupils' kitchen, 16 changing room, 17 laundry, 18 housekeeper's room, 19 gymnasium, 20 changing room, 21 showers, 22 flats, 23 standard (general subjects) classes, 24 special subjects, 25 smaller lecture-room, 26 natural history classes, 27 laboratory, 28 club room, 29 auditorium (lecture-room) and social hall, 30 stage, 31 cloakroom, 32 café, 33 doctor, 34 dentist, 35 commercial class, 36 art classroom, 37 commercial art, 38 modelling.

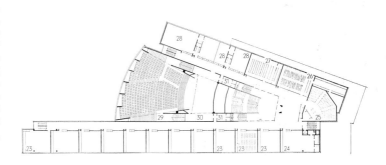

3. Über den Haupteingang schiebt sich der große Hörsaal, dessen funktionell bedingte Form von außen ablesbar ist. Seine über dem Dach liegenden, verkleideten Gitterträger setzen belebende Akzente und lockern die Baumasse auf. Die verglaste Treppe rechts im Bild führt zu den Klassenzimmern der Volksschule, die jedoch auch über den Haupteingang zugänglich sind.

4. Durch die beträchtliche Auskragung des Hörsaales entsteht ein geschützter Eingangsbereich, den die plastisch geformten Stützen in Abschnitte gliedern.

5. Blick in das Auditorium mit der ansteigenden, kreisförmig angeordneten Bestuhlung. Die klare Gliederung des Raumes wird durch die maßvolle Anwendung plastischer Mittel noch gesteigert.

6. Der Speisesaal liegt neben der Eingangshalle im Erdgeschoß. Der Deckensprung in der Fensterzone weitet optisch den Raum und sorgt für zusätzlichen Lichteinfall.

7. Schnitt und Grundrisse von Erdgeschoß (unten), erstem (Mitte) und zweitem Obergeschoß. Legende: 1 Garderobe, 2 Lehrerzimmer, 3 Schuldirektor, 4 Büro, 5 Unterrichtsmittel, 6 Hausmeister, 7 Bibliothek der Volkshochschule, 8 Speisesaal der Volkshochschule, 9 Küche, 10 Holzarbeitsraum, 11 Holzarbeitsmaschinen, 12 Metallarbeitsklasse, 13 Schmiede, 14 Haushaltskomitee, 15 Unterrichtsküche, 16 Umkleideraum, 17 Waschküche, 18 Haushaltsraum, 19 Turnsaal, 20 Umkleideraum, 21 Dusche, 22 Wohnungen, 23 Normalklasse, 24 Spezialklasse, 25 Kleiner Hörsaal, 26 Naturkundeklasse, 27 Labor, 28 Klubraum, 29 Auditorium und Festsaal, 30 Bühne, 31 Garderobe, 32 Café, 33 Arzt, 34 Zahnarzt, 35 Handelsklasse, 36 Kunstklasse, 37 Graphik, 38 Modellieren.

University school of sociology at Tampere. 1958-60
Architect: Toivo Korhonen

Soziologische Hochschule in Tampere. 1958-60
Architekt: Toivo Korhonen

1. View of access side with main entrance. The overhead beams above the roof plane of the large auditorium break the deliberate horizontality of the block.
2. Aerial view. The broad main wing holds the concert hall, lecture-rooms and library.

1. Blick auf die Zugangsseite mit dem Haupteingang. Die über dem Dach liegenden Gitterträger des Auditorium maximum wirken optisch als Unterbrechung und gliedernde Akzente der betont horizontalen Bewegung des Baukörpers.
2. Luftaufnahme. Im breiten Hauptflügel sind Konzertsaal, Auditorien und Bibliothek untergebracht.

The school building stands on a slight elevation in a zone reserved for public buildings. The main entrance adjoining the two-storey hall and cloakrooms lies where its wings intersect to form a cross. A broad staircase links the ground and upper floors. The cruciform plan was chosen because it facilitates internal circulation. The wider of the two wings contains the auditorium (which also serves as a concert hall and is reached from the upper storey) and a group of large lecture-rooms above the main entrance. The gymnasium and associated clubrooms adjoin the auditorium. The library, too, is on the upper floor of the principal wing. The library, the foyer of the lecture-rooms and the restaurant (in front of the gymnasium) have glazed fronts to storey-height. The other, narrower, wing accommodates teaching-staff rooms, research rooms, and offices.

Das Hochschulgebäude steht auf einem flachen Hügel, in einem Gebiet, das für öffentliche Bauten reserviert ist. Im Schnittpunkt seiner sich kreuzförmig durchdringenden Flügel liegt der Haupteingang mit der anschließenden, zweigeschossigen Halle und den Garderoben. Eine breite Treppe verbindet Erd- und Obergeschoß. Der kreuzförmige Grundriß wurde gewählt, da er die günstigste Führung und Verteilung des Verkehrs im Gebäudeinnern ermöglicht. Im breiteren der beiden Flügel befindet sich das vom Obergeschoß aus zugängliche Auditorium, das auch als Konzertsaal dient, und über dem Haupteingang eine Gruppe großer Vorlesungssäle. Der Gymnastiksaal mit den dazugehörigen Klubräumen schließt sich an das Auditorium an. Auch die Bibliothek ist im Obergeschoß des Hauptflügels untergebracht. Die Bibliothek, die Halle vor den Auditorien und das vor dem Gymnastiksaal liegende Restaurant sind geschoßhoch verglast. Der zweite, schmälere Flügel enthält Instituts-, Forschungs- und Büroräume.

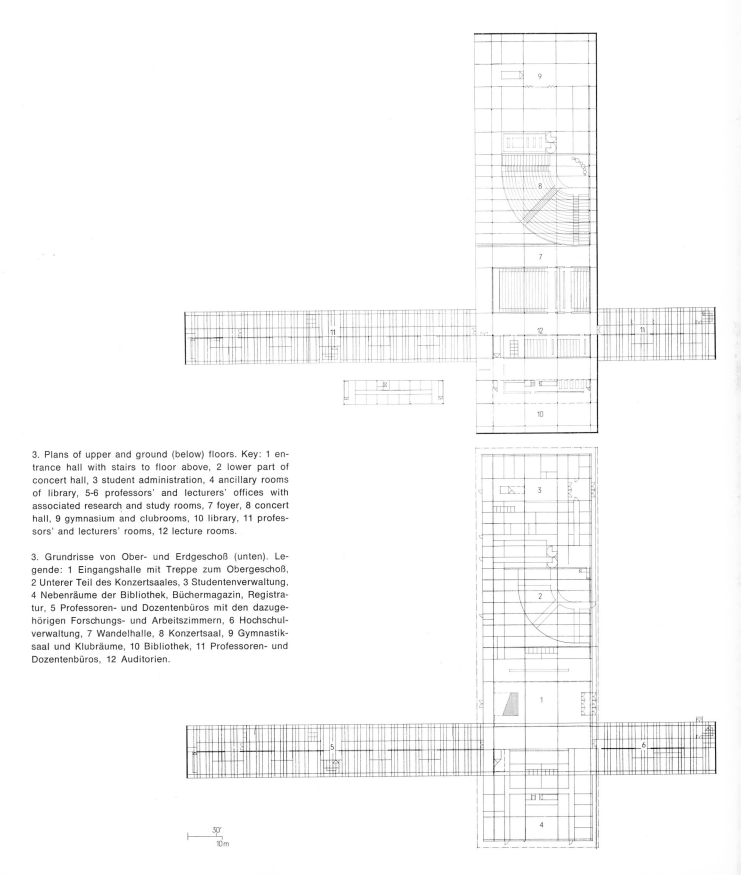

3. Plans of upper and ground (below) floors. Key: 1 entrance hall with stairs to floor above, 2 lower part of concert hall, 3 student administration, 4 ancillary rooms of library, 5-6 professors' and lecturers' offices with associated research and study rooms, 7 foyer, 8 concert hall, 9 gymnasium and clubrooms, 10 library, 11 professors' and lecturers' rooms, 12 lecture rooms.

3. Grundrisse von Ober- und Erdgeschoß (unten). Legende: 1 Eingangshalle mit Treppe zum Obergeschoß, 2 Unterer Teil des Konzertsaales, 3 Studentenverwaltung, 4 Nebenräume der Bibliothek, Büchermagazin, Registratur, 5 Professoren- und Dozentenbüros mit den dazugehörigen Forschungs- und Arbeitszimmern, 6 Hochschulverwaltung, 7 Wandelhalle, 8 Konzertsaal, 9 Gymnastiksaal und Klubräume, 10 Bibliothek, 11 Professoren- und Dozentenbüros, 12 Auditorien.

4. View into large auditorium with its steeply raked, circular, rows of seating.
5. In the library reading-room, extending the full width of the building, rooflights provide adequate natural lighting.
6. View of glazed hall, in front of lecture-rooms, and of teaching-staff wing.

4. Blick in das große Auditorium mit den steil ansteigenden, kreisförmig angeordneten Bankreihen.
5. Im Lesesaal der Bibliothek, der sich über die ganze Breite des Gebäudeflügels erstreckt, sorgen Oberlichter für ausreichende Helligkeit.
6. Blick auf die verglaste Halle vor den Auditorien und den Institutsflügel (rechts).

1. East view. The steeply rising auditorium building is the dominating element in the architectural composition.
2. Photo of model of the loosely grouped, horizontally disposed, range of buildings.

1. Ansicht von Osten. Der steil aufragende Auditorienbau ist das dominierende Element der baulichen Komposition. Rechts die Unterrichtsbauten.
2. Modellfoto des sehr locker gruppierten, in der Horizontalen entwickelten Komplexes.

The choice of site and organization of the competition held in 1949 lay in the hands of Professor Otto-I. Meurman. Aalto's project won first prize, but the execution of the whole scheme was entrusted to various architects. The main building built by Aalto stands on a hill in the centre of the university, where the principal building of an estate, previously on this site, used to be. Part of the former park remains as a green space round it. The focal point of this university centre is the auditorium building with two large halls (also intended for congresses). Its staircase-like ascending rows of windows suggest from the outside an amphitheatre. All tuition rooms are in adjacent buildings grouped about small internal courts, and here are also found the smaller lecture-rooms, laboratories and professors' rooms. The centre is divided into three principal departments: general, geodetic and architectural. The chief materials are dark red brick, black granite and copper.

Wahl des Geländes und Organisation des 1949 veranstalteten Wettbewerbes lagen in den Händen von Professor Otto-I. Meurman. Aalto erhielt für seinen Vorschlag den ersten Preis, die Ausführung der einzelnen Hochschulbauten jedoch wurde an verschiedene Architekten vergeben. Das von Aalto errichtete Hauptgebäude steht auf einem Hügel im Zentrum der Hochschule, wo sich auch das Hauptgebäude des früher auf diesem Grundstück gelegenen Gutshofes befand. Ein Teil des ehemaligen Parkes blieb als Grünraum beim Hauptgebäude erhalten. Kernstück dieses Hochschulzentrums ist der Hörsaalbau mit den beiden großen, auch für Versammlungen gedachten Auditorien. Seine treppenartig ansteigenden Fensterreihen lassen von außen an ein Amphitheater denken. Alle Forschungs- und Unterrichtsräume sind in Nebengebäuden untergebracht, die sich um kleine Innenhöfe gruppieren. Hier befinden sich auch die kleineren Hörsäle sowie Labors und Räume für die Professoren. Das Zentrum ist in drei Hauptabteilungen gegliedert: eine allgemeine, die geographischgeodätische und die Architekturabteilung. Die dominierenden Materialien sind dunkelroter Ziegel, schwarzer Granit und Kupfer.

3. View of entrance hall which extends the full length of the building and links the approach from the parking lot to the parkside access. The cloakrooms are between the powerful supports of the auditorium.

4. The hall in front of the lecture rooms on the first floor receives natural lighting from round ceiling lights. The very spacious room acquires a coherent pattern from the low parapet barriers of staircase exits.

5. The interpenetrating roof frame and ceiling joists ensure glare-free light for the auditorium.

6. Plans of ground floor and first storey. Key: 1 entrance hall, 2 lecture room, 3 art room, 4 practical-work room, 5 laboratory, 6 library, 7 common rooms, 8 records, 9 professors, 10 assistant staff and lecturers, 11 study rooms, 12 caretaker, 13 secretariat, 14 office, 15 conference room, 16 accounts, 17 stationery shop, 18 kitchen, 19 restaurant for teaching staff, 20 student's cafe, 21 air-raid shelter, 22 flat.

7. The auditorium building with its ribbon windows which light the lecture-rooms.

3. Blick in die Eingangshalle, die über die ganze Gebäudetiefe reicht und den Zugang von den Parkplätzen mit dem Zugang auf der Parkseite verbindet. Zwischen den kräftigen Stützpfeilern die Garderoben.

4. Die Halle vor den Auditorien im ersten Obergeschoß erhält durch kreisrunde Oberlichter Tageslicht. Der sehr tiefe Raum wird durch die niedrigen Brüstungen der Treppenabgänge gegliedert.

5. Die einander durchdringenden Dachbinder und Deckenunterzüge sorgen für blendungsfreie Ausleuchtung und geben dem Hörsaal seine besondere Wirkung.

6. Grundrisse von Erdgeschoß und erstem Obergeschoß. Legende: 1 Eingangshalle, 2 Hörsaal, 3 Zeichensaal, 4 Übungssaal, 5 Laboratorium, 6 Bibliothek, 7 Sammlungen, 8 Archiv, 9 Professoren, 10 Assistenten und Fachdozenten, 11 Studienzimmer, 12 Hausmeister, 13 Sekretariat, 14 Büro, 15 Konferenzraum, 16 Kasse, 17 Kiosk, 18 Küche, 19 Restaurant für den Lehrkörper, 20 Studentencafé, 21 Luftschutzraum, 22 Wohnung.

7. Das Auditoriengebäude mit seinen Fensterbändern, über die die Hörsäle belichtet werden.

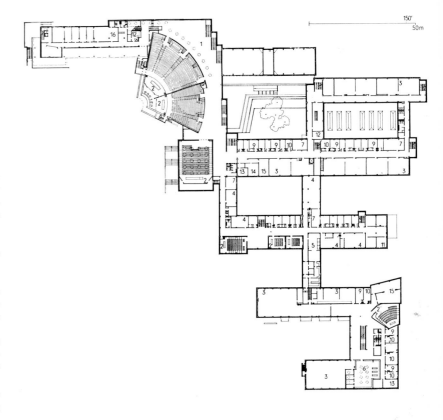

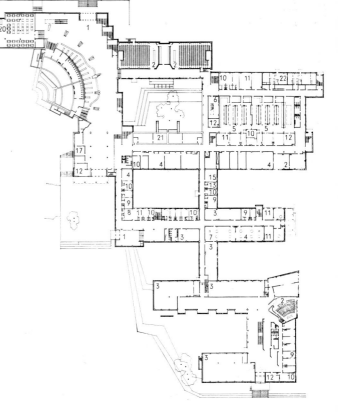

1. View towards cafeteria from South. Behind the high-piled random stone rampert is a large conference room. The projecting star-shaped roof assumes, on the one hand, the movement of the ground and, on the other, presents a strong contrast between its smooth tiered surface and the irregular mass of cyclopean masonry.
2. View of model from above. The two-part division of the building is externally apparent from the restaurant's raised roof.
3. The vertical and horizontal stepped treatment translates the building into massive sculpture in movement.
4. Plan. Key: 1 foyer, 2 large conference and lecture hall, 3 stage, 4 property room, 5 public restaurant, 6 meal service, 7 kitchen, 8 stores, 9 goods delivery, 10 conference room, 11 cafeteria, 12 students' restaurant, 13 buffet, 14 restaurant with dance floor.

1. Blick von Süden auf die Cafeteria. Hinter dem hochaufgeschichteten Wall aus Bruchsteinen ein großer Konferenzraum. Das sternförmig ausgreifende Dach nimmt einerseits die Bewegung des Geländes auf und setzt sich andererseits mit seinen glatten, horizontal strukturierten Flächen kräftig gegen die regellos aufeinander getürmte Zyklopenmauer ab.
2. Aufsicht auf das Modell. Die Zweiteilung des Gebäudes wird durch die Anhebung des Daches über dem Restaurantbereich nach außen sichtbar.
3. Vertikale und horizontale Stufung machen das Gebäude zu einer bewegten Großplastik.
4. Grundriß. Legende: 1 Foyer, 2 Großer Konferenz- und Vortragssaal, 3 Bühne, 4 Requisitenraum, 5 Öffentliches Restaurant, 6 Anrichten und Servieren der Speisen, 7 Küche, 8 Vorratsräume, 9 Warenanlieferung, 10 Konferenzraum, 11 Cafeteria, 12 Studentenrestaurant, 13 Buffet, 14 Restaurant mit Tanzfläche.

The students' union is the cultural and social centre for students of the technical university. The result of a two-stage competition in 1961, it stands on a rocky knoll amid fairiy dense trees which have been carefully preserved. The rugged site largely decided the formal conception of both the inside and outside of the building, which blends with its environment. The plan divides the built-over surface into two large zones. While the one comprising the public rooms emphasizes and reflects the formation and movement of the site, the rooms in the administrative part are disposed on purely functional lines. In the public zone the restaurant rooms occupy the greater part of the area. The administrative zone accommodates in particular the offices, kitchens, store rooms, technical services and cloakrooms. The external cladding of the building is cooper sheet. The exposed reinforced concrete construction has been left board-marked. Some wall surfaces and the ceilings are lined with wood boards.

Das Studentenhaus ist das kulturelle und soziale Zentrum für die Studenten der Technischen Hochschule. Es entstand, als Ergebnis eines Zweistufenwettbewerbes aus dem Jahre 1961, auf einer felsigen Hügelkuppe mit relativ dichtem Baumbestand, der sorgfältig geschont wurde. Das urwüchsige Gelände bestimmte innen und außen weitgehend die formale Gestaltung des Gebäudes, das mit seiner Umgebung verwächst. Der Grundriß gliedert die überbaute Fläche in zwei große Bereiche. Während im öffentlichen, für das Publikum bestimmten Bereich die Bewegung und Struktur des Geländes innen fortgesetzt und wiederholt werden, erfolgte im Wirtschaftsteil die Raumdisposition nach rein funktionalen Gesichtspunkten. Innerhalb des öffentlichen Bereiches nehmen die Restauranträume den größten Teil der Grundfläche ein. Im Wirtschaftsteil sind vorwiegend Büros, Küchen, Vorratsräume, technische Räume und Garderoben untergebracht. Das Gebäude ist außen mit Kupferblech verkleidet. Die Betonkonstruktion wurde innen schalungsroh belassen. Einzelne Wandteile und die Decken sind mit Holzriemen verschalt.

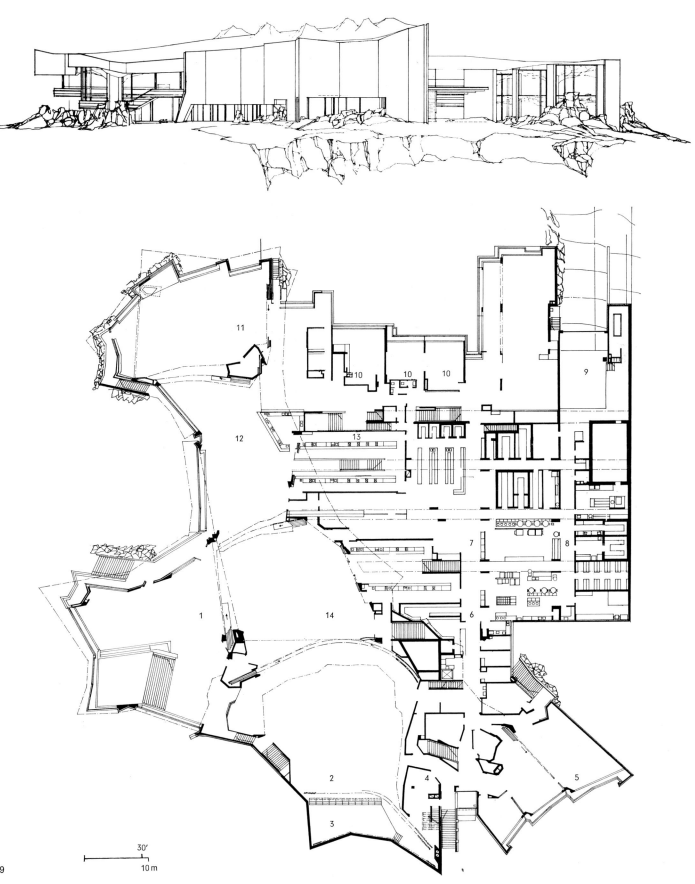

30'

10 m

5. Foyer of the large conference and lecture hall. Above the stone wall extending into the room, concrete joists (between which are hung the timber-lined ceilings) spread like the branches of trees from the vertical supports.

5. Das Foyer vor dem großen Konferenz- und Vortragssaal. Über der Steinmauer, die in den Raum hineinwächst, breiten sich wie die Äste eines Baumes die von der Stütze ausgehenden Beton-Unterzüge, zwischen denen die holzverschalte Decke hängt.

6. Main entrance on the South side.
7. View into the cafeteria from the students' restaurant. Polygonal figures characterize ground plan and wall-treatment.
8. The projecting wings form a succession of intimate open-air spaces, which bring the landscape into the building.

6. Haupteingang auf der Südseite.
7. Blick aus dem Studentenrestaurant in die Cafeteria. Polygonale Brechungen in Grundriß und Wandaufbau kennzeichnen den Raum.
8. Die ausgreifenden Gebäudeflügel bilden eine Reihe von intimen Höfen, durch die die Landschaft in das Gebäude hineingeführt wird.

1. Aerial view with river in foreground. Between the offices and workshops (left) and the auditorium (right) stands the vertical feature of the stage tower.
2. View of the riverbank promenade and the foyer.

1. Luftaufnahme mit dem Fluß im Vordergrund. Zwischen Büros und Werkstätten, links im Bild, und Zuschauerraum mit Foyer, rechts, schiebt sich der Bühnenturm.
2. Blick auf Strandpromenade und Foyer.

The project which won a first prize in a competition in 1955, was only partly carried out. The theatre stands in a parklike hilly landscape on a riverbank. The plan is so contrived that the stage tower is the dominant feature at the centre of the scheme, dividing the public from the private realms of the theatre. The foyer round the auditorium opens on to the river and grounds on either side of the building. The main entrance is under the projecting foyer storey on the East side. Next to the main stage there is extensive wing space connected to the paint-shop and scenery and property stores. The offices and workshops mostly face North and East and, thanks to the stepped plan, all have natural lighting. The elevations are partly faced with ceramic panels, and partly with copper.

Der in dem 1955 ausgeschriebenen Wettbewerb mit einem ersten Preis ausgezeichnete Entwurf wurde nur teilweise verwirklicht. Das Theater steht in einer parkartigen Hügellandschaft am Ufer eines Flusses. Der Grundriß ist so angelegt, daß das Bühnenhaus als Dominante im Zentrum der Anlage steht und die Räume für das Publikum vom theaterinternen Bereich trennt. Die Foyers um den Theatersaal öffnen sich zum Fluß und zu den Anlagen auf beiden Seiten des Gebäudes. Der Haupteingang liegt unter dem vorgezogenen Foyergeschoß an der Ostseite. Neben der Hauptbühne befindet sich eine Seitenbühne, an die sich Malerwerkstatt, Kulissen- und Möbellager anschließen. Die Büros und Werkstätten sind in der Hauptsache nach Norden und Osten orientiert und haben, durch die gestaffelte Bauweise, alle Tageslicht. Die Fassaden sind teils mit Keramikplatten, teils mit Kupfer verkleidet.

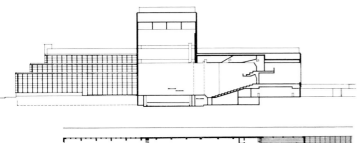

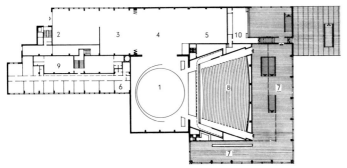

3. Section and plan of the first floor. Key: 1 stage, 2 carpenter's shop, 3 paint shop, 4 wings, 5 scenery store, 6 administration, 7 foyer, 8 auditorium, 9 wardrobe, 10 fitting room.
4. By exploiting a vertical and horizontal stepped layout the building's mass appears diminished and its sculptural qualities are enhanced.
5. The ground floor cloakroom acquires a lively and coherent pattern from light and dark surfaces.
6. View into auditorium.
7. Foyer on first floor.

3. Schnitt und Grundriß des ersten Obergeschosses. Legende: 1 Bühne, 2 Schreiner, 3 Maler, 4 Seitenbühne, 5 Kulissenlager, 6 Verwaltung, 7 Foyer, 8 Zuschauerraum, 9 Schauspielergarderobe, 10 Schneider.
4. Durch die vertikale und horizontale Staffelung der Bauglieder wird das Gebäudevolumen optisch verringert.
5. Die Garderobenhalle im Erdgeschoß wird durch den Wechsel von hellen und dunklen Flächen belebt.
6. Blick in den Zuschauerraum.
7. Das Foyer im ersten Obergeschoß.

Cultural centre at Helsinki. 1955-58
Architect: Alvar Aalto

Kulturhaus in Helsinki. 1955-58
Architekt: Alvar Aalto

The "house of culture" (Kulttuuritalo) serves as a centre for the cultural work of various trade-union organizations. The building comprises three distinct parts: offices, lecture and conference rooms, a concert hall. The office part has five storeys with 110 offices, meeting rooms and two flats. In the lecture and conference room section (in the middle of a U-shaped complex) are a lecture hall, study rooms, discussion rooms, a library and a records room. The concert and congress hall is the main feature of the group. The hall, with 1500 seats and a stage 200 m², is primarily intended for concerts, but is also used for lectures. The various parts of the building are linked together along the street by a canopy 60 m long, under which are the main entrances. The free asymmetrical form of the hall entailed the development of a new facing element, a wedge-shaped brick, with which all the curves of the irregular exterior could be realized.

Das Haus der Kultur (Kulttuuritalo) dient als Zentrum für die kulturelle Arbeit verschiedener Gewerkschaftsorganisationen. Der Gebäudekomplex besteht aus drei deutlich voneinander abgesetzten Trakten, einem Büroteil, dem Vorlesungs- oder Konferenzteil und dem Konzertsaal. Der Büroteil umfaßt fünf Geschosse mit 110 Büros, Besprechungsräumen und zwei Wohnungen. Im Vorlesungs- und Konferenztrakt in der Mitte der U-förmigen Anlage sind Hörsaal, Studienräume, Besprechungsräume, Bibliothek und Archiv untergebracht. Der Konzert- und Kongreßsaal ist der Hauptteil der Gebäudegruppe. Der Saal hat 1500 Sitzplätze und eine zweihundert Quadratmeter große Bühne. Er ist in erster Linie für Konzerte, aber auch Vorträge gedacht. Die verschiedenen Bauteile des Gebäudekomplexes sind längs der Straße durch ein sechzig Meter langes Vordach, unter dem auch die Haupteingänge liegen, verbunden. Die asymmetrisch freie Form des Saales machte die Entwicklung eines neuen Fassadenelementes, eines keilförmigen Ziegels notwendig, mit dem sich alle Kurven der gekrümmten Außenwand mauern ließen.

1. View from the street. Left, the concert hall; right, the office block. The concert hall entrance lies under the canopy.
2. The detail clearly illustrates the lively movement of the façade.
3. Section and plan of the first floor. Key: 1 concert hall, 2 stage, 3 lecture room, 4 group meeting room, 5 library, 6 records, 7 office, 8 common room, 9 chair stack.
4, 5. View into concert hall. The lower (level) rows of seats can be dismantled. The walls are faced with acoustic tiles. The wood-lined ceiling and wall meet in an uneven flowing line.

1. Ansicht von der Straße. Links der Konzertsaal, rechts der Büroteil. Der Eingang zum Konzertsaal liegt unter dem Vordach.
2. Die Detailansicht läßt deutlich Schwung und Bewegung der Fassade erkennen.
3. Schnitt und Grundriß des ersten Obergeschosses. Legende: 1 Konzertsaal, 2 Bühne, 3 Vortragssaal, 4 Gruppenraum, 5 Bibliothek, 6 Archiv, 7 Büro, 8 Gemeinschaftsraum, 9 Stuhlmagazin.
4, 5. Blick in den Konzertsaal. Die unteren, nicht ansteigenden Stuhlreihen sind demontabel. Die Wände wurden mit Akustikplatten verkleidet. Holzverschalte Decke und Wand treffen sich in einer bewegten, fließenden Linie.

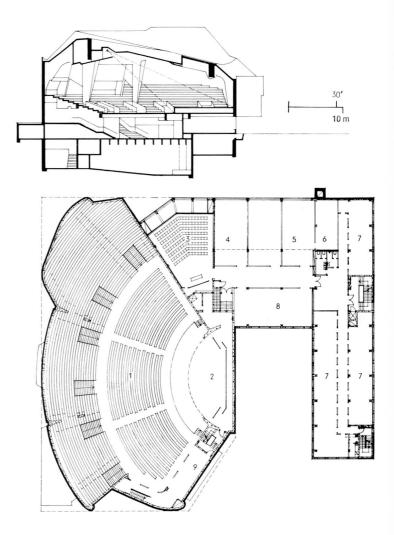

30'
10 m

City theatre in Helsinki. 1964-67
Architect: Timo Penttilä

Stadttheater in Helsinki. 1964-67
Architekt: Timo Penttilä

The scheme won first prize in a competition held in 1960. Standing in a park not far from the projected city centre, the theatre has two stages, one large house with about 950 seats; one small, the studio theatre, with seating for about 300. All public rooms extend in a serpentine band along the entrance side. From the foyer and cloakroom lobby of the large theatre one looks South on to the park and the Töölö lake. The foyer and cloakroom lobby of the small theatre, however, have no windows. Like the studio stage, they have an enclosed, intimate atmosphere. A joint box-office separates the cloakrooms of both theatres. On the second floor there are two cafés and another foyer, which serves the boxes and circle rows. All principal storage and workshop facilities of both houses are at stage level. Actors' dressing rooms, offices and further store rooms are on upper floors. A large car park adjoins the building on the North side. The façades of the r. c. structure are clad with incised ceramic slabs.

Das Projekt erhielt in dem Wettbewerb des Jahres 1960 den ersten Preis. Das Theater, das in einem Park unweit des geplanten neuen Stadtzentrums liegt, hat zwei Bühnen; ein Großes Haus mit rund 950 und ein Kleines Haus, die Studiobühne, mit rund 300 Plätzen. Alle Publikumsräume sind in einem bandartigen Streifen auf der Eingangsseite zusammengefaßt. Aus den Foyers und der Garderobenhalle des Großen Hauses blickt man nach Süden auf den Park und den Töölö-See. Foyer und Garderobenhalle des Kleinen Hauses dagegen haben keine Fenster. Analog zum Charakter der Studiobühne sind sie geschlossen und intim gestaltet. Eine gemeinsame Kassenhalle trennt die Garderoben der beiden Theater voneinander. Im zweiten Obergeschoß befinden sich zwei Cafés und ein zweites Foyer, das in Verbindung mit den Logen steht. Alle wichtigen Lagerräume und Werkstätten der beiden Theater liegen auf Bühnenniveau. Die Schauspielergarderoben, Büros und weitere Lagerräume sind in den oberen Geschossen untergebracht. Im Norden schließt sich an das Gebäude ein großer Parkplatz an. Die Fassaden des Stahlbetonbaues wurden mit Keramikspaltplatten verkleidet.

1, 2. East view and entrance front. The building is adapted to the falling site, so that the top floor meets the slope at ground level. The stepped contours of successive storeys and frequent changes in alignment create a lively and varied sculptural effect, each element vying with the dominance of the stage tower.

3. The theatre looks single-storeyed from the West. The continuous glazed front stresses the monumentality of the stage tower.

4. Ground floor plan. Key: 1 box office lobby, 2 cloakroom lobby, 3 large theatre, 4 large theatre stage, 5 wing space, 6 backstage space, 7 small theatre stage, 8 scenery store, 9 paint shop, 10 carpenter's shop, 11 car access-ramp, 12 property store, 13 artists' rest rooms, 14 stage hands.

1, 2. Ostansicht und Eingangsfront. Das Gebäude ist so in das fallende Gelände eingefügt, daß sich das oberste Geschoß ebenerdig an den Hang anschließt. Höhenstufung der Geschosse und häufiger Richtungswechsel der Fassaden schaffen eine bewegte Großplastik, deren Elemente zur Dominante des Bühnenturmes hinstreben.

3. Von Westen gesehen scheint das Theater nur eingeschossig. Die durchgehende Glasfront betont die Monumentalität des Bühnenturmes.

4. Grundriß Erdgeschoß. Legende: 1 Kassenhalle, 2 Garderobenhalle, 3 Großes Haus, 4 Bühne des Großen Hauses, 5 Seitenbühne, 6 Hinterbühne, 7 Bühne des Kleinen Hauses, 8 Kulissenlager, 9 Malerwerkstatt, 10 Schreinerwerkstatt, 11 Zufahrtsrampe, 12 Requisitenlager, 13 Aufenthaltsräume für Künstler, 14 Bühnenarbeiter.

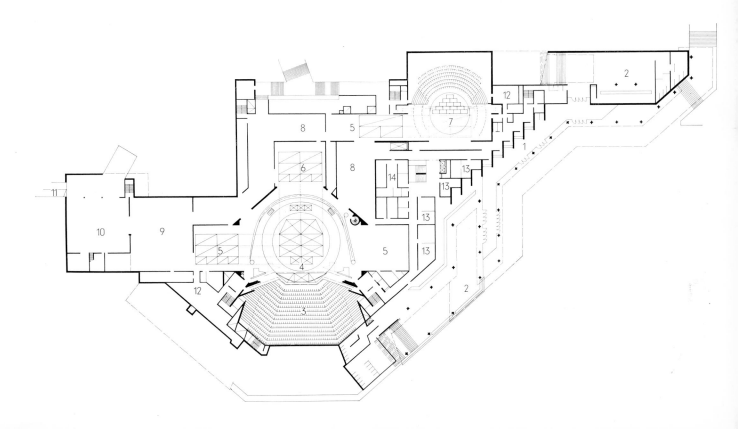

5. The front of the building is recessed at the entrance and the floor deck above is cantilevered outward to form a rain shield. The powerful columns stand, in some cases, in front and, in others, behind the façade.

6, 7. From the cloakroom lobby (6) a broad staircase leads to the upstairs foyer (7). The way in which the rooms flow into one another is clearly shown.

8. Cloakroom foyer and lobby of the small house.

9. View towards the entrance of the small theatre.

5. Im Eingangsbereich ist die Gebäudefront buchtartig zurückgenommen und die Geschoßdecke zum Schutz gegen Regen weit ausgekragt. Die kräftigen Stützen stehen teils vor, teils hinter der Fassade.

6, 7. Von der Garderobenhalle des Großen Hauses (Bild 6) führen breite Treppen zu den Foyers der Obergeschosse (Bild 7). Das Ineinanderfließen der Räume wird überzeugend verdeutlicht.

8. Garderobenhalle und Foyer des Kleinen Hauses.

9. Blick auf den Eingang zum Kleinen Haus.

10. The auditorium of the large theatre reflects the variety and liveliness of form which the exterior of the building displays. Above the steeply rising rows of stall seats reaching in front to the stage edge, the "circle" (resting on heavy raked beams) thrusts forward its irregular, undulating silhouette.

11. The small house recalls the theatres of antiquity in the concentric rows of seats slanted about an almost circular stage.

10. Der Zuschauerraum des Großen Hauses ist ähnlich bewegt und plastisch gestaltet wie die Außenfront des Gebäudes. Über die steil ansteigenden Stuhlreihen des Parketts, die dicht an die Bühne heranrücken, kragt der Rang, der auf kräftigen Trägern ruht, in entschiedenem Auf und Ab, Vor und Zurück weit aus.

11. In der konzentrischen Anordnung der ansteigenden Sitzplätze um eine annähernd kreisförmige Bühne in Höhe der ersten Stuhlreihe erinnert das Kleine Haus an ein antikes Theater.

Project for an opera house at Essen. 1959
Architect: Alvar Aalto

Entwurf für ein Opernhaus in Essen. 1959
Architekt: Alvar Aalto

1. View of South side of model. The line, which climbs against the slope of the ground, derives from enclosing the stage tower in the building.
2. Section.

1. Modellansicht Südseite. Die ansteigende, entgegen dem Geländeabfall verlaufende Dachlinie ergibt sich aus der Einbindung des Bühnenturms in das Gebäude.
2. Längsschnitt.

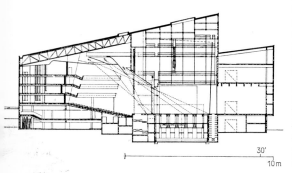

The assessors of the competiton held in 1959 unanimously recommended that Alvar Aalto's design should be built. The opera house is to be erected in the city gardens. A two-storey car park adjoins the entrance driveway on the North side. Vehicular and pedestrian traffic are completely segregated. In the entrance area the rooms flow into one another, and the effect of this on the visitor is step by step to quicken the sense of splendid occasion. From the entrance hall, with cloakrooms on either side, broad staircases lead to the magnificent foyer, irregular and asymmetrical in shape, and divided by three galleries. The auditorium, with three tiers of seats above, encloses the stage amphitheatrically in an approximate semicircle. The raked stalls have 900 seats, the three upper tiers 500. A second (smaller) theatre holding 270 people, on the South side of the building, is intended for experimental productions. The irregular external form of the building is countered by the even slope of the roof, under which the stage tower is concealed. The elevations, vertical in emphasis, are faced with natural stone.

Alvar Aaltos Entwurf wurde vom Preisgericht des 1959 veranstalteten Wettbewerbs einstimmig zur Ausführung empfohlen. Das Opernhaus soll im Stadtgarten errichtet werden. An die Vorfahrt auf der Nordseite schließt sich ein zweigeschossiges Parkgebäude an. Auto- und Fußgängerverkehr sind vollständig voneinander getrennt. Im Eingangsbereich fließen die Räume ineinander. Dieser Raumfluß soll der sich stufenweise steigernden, festlichen Erwartung des Besuchers Ausdruck geben. Von der Eingangshalle mit den Garderoben auf beiden Seiten leiten breit angelegte Treppen in das festliche Foyer, dessen geschwungene, asymmetrische Form durch drei Galerien gegliedert wird. Der Zuschauerraum mit den drei Rängen umgibt die Bühne amphitheatralisch in annähernder Halbkreisform. Das ansteigende Parkett bietet 900 Menschen Platz, die Ränge fassen 500 Zuschauer. Als Experimentierbühne ist der zweite, der kleine Theatersaal für 270 Besucher auf der Südseite des Gebäudes gedacht. Die bewegte äußere Form des Baues wird durch das ansteigende Dach aufgefangen. Der Bühnenturm ist in das Gebäude integriert. Natursteine verkleiden die Fassade und geben ihr eine vertikale Struktur.

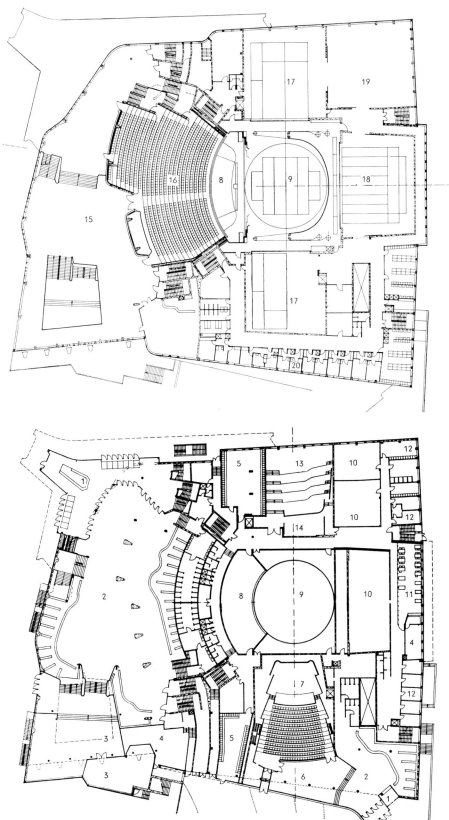

3. Plans of upper storey and ground floor (below). Key:
1 box-office, 2 entrance hall, 3 restaurant, 4 kitchen,
5 musicians' dressing-room, 6 foyer of small theatre,
7 small theatre, 8 orchestra, 9 principal stage, 10 store
room, 11 canteen, 12 staff rooms, 13 orchestra rehearsal
room, 14 instruments, 15 foyer, 16 large theatre auditorium, 17 wing space, 18 backstage space, 19 storage,
20 artists' dressing-room.
4. The irregular, boxlike, tiers of seats project into the
auditorium. Their smooth marble fronts make a lively
contrast with the dark sharply defined multiple divisions
of wall and ceiling.

3. Grundrisse von Obergeschoß und Erdgeschoß (unten).
Legende: 1 Kasse, 2 Eingangshalle, 3 Restaurant, 4
Küche, 5 Musikergarderobe, 6 Foyer zum kleinen Theatersaal, 7 Kleiner Theatersaal, 8 Orchester, 9 Hauptbühne, 10 Lagerraum, 11 Kantine, 12 Personalräume,
13 Orchesterprobenraum, 14 Instrumentenraum, 15 Foyer,
16 Zuschauerraum Großes Haus, 17 Seitenbühne, 18 Hinterbühne, 19 Magazin, 20 Schauspielergarderoben.
4. Die geschwungenen, logenartigen Ränge wachsen in
den Zuschauerraum hinein. Ihre glatten Marmorbrüstun-
gen kontrastieren lebhaft mit den dunklen, stark gegliederten Wand- und Deckenflächen.

1. Interior view. Thanks to the glazed external walls, the roof appears to float, and this increases the sense of space.
2. Entrance area, characterized by the exposed r. c. load-bearing elements. The open staircase to the upper seats relieves the strictly functional space.
3. View of entrances in one of the narrower sides of the stadium. The inward-curving sharply defined glass curtain is placed in front of the load-bearing elements.
4. Section and plans of entrance floor (left) and second storey. Key: 1 playing area, 2 open stage, 3 toilets, 4 power control, 5 cleaning equipment, 6 kiosk, 7 store room, 8 ventilation, 9 pay office, 10 V.I.P. entrance, 11 technical room, 12 press entrance, 13 spectators, 14 seats, 15 standing room, 16 press, 17 control room, 18 lighting (controller), 19 sound (controller).

1. Innenansicht. Die verglasten Außenfronten lassen das Dach abgehoben erscheinen und weiten den Raum.
2. Der Eingangsbereich, dessen Charakter die konstruktiv tragenden Sichtbetonelemente bestimmen.
3. Blick auf die Eingänge in der Schmalfront der Halle. Die nach innen gekrümmte, stark gegliederte Glasfassade ist vor die tragenden Elemente gesetzt.
4. Querschnitt und Grundrisse von Eingangsgeschoß (links) und zweitem Obergeschoß. Legende: 1 Spielfeld, 2 Offene Bühne, 3 Toilette, 4 Kraftzentrale, 5 Putzraum, 6 Kiosk, 7 Lagerraum, 8 Lüftung, 9 Kasse, 10 Zugang für Ehrengäste, 11 Technischer Raum, 12 Zugang für Reporter, 13 Zuschauer, 14 Sitzplätze, 15 Stehplätze, 16 Reporter, 17 Kontrollraum, 18 Beleuchter, 19 Tonmeister.

The sports "hall" stands near the city centre, a near neighbour to the Olympic stadium, a covered swimming-pool and several sports grounds. As well as ice-hockey, figure skating and ice revues, the hall will accommodate basket-ball, volleyball, handball, tennis tournaments, and even boxing and wrestling. In addition the building can be used for congresses and large gatherings. The hall has 12,000 seats, which can be increased to 14,500 by putting seats on the playing area. A close-mesh network of staircases ensures the quick and smooth entry and exit of spectators. Stressed steel cables, 58mm thick and 5m apart, carry the unsupported roof. These are anchored to the reinforced concrete elements on which the stands rest.

Die Sporthalle liegt in der Nähe des Stadtzentrums, unmittelbar neben dem Olympiastadion, dem Schwimmstadion und mehreren Sportplätzen. Neben Eishockey, Eiskunstlauf und Eisrevue sollen in der Halle Basketball-, Volleyball- und Handballspiele, Tennisturniere und auch Box- und Ringkämpfe stattfinden. Darüber hinaus kann der Bau auch für Kongresse und Versammlungen verwendet werden. Die Halle hat 12 000 Sitzplätze, deren Zahl durch die Bestuhlung des Spielfeldes auf 14 500 erhöht werden kann. Für die schnelle und reibungslose Zu- und Abführung der Zuschauer sorgt ein engmaschiges Netz von Treppen. 58 mm dicke, im Abstand von jeweils fünf Metern über die Halle gespannte Stahltrossen tragen das stützenfreie Dach. Als Verankerung für diese Kabel dienen die Stahlbetonelemente, auf denen die Tribünen ruhen.

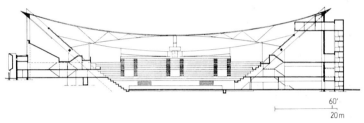

60'
20 m

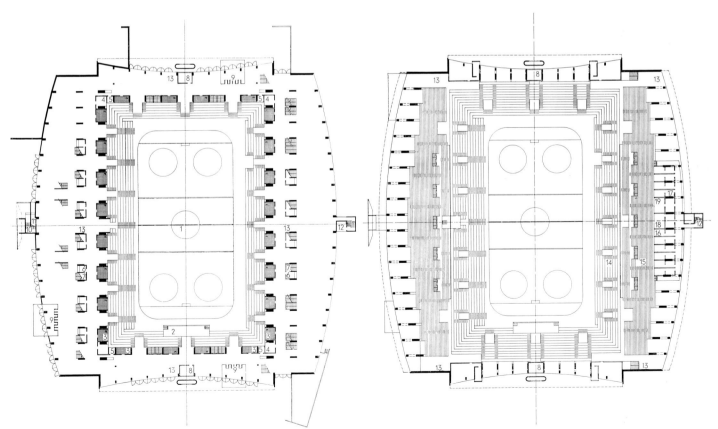

Swimming stadium at Imatra. 1965-66
Architect: Einari Teräsvirta

Schwimmhalle in Imatra. 1965-66
Architekt: Einari Teräsvirta

The covered swimming pool was built as the first phase of a larger sports programme, which will include a sports hall, bowling alleys, facilities for weight-lifting, boxing, etc., a fifty-metre open-air pool and a restaurant. The building, part of the plan for the new centre of Imatra, can in summer be opened on to the proposed riverside open-air bath by lowering a glass wall. The dimensions chosen for the pool are big enough to permit a separate plunge-bath. The (7.5m high) spring-board stands in the middle of the cross-lit hall, where the vaulted roof is at its highest. The ceiling was lined with wood for acoustical reasons. The laminated timber beams carrying the roof have a span of 40m.

Die Schwimmhalle wurde als erster Bauabschnitt einer größeren Sportanlage errichtet. Hinzu kommen noch eine Sporthalle, Kegelbahnen, ein Übungssaal für Schwerathleten, ein Fünfzig-Meter-Freibecken und ein Restaurant. Das Gebäude, das städtebaulich an Imatras neues Zentrum angeschlossen ist, kann im Sommer durch eine versenkbare Glaswand zum geplanten Freibad am Fluß hin geöffnet werden. Die Maße für das Schwimmbecken sind so groß gewählt, daß sich ein Sprungbecken abtrennen läßt. Der siebeneinhalb Meter hohe Sprungturm steht in der Mitte der zweiseitig belichteten Halle, da dort die notwendige Raumhöhe durch die Wölbung des Hallendaches gegeben ist. Aus akustischen Erwägungen wurde die Decke mit Holzriemen verschalt. Die Schichtholzbalken, die das Dach tragen, haben eine Spannweite von 40 Metern.

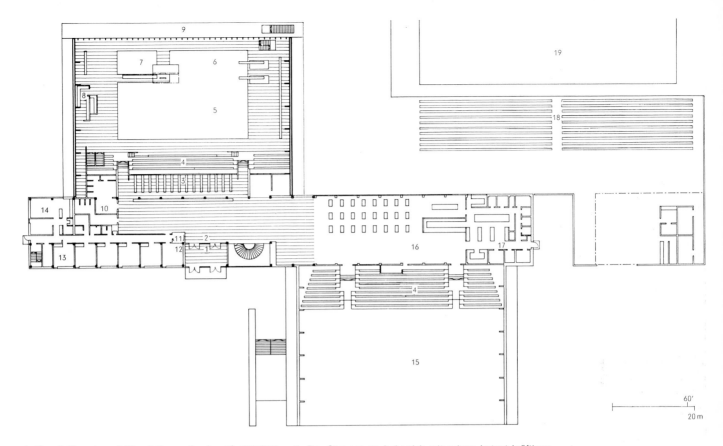

1. The deliberate solidity of the spring-board structure stands out against the delicate filigree of the glazed wall, the lower elements of which can be lowered.
2. The simply composed entrance hall is reached via a glazed porch.
3. Ground floor plan. Key: 1 porch, 2 entrance hall, 3 cloakroom, 4 spectators, 5 swimming pool, 6 plunge bath, 7 learners' pool, 8 bath superintendant, 9 veranda, 10 WC, 11 pay-desk, 12 office, 13 guest rooms, 14 flat, 15 ball game hall, 16 restaurant, 17 kitchen, 18 spectators' stand for open-air pool, 19 open-air pool.
4. View of spectators' seats on South side of hall.
5. General view, with range of guest rooms (left) in front of hall, and main entrance.

1. Der Sprungturm hebt sich mit seinen betont kräftigen Formen deutlich vom zarten Filigran der Glasfront ab, deren untere Elemente versenkt werden können.
2. Die klar gegliederte Eingangshalle erreicht man über einen gläsernen Windfang.
3. Erdgeschoßgrundriß. Legende: 1 Windfang, 2 Eingangshalle, 3 Garderobe, 4 Zuschauer, 5 Schwimmbecken, 6 Sprungbecken, 7 Lehrschwimmbecken, 8 Bademeister, 9 Balkon, 10 WC, 11 Kasse, 12 Büro, 13 Gästeräume, 14 Wohnung, 15 Ballspielhalle, 16 Restaurant, 17 Küche, 18 Tribüne für das Freibad, 19 Freibad.
4. Blick auf die Zuschauerränge auf der Südseite.
5. Gesamtansicht mit dem der Halle vorgelagerten, langgestreckten Gästetrakt (links) und dem Haupteingang.

Military sports centre at Kajaani. 1962-64
Architect: Osmo Lappo, in association with Jaakko Rantanen, Martti Tiula, Harto Helpinen

Militärsportzentrum in Kajaani. 1962-64
Architekt: Osmo Lappo. Mitarbeiter: Jaakko Rantanen, Martti Tiula, Harto Helpinen

1. View from North-West. The long, compact building, enlivened visually by skilful use of structural features, merges with the landscape. The towers contain tent-drying rooms and a staircase.
2. Photo of model with mess hall (above left) and barracks (above right).

1. Ansicht von Nordwesten. Das langgestreckte, kompakte Gebäude wird durch die geschickte Anwendung gestalterischer Mittel optisch aufgelockert und in die Landschaft eingebunden. In den Türmen sind Zelttrockenräume und eine Treppe untergebracht.
2. Modellfoto mit der Kantine (links oben) und der Kaserne (rechts oben).

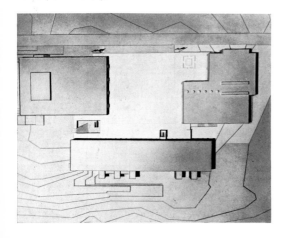

The sports centre is part of a larger scheme, which includes a mess hall and barracks. These three buildings, sited on a hill, are placed round a central square. The ground floor of the sports centre contains storage space and service rooms. Changing rooms, swimming pool and sauna are on the first floor. The swimming pool is 10 x 25m. The three- and five-metre springboards are cantilevered from the side wall. The large gymnasium on the second floor can be divided into two by a curtain. The towerlike constructions on the North side, which provide structural reinforcement, house staircases, air-conditioning plant, apparatus store and drying-rooms for camp equipment. The gymnasium and swimming-pool have natural cross-lighting from windows inserted high up between the roof and ceiling joists. The building is a reinforced concrete structure. The walls of the gymnasium have wood linings over a layer of sound-absorbent material.

Zum Sportzentrum gehören das Sportgebäude, eine Kantine und eine Kaserne. Diese drei Bauten liegen auf einem Hügel und sind einem zentralen Platz zugeordnet. Im Erdgeschoß des Sportgebäudes befinden sich Lager- und technische Räume. Im ersten Obergeschoß liegen Umkleideräume, Schwimmhalle und Sauna. Das Schwimmbecken hat eine Größe von 10 x 25 Metern. Die Drei- und Fünfmeter-Sprungbretter sind aus der Seitenwand ausgekragt. Die große Turnhalle im zweiten Obergeschoß läßt sich mit einem Stoffvorhang in zwei Hallen teilen. In den turmartigen Anbauten auf der Nordseite, die konstruktiv zur Aussteifung der Halle dienen, sind Treppen, Klimaanlage, Gerüstlager und Zelttrockenräume untergebracht. Sport- und Schwimmhalle erhalten über hochliegende, zwischen die Dach- beziehungsweise Deckenunterzüge eingefügte Oberlichter Tageslicht. Das Gebäude ist eine Stahlbetonkonstruktion. Die Wände sind innen mit Holz auf einer schalldämmenden Schicht verkleidet.

3. View of swimming-pool.
4, 6. High-placed windows on opposite sides provide good lighting for the gymnasium. The wood cladding of walls and ceiling gives the austere design warmth.
5. Plans of ground (left) and first floor. Key: 1 stores, 2 mechanical services, 3 oil tank, 4 tent-drying room, 5 changing-room and showers, 6 entrance hall, 7 clothes store, 8 showers, 9 sauna, 10 covered swimming-pool, 11 stairs to springboards, 12 bath superintendant.

3. Blick in die Schwimmhalle.
4, 6. Durch die zweiseitige Belichtung wird eine gute Ausleuchtung der Turnhalle erreicht. Die Holzverkleidung von Wänden und Decke gibt dem formal streng gestalteten Raum Wärme.
5. Grundrisse von Erdgeschoß (links) und erstem Obergeschoß. Legende: 1 Lagerraum, 2 Maschinenraum, 3 Öltank, 4 Zelttrockenraum, 5 Umkleideraum und Dusche, 6 Eingangshalle, 7 Wäschemagazin, 8 Duschraum, 9 Sauna, 10 Schwimmhalle, 11 Treppe zum Sprungturm, 12 Bademeister.

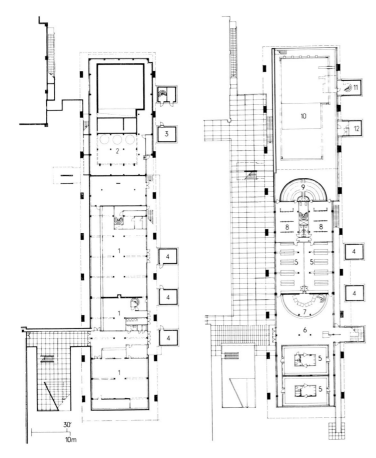

30'
10m

1. South-West view. The main entrance zone of the
principal front is recessed. The prominent mullions give
a vigorous coherence to the façade.

1. Ansicht von Südwesten. Die Fassade ist im Bereich
des Haupteinganges zurückgenommen. Die tiefen Fen-
sterlaibungen bewirken eine kräftige Gliederung der
Gebäudefronten.

The building is the administrative headquarters of one of the largest paper and cellulose
concerns in Finland. It adjoins the classical part of the city and stands at the end of the
Esplanadikatu, a broad park-like road. Immediately behind on a slightly higher level is the
Russian Orthodox church. The scale of this office building derives both its horizontal and
vertical character from the nearby historical buildings, hence its symmetrical, formal
façade. Except for the roof-storey, the plan of the office floors is so arranged that the
large rooms occur on the outside and can be subdivided according to needs. The subsidiary rooms lie on both sides of the central lobby connecting with the offices. The dining-
room is on the top floor. The elevations are faced with white and grey-blue carrara marble.

Das Gebäude ist Sitz der Hauptverwaltung eines der größten Papier- und Zellulosekonzerne
Finnlands. Es schließt sich an den klassizistischen Stadtteil an und steht am Ende der Esplanadikatu, einer breiten parkähnlichen Straße. Unmittelbar dahinter liegt auf etwas hö-
herem Niveau die russisch-orthodoxe Kirche. Die Maße dieses Bürogebäudes sind sowohl
in der Horizontalen wie auch in der Vertikalen von den benachbarten historischen Gebäuden
abgeleitet, wodurch sich die etwas strenge und formale Fassade ergab. Der Grundriß der
Bürogeschosse ist mit Ausnahme des Dachgeschosses so angelegt, daß an den Außenfronten Großräume entstehen, die je nach Bedarf unterteilt werden können. Die Nebenräume liegen zu beiden Seiten des Mittelflures im Anschluß an die Büroräume. Im Dachgeschoß befindet sich der Speisesaal. Die Fassaden sind mit weißem und graublauem
Carrara-Marmor verkleidet.

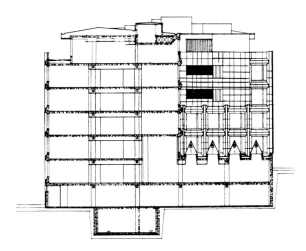

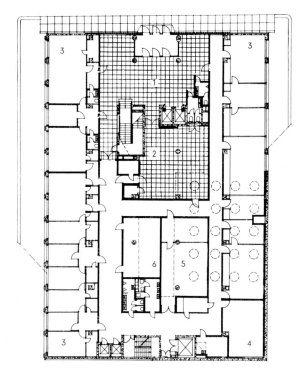

2. Section.
3. Ground floor plan. Key: 1 entrance hall, 2 travel bureau, 3 office, 4 storerooms, 5 common room, 6 stock room.
4. North-East view. The regularity of the building is broken at the back by recessing the façade and retracting the topmost storey.

2. Querschnitt.
3. Erdgeschoßgrundriß. Legende: 1 Eingangshalle, 2 Reisebüro, 3 Büro, 4 Lagerräume, 5 Gemeinschaftsraum, 6 Materialmagazin.
4. Nordostansicht. Die Rückfront des Gebäudes ist durch den Rücksprung der Fassade und das Zurücksetzen des Dachgeschosses aufgelockert.

Shopping centre at Helsinki-Puotinharju. 1964-65
Architect: Erkki Karvinen

Einkaufszentrum in Helsinki-Puotinharju. 1964-65
Architekt: Erkki Karvinen

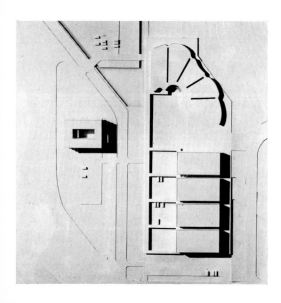

The shopping centre, for an overspill district of 55,000 people, lies about ten kilometres East of Helsinki on the busy main road to Porvoo. It is being built in stages to a competition design of 1962. The first phase comprises a two-storey structure, to which four large stores will be added later. The semi-circular building embraces two sides of a large piazza with pool and children's play space. The ground floor includes conventional and self-service shops, with show windows facing the central piazza. The service road for goods delivery is at the back of the shops and inside the building. Deliveries are also made from here by lifts to the businesses on the floor above. From the central piazza the public reaches this upper storey (of smaller firms, branch banks and cafés) by an escalator and a curved open-air staircase. Passages separate individual groups of shops and lead to the exits at the back of the exposed reinforced concrete building.

Das Einkaufszentrum für ein Einzugsgebiet mit 55 000 Einwohnern liegt etwa zehn Kilometer östlich von Helsinki an der stark befahrenen Hauptstraße nach Porvoo. Es wird nach einem Wettbewerbsentwurf aus dem Jahre 1962 in mehreren Abschnitten errichtet. Als erste Baustufe wurde zunächst eine zweigeschossige Anlage erstellt, an die sich später vier Warenhäuser anschließen sollen. Das halbkreisförmige Gebäude umschließt zwei Seiten eines großen Platzes mit Wasserbecken und Kinderspielplatz. Das Erdgeschoß enthält Großraum- und Selbstbedienungsläden, deren Fronten sich zum Zentralplatz wenden. Die Waren-Anlieferstraße befindet sich auf der Rückseite der Läden und ist in das Gebäude einbezogen. Über Aufzüge werden von hier aus auch die Geschäfte im Obergeschoß beliefert. Das Publikum gelangt über eine Rolltreppe und eine geschwungene Freitreppe vom Zentrumsplatz zu den kleinen Geschäften, den Bankfilialen und den Cafés im Obergeschoß. Passagen trennen einzelne Ladengruppen voneinander und führen zu den Ausgängen auf der Rückseite des Gebäudes, das in Sichtbeton errichtet wurde.

1. View from central piazza. The shopfronts are recessed, so that in bad weather customers can move in the dry from one to the other. In addition appreciable sun-protection is given by the deeply projecting upper floor and roof. The escalator is glazed at upper floor level on the weather side. Below, it is shielded by the extended floor. The curved open-air staircase follows the contour of the floor above.

2. The photo of the model shows the completed shopping centre, as proposed.

3. Section A-A and plans of upper (middle) and ground floors. Key: 1 escalator, 2 play space, 3 kiosk, 4 pool, 5 ramp, 6 goods delivery, 7 shops, 8 loading ramp, 9 garage, 10 storage, 11 passage, 12 shops.

1. Ansicht vom Zentralplatz. Die Ladenfronten sind zurückgenommen, damit bei schlechtem Wetter die Kunden trocken von einem Geschäft zum anderen gelangen können. Darüber hinaus ist durch die Tiefe der Auskragung der Geschoßdecke und des Daches beträchtlicher Sonnenschutz gegeben. Die Rolltreppe ist im Obergeschoß nach der Wetterseite hin verglast, im Erdgeschoßbereich wird sie durch die Geschoßdecke geschützt. Die geschwungene Freitreppe nimmt die Rundung des Deckenausschnittes auf.

2. Das Modellfoto zeigt das Einkaufszentrum im geplanten Endzustand.

3. Schnitt (A-A) und Grundrisse von Obergeschoß (Mitte) und Erdgeschoß. Legende: 1 Rolltreppe, 2 Spielplatz, 3 Kiosk, 4 Wasserbecken, 5 Rampe, 6 Warenanlieferung, 7 Läden, 8 Laderampe, 9 Garage, Lagerraum, 10 Arzt, 11 Passage, 12 Läden.

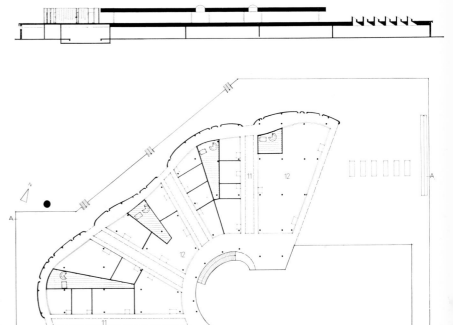

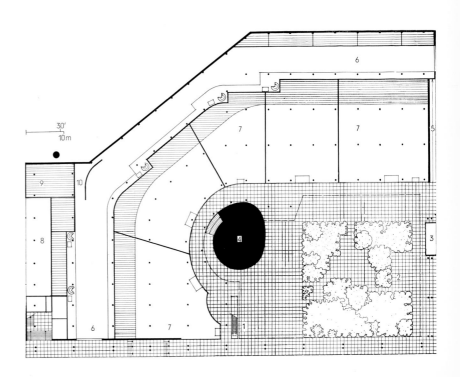

4. View of the shopping street of the upper floor, its semi-circular shape suggesting an intimate enclosed space.

5. A pool with fountains is a feature of the central piazza.

6. In front of the largely blind rear front of the upper storey stretches a broad terrace, from which a few steps lead down to the adjoining grounds. The shell-like reinforced concrete elements which stand clear of the ground break the continuity of the façade.

7. The curved reinforced concrete slab weather-shields on the West side are separated by open slits of light.

4. Blick in die Ladenstraße des Obergeschosses, deren Führung im Halbkreis einen intimen, geschlossenen Raum suggeriert. Im Vordergrund der Abgang zum Untergeschoß.

5. Die gekrümmten Wetterschutz-Betonscheiben auf der Westseite lassen Lichtschlitze offen.

6. Das Wasserbecken mit den Fontänen akzentuiert den Zentralplatz.

7. Vor der weitgehend geschlossenen Rückfront des Obergeschosses liegt eine breite Terrasse, von der aus man über einige Stufen auf das anschließende Gelände gelangt. Die vom Boden abgehobenen, schalenförmigen Betonelemente gliedern und lockern die Fassade auf.

1. General view. The bands of granite-slab cladding stress the building's marked horizontal character.
2. Section.

1. Gesamtansicht. Die mit Granitplatten verkleideten Brüstungsbänder betonen die kräftige horizontale Schichtung des Gebäudes.
2. Querschnitt.

From 1912 the streetscape of Lahti was determined by Pentila's KOP Granite House. Expanding business finally demanded a new building, and the firm invited several architects in 1961 to take part in a competition which was won by Revell. The architect's basic idea was to transfer the banking rooms to the first floor, which is also the highest complete storey of the building. Here the banking hall could easily be given the spacious and central location essential to the smooth operation of customers' business. The middle part of the ground floor was turned into a hall partly open to the street on three sides, whence one climbs by escalator, past shops, a café and the bank show-windows, to the banking hall, which occupies about half of the first floor. The bank offices are placed along the street front of the building. As well as banking accommodation and shops, the building contains offices for rent and flats. The façades are clad with grey granite slabs.

Seit 1912 wird das Straßenbild der Stadt Lahti wesentlich von dem von Pentila geplanten KOP-Granithaus bestimmt. Da sich der Geschäftsverkehr ausweitete, wurde ein Neubau notwendig und die Bank lud 1961 mehrere Architekten zu einem Wettbewerb ein, dessen Ergebnis das neue Bankhaus von Revell ist. Die grundlegende Idee des Architekten war die Verlegung der Bankräume in das erste Obergeschoß, das zugleich das letzte Vollgeschoß des Gebäudes ist. Hier konnte er ohne Schwierigkeiten der Schalterhalle die Weite und zentrale Lage geben, die für eine reibungslose Abwicklung des Kundenverkehrs nötig ist. Der Mittelteil des Erdgeschosses wurde in eine nach drei Seiten zur Straße hin teilweise offene Halle verwandelt. Von hier aus gelangt man, vorbei an Läden, einem Café und den Schaufenstern der Bank, über eine Rolltreppe in die Schalterhalle, die etwa die Hälfte der Grundfläche des ersten Obergeschosses einnimmt. Die Bankbüros sind an die Straßenfront des Gebäudes verlegt. Das Bankgebäude enthält neben Bankräumen und Läden, Mietbüros und Wohnungen. Die Fassaden sind mit grauen Granitplatten verkleidet.

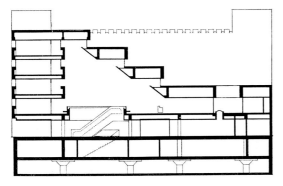

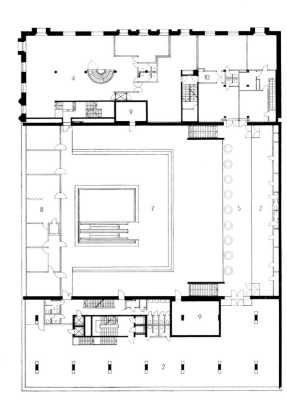

3. View into banking hall. The ceiling slope is interrupted by horizontal light openings extending the whole width of the hall, which obstruct the direct entry of light and prevent dazzle. The progressive reduction in room height from four storeys to one helps visually to guide customers from the escalator (at right) to the bank counters.

4. Ceiling design and furnishing emphasize and enhance the quiet sober atmosphere of the room.

3. Blick in die Schalterhalle. Die Deckenschräge wird von horizontalen, über die ganze Breite der Halle geführten Lichtöffnungen unterbrochen, die direkten Lichteinfall verhindern und für eine blendungsfreie Ausleuchtung sorgen. Die kontinuierliche Abnahme der Raumhöhe von vier auf ein Geschoß leitet den Bankkunden optisch von der Rolltreppe (rechts im Bild) zu den Bankschaltern.

4. Deckengestaltung und Möblierung unterstreichen die kühle und nüchterne Atmosphäre des Schalterraumes.

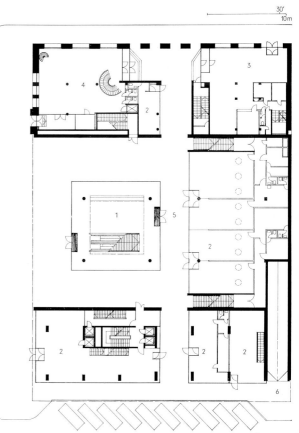

30'
10 m

6. The upper-floor offices are reached by galleries, which are open on the banking-hall side. The low barrier round the escalator shaft is seen in the foreground. The gallery parapets and corresponding oblique ceiling elements repeat inside the building the horizontal conception of the design.

7. The bank is entered through a completely glazed entrance hall in the middle of the open ground floor area, into which one passes by a porch.

6. Die Büros der Obergeschosse werden über Galerien erschlossen, die zur Schalterhalle hin offen sind. Im Vordergrund die Brüstung um den Rolltreppenschacht. Galeriebrüstungen und die damit korrespondierenden schrägen Deckenstreifen wiederholen im Innern optisch die horizontale Gliederung des Gebäudes.

7. Der Zugang zur Bank erfolgt über eine in die Mitte des offenen Erdgeschoßbereiches gestellte, voll verglaste Eingangshalle, die man über einen Windfang betritt.

◁ 5. Plans of first and (below) ground floors. Key: 1 bank entrance hall, 2 shop, 3 chemist, 4 café, 5 passage, 6 ramp to basement floors, 7 banking hall, 8 bank director, 9 staircase, 10 office.

5. Grundrisse des ersten Obergeschosses und des Erdgeschosses (unten). Legende: 1 Eingangshalle der Bank, 2 Laden, 3 Apotheke, 4 Café, 5 Passage, 6 Rampe zu den Untergeschossen, 7 Schalterhalle, 8 Bankdirektor, 9 Tresor, 10 Büro.

Schaumann paper and cellulose factory at Pietarsaari. 1960-62
Architects: Keijo Ström and Olavi Tuomisto

Papier- und Zellulosefabrik Schaumann in Pietarsaari. 1960-62
Architekten: Keijo Ström und Olavi Tuomisto

1. General view from the access road of the vigorously modelled premises.
2. View of the works road and the two circulation "tunnels".

1. Gesamtansicht der lebhaft gegliederten Anlage von der Zufahrt.
2. Blick auf die Werkstraße und die beiden Verkehrstunnel.

The works comprise a paper and cellulose factory with power plant, together with associated and subsidiary departments, e.g., pulping plant, chips silo, glauber's salt store, repair shop, central and paper stores. The buildings, mostly large halls, are organized into two ranges corresponding to the twin production processes and connected by circulation "tunnels", supported on columns. In one of these production sequences the wood is mechanically treated, while the other takes care of most of the chemical processes. In the space between the halls, about 90m wide, bridged by the circulation "tunnels", a pumping station, laboratory and office building are to be erected. r.c. and red brick are the materials used.

Zur Werksanlage gehören eine Papier- und eine Sulfatzellulosefabrik mit Kraftstation, sowie Neben- und Hilfsabteilungen wie Schälstation, Zerkleinerungsanlage, Holzspansilo, Glaubersalzlager, Reparaturwerkstatt, Zentral- und Papierlager. Die Bauten, in der Hauptsache große Hallen, sind in zwei, den beiden Produktionssträngen entsprechenden Zeilen nebeneinander gestellt und durch auf Stützen gestellte Verkehrstunnel miteinander verbunden. Auf einer dieser Produktionsstraßen, die parallel laufen, wird das Holz mechanisch bearbeitet, auf der anderen wickelt sich der größte Teil der chemischen Prozesse ab. In dem zwischen den Hallen verbleibenden etwa 90 Meter breiten Raum, über den die Verbindungstunnel geführt sind, sollen die Pumpenstation, ein Labor und das Verwaltungsgebäude errichtet werden. Als Baumaterial ist Beton und roter Backstein verwendet.

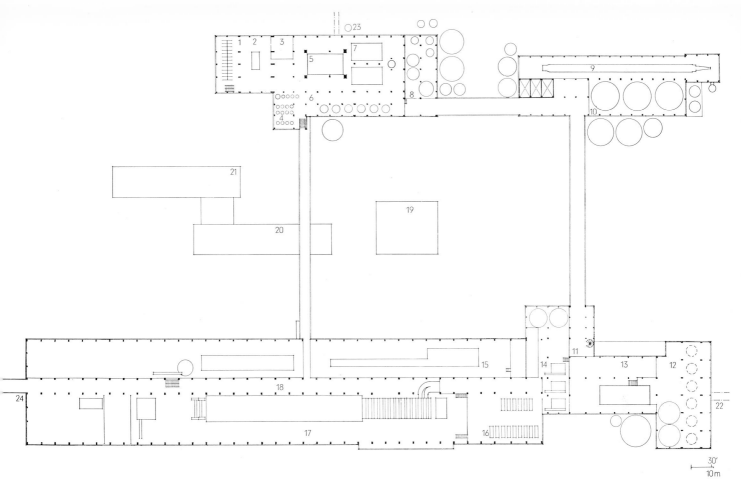

3. General plan. Key: 1 switch apparatus, 2 turbine hall, 3 control, 4 water treatment, 5 soda boiler, 6 evaporation, 7 filters, 8 tall oil department, 9 Mesa drying oven, 10 white liquor department, 11 works management, 12 cooking department, 13 washing, 14 sorting, 15 Kamyr machine, 16 grinding, 17 paper machine, 18 operational control, 19 pumping station, 20 laboratory, 21 administration, 22 chiptransporter, 23 glauber's salt transporter, 24 air shaft to paper department.
4. The large wall surfaces of the halls are divided and relieved by changes in materials and skilfully distributed openings.
5. Production hall.

3. Gesamtgrundriß. Legende: 1 Schaltstation, 2 Turbinenhalle, 3 Leitstand, 4 Wasseraufbereitung, 5 Sodakessel, 6 Eindampfung, 7 Filterstation, 8 Fallölgewinnung, 9 Drehofen, 10 Weißlaugenherstellung, 11 Betriebsleitung, 12 Kocherei, 13 Zellstoffwäsche, 14 Zellstoffsortierung, 15 Kamyr-Maschine, 16 Schleiferei, 17 Papiermaschine, 18 Produktionskontrolle, 19 Pumpenstation, 20 Labor, 21 Verwaltung, 22 Hackschnitzeltransport, 23 Glaubersalztransport, 24 Belüftungstunnel.
4. Die großen Wandflächen der Hallen werden durch Materialwechsel und geschickt verteilte Öffnungen aufgelockert und gegliedert.
5. Produktionshalle.

Works premises for the AGA company at Kilo near Helsinki. 1964-67
Architect: Kurt Simberg

Werkanlagen des AGA-Konzerns in Kilo bei Helsinki. 1964-67
Architekt: Kurt Simberg

In 1964 the AGA company began to transfer its works from Helsinki to the neighbouring district of Espoo. The site of 9.5 hectares, acquired in 1962, has direct rail facilities and the further advantage of lying on two main roads. The first phase comprised gas and heating plants, repair shops and a housing scheme. In phase 2 the administration and welfare buildings, a welding institute and a caretaker's lodge were built. The rooms of the administration building are grouped round a central light well, which on the ground floor also serves as an exhibition hall. In the welding institute sixty apprentices in groups can be trained in welding techniques. The welfare building contains separate dining rooms for office staff, and craftsmen and apprentices. A factory for light metal products is planned as phase 3, adjoining the welfare block. All buildings are of reinforced concrete. The administration building has brick cladding. For the others precast reinforced concrete elements were chosen.

Der AGA-Konzern begann 1964, seine Werkanlagen aus Helsinki in den Nachbarkreis Espoo zu verlegen. Das 1962 erworbene, 9,5 Hektar große Gebiet hat direkten Eisenbahnanschluß und liegt verkehrsgünstig an zwei Hauptstraßen. Der erste Bauabschnitt umfaßte: Gaswerk, Heizzentrale, Garagen mit einer Reparaturwerkstatt sowie eine Wohnsiedlung. Im zweiten Bauabschnitt wurden Verwaltungsgebäude, Sozialgebäude, Schweißinstitut und Pförtnerhaus errichtet. Die Räume des mehrgeschossigen Verwaltungsgebäudes sind um einen zentralen Lichthof gruppiert, der im Erdgeschoß als Ausstellungshalle dient. Im Schweißinstitut können sechzig Lehrlinge in Gruppen auf dem Gebiet der Schweißtechnik ausgebildet werden. Das Sozialgebäude enthält getrennte Speiseräume für Angestellte und für Arbeiter und Lehrlinge. Ein Fabrikationsgebäude für Leichtmetallprodukte ist als dritter Bauabschnitt im Anschluß an das Sozialgebäude geplant. Sämtliche Bauten sind Stahlbetonkonstruktionen. Das Verwaltungsgebäude ist mit Ziegeln verkleidet. Für die anderen Bauten wurden Betonelemente gewählt.

1. General view of administration building. To provide parking space under the building, the entrance floor was raised. This offered the welcome opportunity to design the approach as an impressive broad stairway. Elegant multimullioned ribbon windows and continuous narrow window breasts, the slim columns in front of the entrance floor (recessed near the way-in) and vertical slats in front of the data-processing extension (right) lighten the building's mass.
2. View into the administration building's central entrance hall, which serves as light well and display space for large exhibits.
3. Administration building, section and plans of entrance floor and typical upper floor (right). Key: 1 entrance and exhibition hall, 2 office, 3 dataprocessing centre, 4 cloakroom, 5 W.C, 6 ramp to parking area in basement.
4. Aerial view of the whole works area in its woodland setting. In foreground, the welding institute (right) and low welfare building; behind, the administration block (right), heating and gas plants.

1. Gesamtansicht des Verwaltungsgebäudes. Um Parkraum unter dem Gebäude zu gewinnen, wurde das Eingangsgeschoß angehoben. Damit ergab sich auch die willkommene Möglichkeit, den Zugang als repräsentative, breit angelegte Treppe zu gestalten. Fein unterteilte Fensterbänder und schmale Brüstungsstreifen, die schlanken Säulen vor der im Zugangsbereich zurückgesetzten Front des Eingangsgeschosses und die Vertikallamellen vor der Datenverarbeitungsanlage (rechts) lösen die Baumasse optisch auf.
2. Die zentrale, als Lichthof und Ausstellungsfläche dienende Eingangshalle des Verwaltungsgebäudes.
3. Verwaltungsgebäude, Querschnitt und Grundrisse von Eingangsgeschoß und Normalgeschoß (rechts). Legende: 1 Eingangs- und Ausstellungshalle, 2 Büros, 3 Datenverarbeitungszentrale, 4 Garderobe, 5 Toiletten, 6 Rampe zur Parkfläche im Untergeschoß.
4. Luftaufnahme des gesamten, in Wald eingebetteten Werkgeländes. Im Vordergrund das Schweißinstitut (rechts) und der Flachbau des Sozialgebäudes; dahinter Verwaltungsgebäude (rechts), Heizzentrale und Gaswerk.

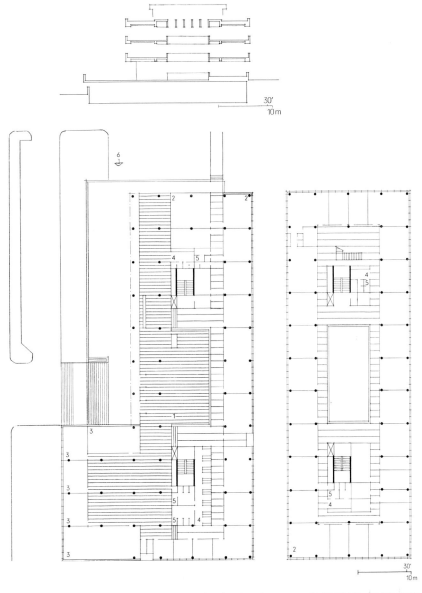

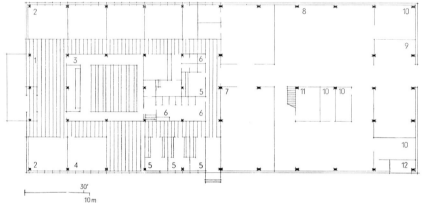

5. Welding institute. The higher building, with its encircling band of top lighting, contains workshops and machine shops.

6. The welding institute is faced with large Eternit panels, their width determined by that of the windows. The façades thus have an overall vertical emphasis.

7. Welding institute, plan. Key: 1 entrance hall, 2 office, 3 lecture hall, 4 laboratory, 5 changing-room, 6 toilets, 7 demonstration room, 8 welding shop, 9 cutting shop, 10 store, 11 machine shop, 12 transformer room.

8. Welfare building, plan. Key: 1 entrance hall, 2 doctor, 3 kiosk, 4 cloakroom, 5 kitchen, 6 dining-rooms.

5. Schweißinstitut. In dem erhöhten Gebäudeteil mit dem umlaufenden Oberlichtband liegen Werkstätten und Maschinenräume.

6. Das Schweißinstitut ist mit großformatigen Eternitplatten verkleidet, deren Breite auf die der Fenster abgestimmt ist, so daß sich eine durchgehende vertikale Strukturierung der Fassade ergibt.

7. Schweißinstitut, Grundriß. Legende: 1 Eingangshalle, 2 Büros, 3 Vorlesungssaal, 4 Labor, 5 Umkleideraum, 6 Toiletten, 7 Vorführraum, 8 Schweißwerkstatt, 9 Schneidewerkstatt, 10 Lager, 11 Maschinenraum, 12 Transformatorenraum.

8. Sozialgebäude, Grundriß. Legende: 1 Eingangshalle, 2 Arzt, 3 Kiosk, 4 Garderobe, 5 Küche, 6 Speiseräume.

9. View of passage linking the two dining-rooms. Right, buffet; left, cloakrooms.
10. Entrance hall of welfare building. In background, way to dining-rooms and buffet. The grid pattern of the ceiling is partly reflected on the floor. The character of the cheerful, simply composed room is defined by a rhythmic alternation of light and dark materials.
11. Office-staff dining-room.

9. Blick in den Flur, der die beiden Speisesäle verbindet. Rechts das Buffet, links die Garderoben.
10. Die Eingangshalle des Sozialgebäudes. Im Hintergrund der Zugang zu den Speisesälen und zum Buffet. Der Raster der Deckenverkleidung wiederholt sich im Fußboden. Der Raumcharakter wird durch den rhythmischen Wechsel heller und dunkler Materialien bestimmt.
11. Speisesaal der Angestellten.

Hosiery factory for Kudeneule Ltd. at Hanko. 1954-56
Architect: Viljo Revell

Trikotagenfabrik Kudeneule AG. in Hanko. 1954-56
Architekt: Viljo Revell

1. The production hall (left), and the office wing meeting it at right angles, enclose a slab-paved courtyard.
2. Site plan. The housing scheme is to the North-East, close to the factory.

1. Die Fabrikationshalle (links) und der rechtwinklig ansetzende Büroflügel umschließen einen plattenbelegten Hof mit Wasserbecken.
2. Lageplan. Die Wohnbauten liegen nordöstlich dicht bei der Fabrik.

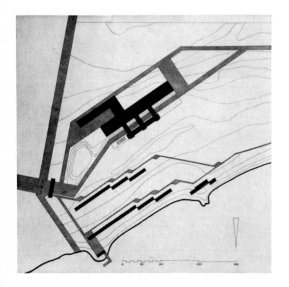

In a competition held in 1953 Revell's design won first prize. The brief required a factory with production hall, power plant, offices, staff common rooms, storage and housing. The architect was particularly concerned to achieve a logically evolving spatial sequence conforming to the production process, and humane, close-to-nature working conditions. In addition the scheme had to be realized in stages and functionally flexible. The site lies outside Hanko on the shores of the Gulf of Finland. Phase 1 entailed the construction of the production hall, followed next by the power plant, offices and staff common rooms, with the storage hall (adjoining the power plant) as phase 3. All buildings have reinforced concrete skeleton frame construction. The elevations are faced with aluminium.

In dem Wettbewerb des Jahres 1953 erhielt Revells Vorschlag den ersten Preis. Gefordert war eine Fabrikanlage mit Produktionshalle, Kraftzentrale, Büros, Gemeinschaftsräumen, Lager und eine Wohnsiedlung. Der Architekt bemühte sich vor allem, eine dem Produktionsablauf folgende, rational gegliederte Raumfolge und menschenwürdige Arbeitsplätze mit betonter Naturnähe zu schaffen. Darüber hinaus sollte die Anlage in Etappen ausführbar und in der Nutzung flexibel sein. — Das Grundstück liegt außerhalb Hankos am Strand des Finnischen Meerbusens. Als erster Bauabschnitt wurde die Produktionshalle errichtet. Es folgten Kraftzentrale, Büros und Gemeinschaftsräume und als dritter Bauabschnitt die Lagerhalle, die sich an die Kraftzentrale anschließt. Alle Gebäude sind in Stahlbeton-Skelettbauweise errichtet. Die Fassaden erhielten eine Verkleidung aus Aluminiumplatten.

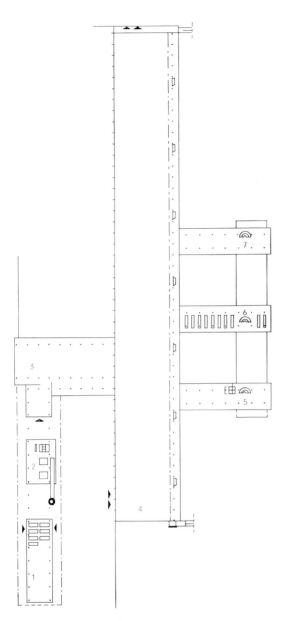

3. Plan of intermediate floor. Key: 1 store-room, 2 heating plant, 3 dye-shop, 4 production hall, 5 office wing, 6 changing-room, 7 special departments.

4. The continuous glazed front of the production hall overlooks the "valley". In the background stretches the office wing, its light openings (only slightly varied by a cill-height bar) extend the ribbon window of the production hall.

5. View of entrance hall.

6. The simply-designed offices are lit from two sides.

3. Grundriß des Zwischengeschosses. Legende: 1 Lagerraum, 2 Heizzentrale, 3 Färberei, 4 Fabrikationshalle, 5 Büroflügel, 6 Umkleideraum, 7 Spezialabteilungen.

4. Die Fabrikationshalle ist über eine durchlaufende Fensterfront zur Talseite geöffnet. Im Hintergrund ein Büroflügel, dessen Lichtöffnungen das Fensterband der Fabrikationshalle fortführen.

5. Blick in die Eingangshalle.

6. Die Büroräume werden von zwei Seiten belichtet.

Cemetery chapel at Kemi. 1959-60
Architect: Osmo Sipari

Friedhofskapelle in Kemi. 1959-60
Architekt: Osmo Sipari

From the road a long low wall leads to the main entrance of the chapel, of which the sides continue the line of the pitched roof to the ground. The lower part of the chapel wall on the cemetery side is glazed, so that inside and outside space become one. The surface of the same wall above is divided by vertical slats, which are set obliquely on plan to allow diffused light to enter. On the opposite, lower, side of the room there is a gallery reached from the porch by a staircase. The sacristy, relatives room, funeral chapel and other dependent rooms are directly connected to the chapel. The wood-lined ceiling, low concrete walls and lime-washed brick sides give the chapel, which has r.c. load-bearing elements, its particular quality.

Von der Straße leitet eine lange, niedrige Mauer zum Haupteingang der Kapelle, deren Seitenwände die Linie des Pultdaches bis zum Erdboden führen. Die friedhofseitige Wand des Andachtsraumes ist im unteren Bereich verglast: Außen- und Innenraum durchdringen einander. Die darüberliegende Wandfläche wurde durch schräg gestellte Vertikallamellen geschlossen, die ein diffuses Licht einfallen lassen. Auf der gegenüberliegenden niedrigen Raumseite befindet sich die Empore, die man vom Windfang aus über eine Treppe erreicht. Direkt an die Kapelle schließen sich die Sakristei, der Warteraum für die Hinterbliebenen, der Aufbahrungsraum und andere Nebenräume an. Holzverschalte Decke, niedrige Betonmauern und weißgeschlämmte Backsteinwände geben der Kapelle, deren tragende Teile aus Stahlbeton sind, ihr charakteristisches Gepräge.

1. View of altar wall of chapel. Left, the gallery. The character of the very simply handled room is determined by its clear lines and the harmony of wood, stone and concrete.
2. Door to the cemetery under the slatted wall.
3. Plan. Key: 1 chapel, 2 sacristy, 3 waiting-room for bereaved, 4 mortuary, 5 room for wreaths, 6 cloakroom.
4. East view. One of the walls running parallel to the altar side leads along the cemetery path up to, and under, the low belfry, which repeats in modified form the theme of the r.c. frame and vertical slats from the main front of the chapel.

1. Blick auf die Altarwand der Kirche. Links die Empore. Der Charakter des sehr schlicht gehaltenen Raumes wird durch die klare Linienführung und den Zusammenklang von Holz, Backstein und Beton bestimmt.
2. Das Portal zum Friedhof unter der Lamellenwand.
3. Grundriß. Legende: 1 Kapelle, 2 Sakristei, 3 Warteraum für Hinterbliebene, 4 Aufbahrungsraum, 5 Kranzraum, 6 Garderobe.
4. Ostansicht. Eine zur Altarwand parallel laufende Mauer führt längs des Weges zu den Grabstätten bis unter den niedrigen Glockenturm, der das Motiv des Betonrahmens und der Vertikallamellen von der Hauptfront der Kapelle in abgewandelter Form wiederaufnimmt.

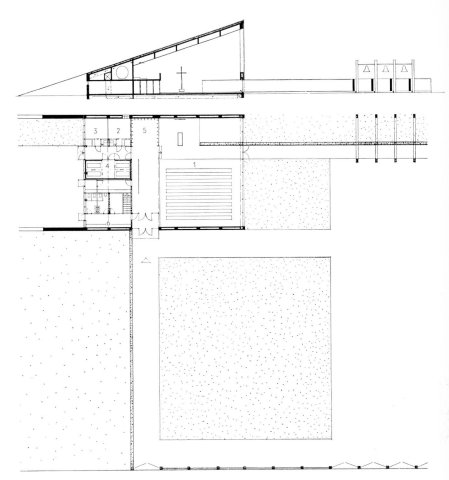

Cemetery chapel at Imatra. 1961-62
Architects: Jaakko Kontio and Kalle Räike

Friedhofskapelle in Imatra. 1961-62
Architekten: Jaakko Kontio und Kalle Räike

The cemetery extensions included a new main entrance and the provision, not far away from it, of a chapel. The entrance, flanked by a bell tower, leads to an inner court, in which mourners assemble. From here one proceeds, through the anteroom and waiting-room for the bereaved, to the chapel. The clients' wish for a steep, snow-free, roof persuaded the architects to make its form a principal feature. The chapel itself is completely enclosed and is lit only by a large corner gable window. The light entering diagonally at a steep angle is concentrated on to the altar in the opposite corner. The diagonal placing of the chapel's pews is also determined by these lighting conditions and by the doors at the other two corners. The ground plan is thus divided into two almost equal-sized triangles of the altar and seating areas, between which a broad corridor extends from door to door. The dependent rooms, which adjoin the chapel to the North-East, have a separate entrance. The roof is copper-covered. The walls are lime-washed brick masonry. The bell tower is concrete.

Bei der Erweiterung des Friedhofs legte man einen neuen Haupteingang an und errichtete nicht weit davon entfernt die Kapelle. Der vom Glockenturm flankierte Zugang führt zu einem Innenhof, in dem sich die Trauergemeinde versammelt. Von diesem Hof gelangt man über die Vorhalle und den Warteraum für die Hinterbliebenen in die Kapelle. Der Wunsch des Bauherrn nach einem steilen, schneefreien Dach kam der Absicht der Architekten, die Kapelle durch die Dachform zu akzentuieren, entgegen. Der Raum ist rundum geschlossen und hat nur ein großes, übereck geführtes Giebelfenster. Das steil in der Raumdiagonalen einfallende Licht wird auf den Altar in der gegenüberliegenden Ecke konzentriert. Auf diese Belichtungsverhältnisse und die in den beiden verbleibenden Ecken befindlichen Zugänge ist auch die diagonale Stellung der Kirchenbänke abgestimmt. Der Grundriß wird so in die zwei, fast gleich großen Dreiecke des Altarbereichs und der Bestuhlung zerlegt, zwischen denen ein breiter Durchgang von Tür zu Tür verbleibt. Die Nebenräume, die sich an die Nordostfront der Kapelle anschließen, haben einen separaten Eingang. Decke und Dachkonstruktion sind aus Holz. Das Dach wurde mit Kupfer abgedeckt. Die Wände sind aus weiß geschlämmtem Ziegelmauerwerk, der Glockenturm ist aus Beton.

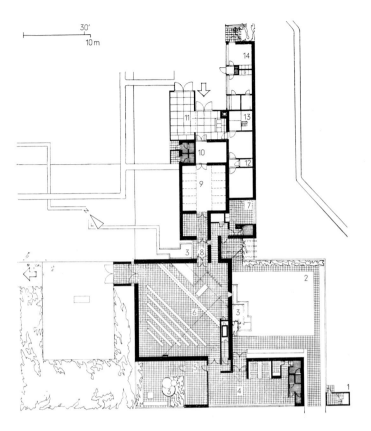

1. General view from the entrance side. The bell tower (right) acts as a visual foil to the movement of the roof.
2. View of the inner court with its pool.
3. Plan. Key: 1 bell tower, 2 internal court, 3 pool, 4 anteroom, 5 waiting-room, 6 chapel, 7 sacristy, 8 preparation room, 9 mortuary, 10 entrance hall, 11 equipment room, 12 cold chamber, 13 heating, 14 supervisor.
4. The dark-toned wood of the exposed roof truss and ceiling contrasts simply with the lime-washed brick walls. The glazing bars of the gable window (composed of two triangles) repeat the dominant diagonal pattern.
5. A free-standing, segmented partition encloses an open-topped sacristy, which forms a part of the altar area.

1. Gesamtansicht von der Eingangsseite. Der Glockenturm (rechts) fängt die Bewegung des Daches optisch auf.
2. Blick in den Innenhof mit dem Wasserbecken.
3. Grundriß. Legende: 1 Glockenturm, 2 Innenhof, 3 Wasserbecken, 4 Vorhalle, 5 Warteraum, 6 Kapelle, 7 Sakristei, 8 Vorbereitungsraum, 9 Aufbahrungsraum, 10 Eingangshalle, 11 Geräteraum, 12 Kühlraum, 13 Heizraum, 14 Aufseher.
4. Der dunkle Holzton der sichtbar belassenen Dachkonstruktion und der Decke kontrastiert lebhaft mit den weißgeschlämmten Backsteinwänden. Die Sprossen des aus zwei Dreiecken zusammengesetzten Giebelfensters wiederholen das Motiv der Diagonalteilung.
5. Eine frei stehende, stark gegliederte Wand umschließt die nach oben offene Sakristei, die in den Altarbereich einbezogen ist.

With this original design the architect won first prize in a competition held in 1963. The triangular plan is formed by three slab walls which reach out into the surroundings and link them to the chapel. A tubular steel space structure carries the roof, raising it high enough over the otherwise blind construction beneath to provide a broad continuous ribbon of natural light for the interior. The path to the burial ground is flanked by one of the three walls, at the end of which stands the bell tower. The chapel's r. c. walls are painted white. The roof rests on three supports in the angles of the interior.

1. General view showing doorway to cemetery. The transparent tracery of the roof rises weightless over the long low walls.

1. Gesamtansicht mit dem Portal zum Friedhof. Über niedrige, langgestreckte Mauern erhebt sich schwerelos das durchsichtige Filigran der Dachkonstruktion.

Mit diesem eigenwilligen Entwurf errang der Architekt in dem 1963 durchgeführten Wettbewerb den ersten Preis. Die dreieckige Grundrißfigur wird von drei Mauerscheiben gebildet, die die Kapelle weit ausgreifend mit der Umgebung verbinden. Eine räumliche Tragkonstruktion aus Stahlrohren hebt das Dach so weit über den geschlossenen Unterbau, daß ein breites umlaufendes Oberlichtband entsteht, über das der Innenraum Tageslicht erhält. Das einzige »Schmuckelement« ist ein schlichtes, an die glatte Wand gehängtes Holzkreuz. Der Weg zu den Gräbern wird von einer der drei Mauerscheiben, an deren Ende der Glockenturm steht, flankiert. Die Betonwände der Kapelle sind weiß gestrichen. Das freitragende Dach ruht auf drei Stützen in den Ecken des Innenraumes.

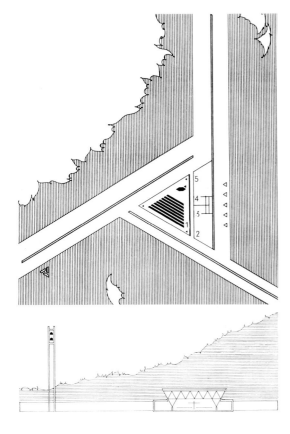

2. Plan and section. Key: 1 chapel, 2 anteroom, 3 waiting-room for bereaved, 4 sacristy, 5 mortuary.

3. The long wall leads to the entrance.

4. The chapel and tall, distantly placed, bell tower, which (like the chapel) is triangular in plan and linked to it by the wall.

5. View towards altar wall. In background, doorway to cemetery. Climbing plants brighten the simple geometry of the room, in which the intersecting lines of the roof construction cast a lively multiplicity of shadow.

2. Grundriß und Schnitt. Legende: 1 Kapelle, 2 Vorraum, 3 Warteraum für die Hinterbliebenen, 4 Sakristei, 5 Leichenraum.

3. Der Zugang erfolgt entlang der weit ausgreifenden Mauer.

4. Kapelle und der weitab gestellte, hohe Glockenturm, der wie die Kapelle einen dreieckigen Grundriß hat und durch die Mauer mit der Kapelle verbunden ist.

5. Blick auf die Altarwand. Im Hintergrund das Portal zum Friedhof. Rankgewächse beleben den geometrisch klar gegliederten, kühlen Raum, in den die sich überschneidenden Linien der Dachkonstruktion ein lebendiges Schattenmuster werfen.

Cemetery chapel at Järvenpää. 1956-57
Architects: Tarja and Esko Toiviainen

Friedhofskapelle in Järvenpää. 1956-57
Architekten: Tarja und Esko Toiviainen

1. General view from South. The band of top-lighting raises the chapel roof above the long brick front, about 3 m in height.
2. West front with open entrance zone.
3. The pergola-like continuation of the structural skeleton into the forecourt, with its lively pattern of plants and varied paving, marries the building organically to the woodland setting.

1. Gesamtansicht von Süden. Das Oberlichtband hebt das Kapellendach über die mit Backsteinen ausgefachte, rund drei Meter hohe Längsfront.
2. Die Westfront mit dem offenen Eingangsbereich.
3. Die pergolaartige Fortführung des konstruktiven Gerüstes in den lebendig gestalteten Vorhof läßt den Bau organisch in die lichte Waldlandschaft übergehen.

The chapel stands on a pine clad hill, and serves also as a meeting room for lay purposes. It is approached by a forecourt, which is partly covered. One enters first an anteroom, accommodating wreaths and open to the forecourt through a continuous glass front. The chapel itself, where the catafalque stands on the central access in front of the altar, can be combined with the choir by pushing back a folding partition. For parish meetings the catafalque sinks into the floor. The chapel is lit by a large window in the long front and by a continuous band of top-lighting. Behind the altar wall there is a waiting-room for the bereaved. The basement contains a sacristy, mortuary, cloakroom and various other dependent rooms.

Die Kapelle liegt auf einem tannenbewachsenen Hügel. Sie dient auch als Versammlungsraum für profane Zwecke. Der Zugang erfolgt über einen Vorhof, der zum Teil überdacht ist. Zunächst betritt man einen Vorraum, der als Kranzraum dient und über eine durchgehende Glasfront optisch zum Vorhof geöffnet ist. Der Andachtsraum, in dessen Mittelachse vor der Altarwand die Katafalk steht, läßt sich bei Bedarf durch Zurückschieben einer Faltwand mit dem Chorraum verbinden. Bei Gemeindeversammlungen wird der Katafalk im Boden versenkt. Die Belichtung des Raumes erfolgt über ein großes Fenster in der Längsfront und ein rundumlaufendes Oberlichtband. Hinter der Altarwand liegt der Warteraum für die Hinterbliebenen. Im Untergeschoß befinden sich Sakristei, Leichenhalle, Garderobe und verschiedene andere Nebenräume.

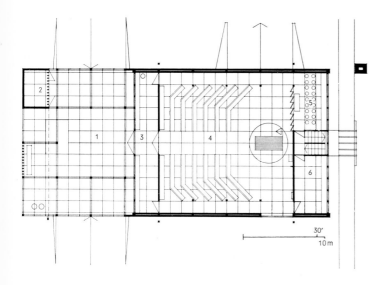

4. Ground floor plan. Key: 1 forecourt, 2 store-room,
3 anteroom, 4 chapel, 5 choir, 6 waiting-room for the
bereaved.
5. View of the simple chancel. Right, folding partition in
front of choir space.
6, 7. Features of the altar area (with catafalque) are the
cylindrical light fittings and picture.

4. Grundriß des Erdgeschosses. Legende: 1 Vorhof,
2 Abstellraum, 3 Vorraum, 4 Kapelle, 5 Chor, 6 Warteraum für die Hinterbliebenen.
5. Blick auf die schlichte Kanzel. Rechts die Faltwand
zum Chorraum.
6, 7. Der Altarbereich mit dem Katafalk ist durch den
kreisförmigen Leuchter und das Gemälde betont.

Kaleva church at Tampere. 1964-66
Architects: Raili Paatelainen and Raima Pietilä

Kaleva-Kirche in Tampere. 1964-66
Architekten: Raili Paatelainen und Raima Pietilä

1. General view of the freely, sculpturally, composed building, on which the tiny cruciform bell tower rides like a turret. The reinforced concrete slabs, arched inwards, form broad ribs, into which narrow vertical ribbon windows are inserted. The prominent slab wall (right) leads to the main entrance.
2. The curved external walls and bell tower are floodlit at night. From the road, therefore, the church affords a striking experience in the architecture of light.

1. Gesamtansicht des plastisch frei geformten Baukörpers, auf dem wie ein Dachreiter der kleine kreuzförmige Glockenturm sitzt. Die nach innen gewölbten Betonscheiben bilden breite Rippen, in denen schmale Fensterbänder hochgeführt sind. Die weit ausgreifende Scheibe (rechts) leitet zum Haupteingang.
2. Die gekrümmten Außenwände und der Glockenturm werden in der Nacht angestrahlt. So erlebt man die Kirche von der Straße her als eindrucksvolle Lichtarchitektur.

This hill-top church derives from a competition design awarded first prize in 1959. It stands as a foil to Lars Sonck's cathedral in the extension of the axis of the main road to the East. The nave has space for 1050 people and for 80 in the choir at the side. The rooms of the parish centre are in an annexe on the South side. The basement contains a large parish hall and technical services. The walls consist of irregular curved slabs, differing from the original design which was modified for reasons of conventional preference. The architect had provided for double r. c. shells, but only the inner one was retained, the outer being replaced by a masonry skin. The floor is paved with sandcoloured bricks. Ceiling, seats, organ screen and altar rail are wood.

Diese Kirche auf der Kuppe eines Hügels entstand nach einem mit dem ersten Preis ausgezeichneten Entwurf aus dem Jahre 1959. Sie steht als Gegenstück zu Lars Soncks Dom in der Verlängerung der Achse der Ausfallstraße nach Osten. Das Kirchenschiff bietet 1050 und ein Seitenchor 80 Personen Platz. In einem Anbau auf der Südseite sind die Räume des Gemeindezentrums untergebracht. Im Untergeschoß befinden sich ein großer Gemeindesaal und technische Räume. Die Wände bestehen aus unregelmäßig gekrümmten Wandscheiben, die jedoch nicht mehr ganz dem ursprünglichen Entwurf entsprechen, der aus konventionellen Überlegungen heraus abgeändert wurde. Der Architekt hatte doppelte Betonschalen vorgesehen, von denen man nur die inneren beibehielt, die äußeren aber durch eine Vormauerung ersetzte. Der Boden ist mit sandfarbenen Klinkern belegt. Decke, Bänke, Orgelprospekt und Altarschranke bestehen aus Holz.

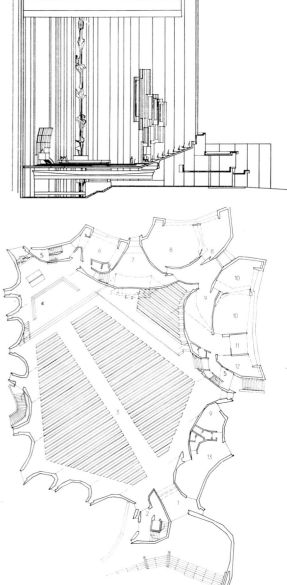

3. View from the nave towards the main and (left) secondary entrances.

4. The nave with the altar precinct (left), the organ, and the ascending choir tapering like a funnel. The organ screen, with its elements of different sizes, is an important design factor.

5. Section and plan. Key: 1 main entrance, 2 staircase to bell tower, 3 nave, 4 altar precinct, 5 secondary entrance, 6 vestry, 7 chapel, 8 meeting room, 9 anteroom, 10 parish hall, 11 kitchen, 12 choir room, 13 cloakroom.

6. View from the altar towards the chancel and seats in the nave. The lighting is contrived in recesses, so that the wall slabs are floodlit and reflect this light in their turn.

3. Blick aus dem Schiff auf Haupt- und Nebeneingang (links).

4. Das Hauptschiff mit dem Altarbezirk (links), der Orgel und dem ansteigenden Chor, der sich trichterförmig verjüngt. Der Orgelprospekt wirkt mit seinen unterschiedlich großen Elementen, die in der Höhe gestuft angeordnet sind, als raumgestaltendes Element.

5. Querschnitt und Grundriß. Legende: 1 Haupteingang, 2 Treppenhaus des Glockenturmes, 3 Hauptschiff, 4 Altarbezirk, 5 Nebeneingang, 6 Sakristei, 7 Kapelle, 8 Versammlungsraum, 9 Vorraum, 10 Gemeindesaal, 11 Küche, 12 Chorzimmer, 13 Garderobe.

6. Blick vom Altar zur Kanzel und auf das Gestühl im Kirchenschiff. Die Raumbeleuchtung ist in den Nischen so angeordnet, daß die Mauerscheiben angestrahlt werden, die ihrerseits wieder das Licht reflektieren.

1. The two chapels rise conspicuously from the long low group of buildings. The overlap of the large chapel's roof increases with height. The massive flat roof of the small chapel is carried on four supports. Its solidarity offers a contrast to the large chapel's reinforced concrete parabola.
2. Photo of model.

1. Von dem langgestreckten Gebäudekomplex heben sich die beiden Kapellen deutlich ab. Der Dachüberstand der großen Kapelle wächst mit zunehmender Höhe. Das Flachdach des kleinen Kapellenraumes wird von vier Außenstützen getragen und wirkt optisch als Gegengewicht zur Betonparabel der großen Kapelle.
2. Modellfoto.

The building stands in the middle of a newly laid-out cemetery East of Tampere, planned by architects Rauhala and Meller. The two chapels are placed left and right of a central entrance hall, connected to both sacristies and mortuaries and the mourners' waiting-room. The large chapel has a parabolic r. c. shell roof. The side walls are glazed from floor to eaves, opening the room on to the two internal courts which have large pools. The small chapel, largely closed to the outside, has as its only light source a continuous narrow ribbon window under the roof. The basement containing dependent rooms is linked to the ground floor by lift and staircase. Concrete is the dominant material inside and out. The ceilings of the entrance hall and small chapel are lined with wood.

Das Gebäude steht in der Mitte eines neu angelegten Friedhofs östlich von Tampere, der von den Architekten Rauhala und Meller geplant wurde. Die beiden Kapellenräume liegen links und rechts der zentralen Eingangshalle, an die sich die beiden Sakristeien, die Aufbahrungsräume und der Warteraum für die Hinterbliebenen anschließen. Die große Kapelle wird von einer parabolischen Dachschale aus Beton überspannt. Die Seitenwände sind vom Boden bis zur Dachunterkante verglast und öffnen den Raum zu den beiden Innenhöfen mit den großen Wasserbecken. Der kleine, nach außen weitgehend geschlossene Kapellenraum hat als einzige Lichtquelle ein unter dem Dach rundum laufendes Oberlichtband. Das Untergeschoß, das Nebenräume enthält, ist durch einen Aufzug und Treppen mit dem Erdgeschoß verbunden. Das bestimmende Material ist innen und außen Beton. Die Decken der Eingangshalle und der kleinen Kapelle sind mit Holz verschalt.

3. Section and plan. Key: 1 large chapel, 2 small chapel, 3 entrance hall and cloaks, 4 internal court, 5 sacristy, 6 waiting-room for bereaved, 7 mortuary, 8 exit to cemetery.

4. View into waiting-room with storey-high glazing on cemetery side.

5. The steep vaulted shell roof dominates the simple, almost ascetic, interior. The ceiling is faced with sound-absorbent material; the floor is paved with large re-constructed stone slabs.

6. The small chapel's walls are composed of large r.c. blocks. The projecting roof and continuous band of top-lighting give a sense of greater space.

3. Längsschnitt und Grundriß. Legende: 1 Große Kapelle, 2 Kleine Kapelle, 3 Eingangshalle und Garderobe, 4 Innenhof, 5 Sakristei, 6 Warteraum für Hinterbliebene, 7 Aufbahrungsraum, 8 Ausgang zum Friedhof.

4. Blick in den Warteraum, der zum Friedhof hin raumhoch verglast ist.

5. Die steile Wölbung der Dachschale bestimmt den schlichten, fast asketischen Innenraum. Die Decke ist mit schallschluckendem Material verkleidet, der Boden mit großformatigen Kunststeinplatten belegt.

6. Die Wände des kleinen Kapellenraumes bestehen aus großformatigen Betonsteinen. Durch das auskragende Dach und das umlaufende Oberlichtband wird der Raum optisch erweitert.

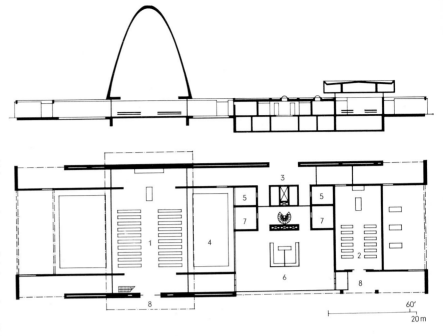

60'
20 m

1. General view of parish centre. Daylight enters the dependent rooms by the ground floor glazed front.
2. The main door enclosed in a concrete frame forms a solid block in the glazed front of the entrance hall.

1. Gesamtansicht vom Gemeindezentrum. Über die Fensterfront im Erdgeschoß erhalten die Nebenräume Tageslicht.
2. Der in einen Betonrahmen gefaßte Haupteingang ist als Block in die Glasfassade der Vorhalle gestellt.

The church stands on a park-like site in the town centre. The nave gives the impression of a largely enclosed space with no connection with the world outside, except for light entering from above over the entrance, and a window at the side concentrating the light and the congregation's attention on the altar. The choir and organ are accommodated in a side gallery. An annexe on the same level contains the parish hall, which can open into the church by means of folding doors. Next to the entrance hall on the ground floor is a roomy cloakroom and other dependent rooms. The church precincts are segregated behind the parish centre, which contains parish rooms, a small chapel, offices and flats. The little bell tower stands apart from the church, near the parish centre.

Die Kirche steht auf einem parkähnlichen Grundstück im Zentrum der Stadt. Das Schiff ist weitgehend geschlossen; die Verbindung zur Außenwelt wird nur durch das an der Eingangsseite von oben einfallende Licht angedeutet. Ein zweites Fenster in der Seitenfront konzentriert das Licht und die Aufmerksamkeit der Gemeinde auf den Altar. Chor und Orgel sind auf einer Seitenempore untergebracht. Auf gleicher Höhe liegt in einem Anbau der Gemeindesaal, den man zum Schiff hin durch Falttüren öffnen kann. Im Erdgeschoß befinden sich neben dem Vorraum eine geräumige Garderobe und weitere Nebenräume. Nach außen wird der Kirchenbereich durch das Gemeindezentrum abgeschlossen, das Gemeindesäle, eine kleine Kapelle, Verwaltungsräume und Wohnungen enthält. Der kleine Glockenturm steht abseits von der Kirche beim Gemeindezentrum.

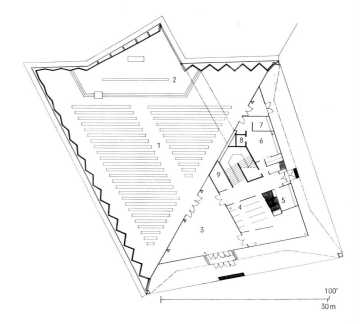

3. Die Verstärkungsrippen der Dachkonstruktion bestimmen den Charakter des zeltartig in die Höhe geführten Innenraumes. Die Orgelempore ist in eine Nische der Seitenfront eingefügt und überkragt zum Teil die Sitzbänke im Schiff.

4. Erdgeschoßgrundriß. Legende: 1 Hauptschiff, 2 Altarbezirk, 3 Vorraum, 4 Garderobe, 5 Warteraum für die Angehörigen, 6 Sakristei, 7 Andachtsraum, 8 Tresor, 9 Besenkammer.

5. Die Räume des Gemeindezentrums sind in einem flachen, langgestreckten Gebäude untergebracht. Rechts der Glockenturm.

3. The stiffening ribs of the roof construction distinguish the soaring, tent-like interior. The organ loft fits into a recess in the side of the church and is partly projected over the nave seats.

4. Ground floor plan. Key: 1 nave, 2 altar precinct, 3 entrance hall, 4 cloaks, 5 waiting room, 6 sacristy, 7 chapel, 8 treasure, 9 cleaning equipment.

5. The rooms of the parish centre are contained in a long low building. Right, the bell tower.

Church and parish centre at Helsinki-Lauttassari. 1957-59
Architect: Keijo Petäjä

Kirche und Gemeindezentrum in Helsinki-Lauttasaari. 1957-59
Architekt: Keijo Petäjä

A terraced path leads to the church, parish centre and chapel, which form a U-shaped group about the church piazza. Reflecting their importance, church and chapel stand out from the complex as separate buildings in their own right. Each has a smaller parish room which can be combined with the church or chapel respectively. Daylight enters through high-placed ribbon windows and, in the case of the church, by a broad and deep glazed front on the East side. The organ loft on this same side is directly accessible from the entrance hall. The range of buildings linking church and chapel include a gymnasium, a workroom and three dwellings. The buildings' façades are partly clad with copper, and partly with sand-blasted slabs of white cement.

Ein terrassierter Zugangsweg führt zu Kirche, Gemeindezentrum und Kapelle, die U-förmig um den Kirchenplatz gruppiert sind. Entsprechend ihrer Bedeutung heben sich Kirche und Kapelle aus der Gesamtanlage als eigene Baukörper heraus. An beide ist ein kleinerer Gemeindesaal angebaut, der in den Sakralraum einbezogen werden kann. Die Belichtung erfolgt über hochliegende Fensterbänder und, bei der Kirche, über eine breite, tief gezogene Fensterfront auf der Ostseite. Die an dieser Fensterfront liegende Orgelempore ist von der Vorhalle aus direkt zugänglich. In dem Gebäudetrakt, der Kirche und Kapelle verbindet, sind unter anderem ein Gymnastiksaal, ein Werkraum und drei Wohnungen untergebracht. Die Gebäudefassaden sind teils mit Kupferblech, teils mit sandbestrahlten Platten aus Weißzement verkleidet.

1. General view from road. The ground is terraced by steps and random stone walls. Left, the church; right, the chapel, with the vertical feature of the slim tower in between.

1. Gesamtansicht von der Straße. Das Gelände ist durch Treppen und Bruchsteinmauern terrassiert. Links die Kirche und rechts die Kapelle, zwischen die als Vertikalakzent der schlanke Kirchturm gesetzt ist.

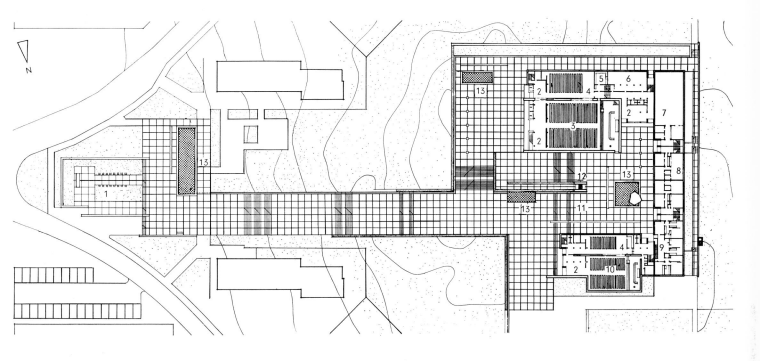

2. Plan. Key: 1 place for meditation near entrance, 2 vestibule, 3 church, 4 parish room (which can be partitioned off), 5 kitchen, 6 parish room, 7 gymnasium, 8 workroom, 9 dwellings, 10 chapel, 11 courtyard, 12 bell tower, 13 pools.

3. View across the courtyard towards the North front of the church and the bell tower. Stone benches at the pool's edge offer an invitation to rest. The huge rock came to light during foundation work.

4. The church is lit by ribbon windows inserted high up in the side walls. The altar precinct receives additional light from narrow slit glazing (right), stretching from floor to ceiling of North front.

2. Grundriß. Legende: 1 Gedenkstätte neben dem Zugang, 2 Vorhalle, 3 Kirche, 4 Abtrennbarer Gemeindesaal, 5 Küche, 6 Gemeindesaal, 7 Gymnastiksaal, 8 Werkraum, 9 Wohnungen, 10 Kapelle, 11 Hof, 12 Glockenturm, 13 Wasserbecken.

3. Blick über den Hof auf die Nordfront der Kirche und den Glockenturm. Am Rande des Wasserbeckens laden steinerne Bänke zum Verweilen ein. Der mächtige Felsbrocken wurde beim Aushub zutage gefördert.

4. Die Kirche wird durch hochliegende Fensterbänder in den Seitenfronten belichtet. Der Altarbereich erhält zusätzliches Licht über den schmalen, bis zur Decke geführten Fensterstreifen (rechts) in der Nordfront.

Chapel of Otaniemi technical university. 1956-57
Architects: Kaija and Heikki Siren

Kapelle der Technischen Hochschule Otaniemi. 1956-57
Architekten: Kaija und Heikki Siren

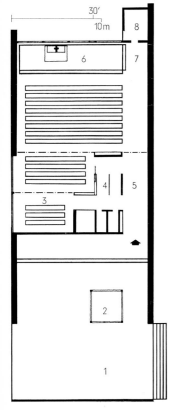

The chapel stands on a hill among rocks, birches and pines, very close to the students' village. The building's history begins with a design commissioned in 1952. The basis of the scheme carried out was a purchased competition entry by the architects of 1954. The chapel comprises a succession of spaces, beginning with a forecourt and leading through a low vestibule to the high nave, the ceiling of which drops again towards the glass altar wall. The view through this wall was the determining factor in the architectural conception of the room — the altar set against the tree-clad hill, and the forms and colours of nature changing with the seasons. Instead of the usual altar decoration a simple cross stands outside before the window wall. To avoid glare and provide the main source of light, the South front of the chapel is completely glazed at the line of transition to the highest part. The club and meeting rooms, which adjoin the chapel, can be incorporated with it by retracting sliding doors. The load-bearing sides of the chapel are of red brick, the lattice beams and roof construction wood.

Die Kapelle steht auf einer Anhöhe inmitten von Felsblöcken, Birken und Tannen, in unmittelbarer Nähe des Studentendorfes. Ihre Baugeschichte beginnt mit einem 1952 bestellten Entwurf. Grundlage der Ausführung war jedoch ein angekaufter Wettbewerbsentwurf der Architekten aus dem Jahre 1954. Die Kapelle besteht aus einer Folge von Räumen, die mit einem Vorhof beginnt und über eine niedrige Eingangshalle zu dem hohen Schiff führt, dessen Decke dann wieder zur Altarwand hin abfällt. Die Altarwand ist aus Glas. Sie bestimmt mit ihrer Aussicht den Raum und war Ausgangspunkt der architektonischen Idee. Altarbild ist der waldbewachsene Hügel, sind die je nach Jahreszeit wechselnden Farben und Formen der Natur. An Stelle des üblichen Altarschmuckes steht außen vor der Glaswand ein schlichtes Kreuz. Um Blendung zu vermeiden und als Hauptlichtquelle ist die Südfront der Kapelle an der Stelle des Übergangs zum hohen Kapellenteil voll verglast. Versammlungs- und Klubraum, die sich an den Sakralraum anschließen, lassen sich durch Schiebetüren mit diesem vereinigen. Die tragenden Seitenwände der Kapelle sind aus rotem Backstein, die Fachwerkträger und die Dachkonstruktion aus Holz.

1. General view, showing the entrance and steps leading up to it. Transparent screens of wooden rods, almost a part of the forest, and projecting slabs of masonry shield the forecourt.

2. Plan. Key: 1 forecourt, 2 bell tower, 3 club room, 4 cloakroom, 5 entrance hall, 6 altar precinct, 7 organ, 8 vestry.

3. View from the nave of the main entrance and glazed South front, against which the spare skeleton of the

roof frame stands out sharply, making the ceiling appear lower and the chapel more intimate. All the materials used, red brick for the floor, wood boards for ceiling and upper walls, are left exposed and untreated.

4. The slender lines of altar, font and pulpit accurately reflect the general architectural intention and do not block the view outside.

5. The altar is raised by three steps. The cross outside the chapel enhances the perspective effect of the room.

1. Gesamtansicht mit dem Eingang, zu dem einige Stufen hinaufführen. Transparente Stabwände aus Rundhölzern — fast noch ein Teil des Waldes — und vorgezogene Mauerscheiben schirmen den Vorhof nach außen ab.

2. Grundriß. Legende: 1 Vorhof, 2 Glockenturm, 3 Klubraum, 4 Garderobe, 5 Eingangshalle, 6 Altarraum, 7 Orgel, 8 Sakristei.

3. Blick aus dem Schiff auf den Haupteingang und die verglaste Südfront, gegen die sich das sparsame Gerüst der Dachkonstruktion abhebt. Es läßt die Decke niedriger erscheinen und verleiht dem Raum größere Intimität. Alle verwendeten Materialien, rote Backsteine für Fußboden und Wände, Holzriemen für Decke und obere Wandfelder, sind naturbelassen.

4. Altar, Taufbecken und Kanzel ordnen sich in ihrer filigranen Leichtigkeit ganz dem architektonischen Gesamteindruck des Raumes unter und behindern nicht den Ausblick in die Landschaft.

5. Der Altar ist um drei Stufen erhöht. Das Kreuz außerhalb der Kapelle vergrößert die perspektivische Wirkung des Raumes.

Vuoksenniska church at Imatra. 1957-59
Architect: Alvar Aalto

Vuoksenniska-Kirche in Imatra. 1957-59
Architekt: Alvar Aalto

1. View from West. Right foreground, part of parsonage, which is linked to the church by a wall. The church tower provides a vertical feature, a foil to the falling roof line.
2. Site plan.

1. Ansicht von Westen. Rechts im Vordergrund ein Teil des Pfarrhauses, das mit der Kirche durch eine Mauer verbunden ist. Der Kirchturm wirkt als vertikaler Akzent, der die abfallende Dachlinie auffängt.
2. Lageplan.

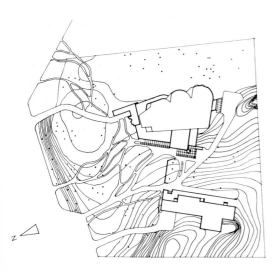

The church has to serve as a parish centre, i. e., the architect had to equip the three large rooms stipulated by the clients to be equally adaptable to church and lay purposes. Aalto solved the problem by making the nave divisible (by mechanically driven sound-proof reinforced concrete sliding partitions) into three halls, of which only the one with the altar is normally used for services. On festival occasions like Christmas or Easter the partitions can be pushed back to form a large hall with 800 to 1000 seats. All three rooms have separate entrances and can be used on their own. Another entrance in the North front, backing closely on the road, is only employed as a rule for funerals and weddings. Light enters through windows placed high up in the serpentine East front, with a shaft in the roof concentrating light on the altar. A low structure, extending in front of the West front, contains further parish rooms. The construction is r. c. combined with load-bearing brick masonry. All walls are fair-faced inside and out, and painted white.

Die Kirche soll zugleich als Gemeindezentrum dienen, das heißt, der Architekt hatte die vom Bauherrn geforderten drei großen Räume so einzurichten, daß sie kirchlichen und weltlichen Zwecken gleichermaßen dienen können. Aalto fand folgende Lösung: Das Kirchenschiff läßt sich durch maschinell gesteuerte, schallsichere Schiebewände aus Beton in drei Säle unterteilen, von denen im Normalfall nur der Raum mit dem Altar für den Gottesdienst gebraucht wird. Bei Festgottesdiensten an Weihnachten oder Ostern läßt sich durch Zurückschieben der Wände eine große Halle mit 800 bis 1000 Sitzplätzen schaffen. Alle drei Räume haben separate Eingänge und können für sich benutzt werden. Ein weiterer Zugang in der dicht an die Straße heranrückenden Nordfront wird im allgemeinen nur bei Begräbnissen oder Hochzeiten benutzt. Die Belichtung erfolgt über hochliegende Fenster in der geschwungenen Ostfront. Zusätzlich dazu ist auf dem Dach ein Lichtschacht untergebracht, der das Licht auf den Altar konzentriert. Auf der Westseite ist der Kirche ein niedriger Bauteil vorgelagert, in dem weitere Gemeinderäume untergebracht sind. Das Gebäude ist eine Stahlbetonkonstruktion in Kombination mit tragenden Backsteinmauern. Alle Innen- und Außenwände sind verputzt und weiß gestrichen.

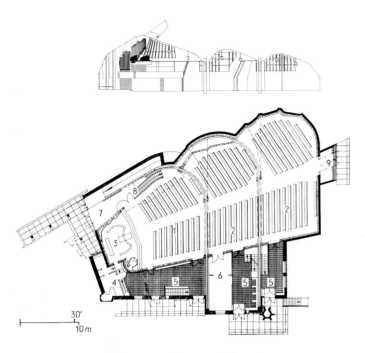

3. Section and plan. Key: 1 nave, 2 rooms which can be partitioned off, 3 altar precinct, 4 vestry, 5 anteroom, 6 dependent room, 7 additional entrance for weddings and funerals, 8 way-up to organ loft, 9 main entrance.
4. The altar wall, gently cambered and downward-sloping for acoustic reasons, the double-storey cantilevered organ loft and the varied movement of the walls create an asymmetrical, organically coherent room directed towards the altar.
5. Wall detail showing the windows stepped along the ceiling line.
6. The tripartite form of the nave is clearly apparent from the curved East front.

3. Längsschnitt und Grundriß. Legende: 1 Kirchenschiff, 2 Abteilbare Räume des Kirchenschiffes, 3 Altarbezirk, 4 Sakristei, 5 Vorraum, 6 Nebenraum, 7 Nebeneingang für Hochzeiten und Beerdigungen, 8 Aufgang zur Orgelempore, 9 Haupteingang.

4. Die aus akustischen Gründen in sanfter Wölbung nach unten geführte Altarwand, die doppelgeschossige, frei auskragende Orgelempore und die bewegten Wandflächen schaffen einen organisch frei gegliederten, auf den Altar konzentrierten Raum.
5. Wanddetail mit gestufter, der Deckenlinie folgender Fenstergruppe.
6. An der gekurten Ostfassade ist die Dreiteilung des Kirchenschiffes deutlich ablesbar.

Proposed new city centre for Helsinki. 1958-65
Architect: Alvar Aalto

Entwurf für ein neues Stadtzentrum von Helsinki. 1958-65
Architekt: Alvar Aalto

With the acceptance by the municipal council of the Aalto plan for the new city centre, fifty years of discussion have reached a happy conclusion. The scheme embraces the central square, Hesperian park with public buildings, the replanning of the bay with the buildings along the shore, the urban quarter of Kamppi on the perimeter of the old city and that of Pasila, which was drawn into the plan fairly late. The placing of the main access road along the East shore of the bay gives arriving travellers a view of the whole city. There are no intersections to impede vehicles, while for the central square a three-level traffic scheme is foreseen. The lowest will serve as parking space, and the terracelike upper storeys will have shops. The public buildings on the edge of Hesperian park are to be partly constructed over the water. The concert and congress hall marks the Southern limit. North of it an opera house, art museum, library and other public buildings are planned. A pedestrians' promenade extends along the shore.

Mit der Annahme des Aaltoschen Planes für das neue Stadtzentrum durch das Stadtparlament wurde eine fünfzigjährige Auseinandersetzung zum glücklichen Abschluß gebracht. Die einzelnen Elemente des Entwurfs sind der Zentralplatz, der Hesperianpark mit den öffentlichen Bauten, die Gestaltung der Bucht mit den Ufergebäuden, das Stadtviertel Kamppi als Abschluß der alten City und das Stadtviertel Pasila, das erst relativ spät in die Planung einbezogen wurde. — Die Führung der Hauptzufahrtsstraße am Ostufer der Bucht verschafft dem Ankommenden einen Blick über die ganze Stadt. Der Verkehr wird kreuzungsfrei geführt. Für den Zentralplatz ist eine dreigeschossige Anordnung der Verkehrsebenen vorgesehen. Die unterste dient als Parkfläche, und die terrassenartigen oberen Stockwerke enthalten Läden. Die öffentlichen Gebäude am Rande des Hesperianparkes sind teilweise über das Wasser hinausgebaut. Den südlichen Abschluß bildet das Konzert- und Kongreßhaus. Geplant sind nördlich davon Oper, Kunstmuseum, Bibliothek und andere öffentliche Bauten. Entlang des Ufers läuft eine Fußgängerpromenade.

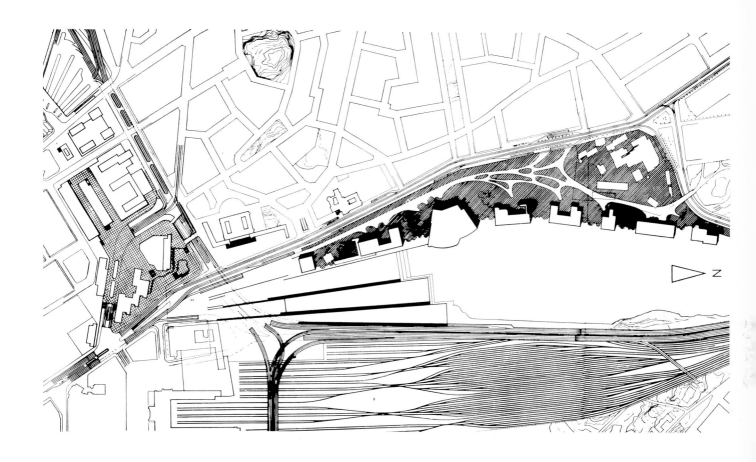

1. Photo of model. View from North of main access road and proposed public buildings round the bay.
2. The concert and congress hall (in background) will be the first building of the new centre. In foreground, the terraced Töölö piazza, and road.
3. Site plan of complete scheme. On West bank of bay, Hesperian park with public buildings.
4. Kamppi residential quarter adjoins the terraces of the Töölö piazza.

1. Modellfoto. Blick von Norden auf die Zufahrtsstraße (links) und die rings um die Bucht geplanten Bauten.
2. Als erstes Gebäude des neuen Zentrums wird das Konzert- und Kongreßhaus (im Hintergrund) gebaut. Im Vordergrund der terrassierte Töölö-Platz und die Straße.
3. Lageplan des Gesamtentwurfes. Am Westufer der Bucht der Hesperianpark mit den öffentlichen Bauten, am Ostufer die neue Straße.
4. An die Terrassen des Töölö-Platzes schließt sich das Wohnviertel Kamppi an.

Rehabilitation proposals for an industrial site in Helsinki. 1964/65
Architect: Erik Kråkström

Entwurf für die Neuordnung eines Industriegeländes in Helsinki. 1964-65
Architekt: Erik Kråkström

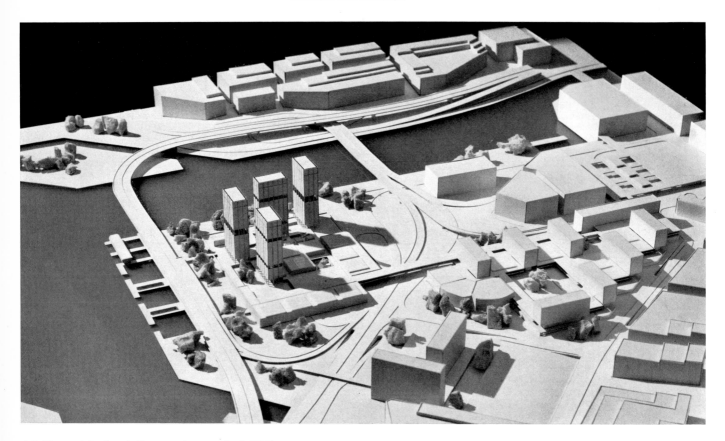

1, 2. The models show both renewal proposals: 1 (1964), 2 (1965).

1, 2. Die Modellansichten zeigen die beiden Neuordnungsvorschläge von 1964 (Bild 1) und 1965 (Bild 2).

This project, sponsored by the Wärtsila concern, enables the possibilities to be studied of a renewal and extension of the premises managed by the Kone ja Silta engineering plant belonging to this firm. Because of its central location and its size of 10.5 hectares the area has a particular importance for the renewal of this part of the city. With his two planning proposals the architect has tried to create a fresh townscape feature and to focus interest on the spot where the inner bay of Helsinki meets the sea. The schemes allow the firm and the municipality enough freedom for future developments. A vertical element, which enriches the silhouette of the city, is introduced into the horizontal succession of public buildings.

Der Wärtsila-Konzern ließ mit diesem Entwurf die Möglichkeiten für eine Erneuerung und Erweiterung der Anlagen untersuchen, die von der zum Konzern gehörenden Maschinenfabrik Kone ja Silta in Helsinki betrieben werden. Durch seine Lage in der Nähe des Stadtzentrums und seine Größe von 10,5 ha gewinnt das Gebiet für die Erneuerung dieses Stadtteiles eine besondere Bedeutung. Mit seinen beiden Planungsvorschlägen versucht der Architekt einen neuen Schwerpunkt im Stadtbild zu schaffen und die Stelle zu betonen, an der die innere Bucht von Helsinki und das Meer zusammentreffen. Die Entwürfe lassen dem Konzern und der Stadt genügend Spielraum für die Weiterentwicklung. In das horizontale Band von öffentlichen Gebäuden längs des Ufers wird eine Vertikalkomponente gestellt, die die Silhouette der Stadt bereichert.

3. Site plan for renewal scheme of 1965.
4. Photo of model. General view from West.

3. Lageplan zum Neuordnungsvorschlag aus dem Jahre 1965.
4. Modellfoto. Gesamtansicht von Westen.

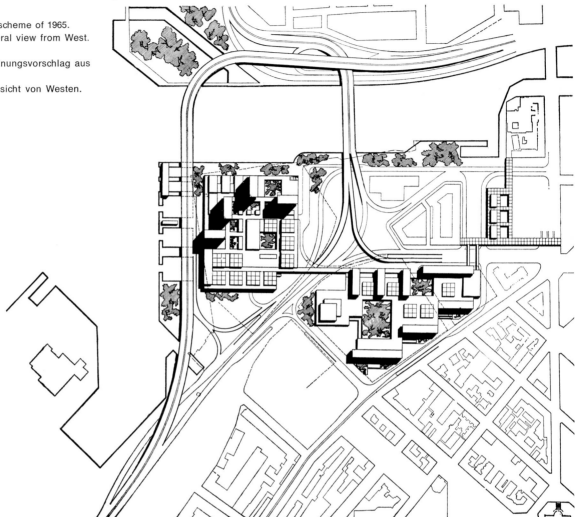

Index of Architects · Verzeichnis der Architekten